T0278277

POLES APART

ADVANCE PRAISE FOR THE BOOK

'The Indian military's steadfast political forbearance, amidst frequent displays of praetorianism, in the neighbourhood, has always confounded analysts. Now, Aditya Sondhi painstakingly undertakes a comparison of the divergent paths along which civil–military relationships have evolved on the subcontinent and offers rationales for the varied impact that encroachment of civilian spaces, by the military, can have on the political destiny of nations. A timely and thought-provoking study'—Admiral Arun Prakash (Retired), former chief of the Naval Staff

'*Poles Apart* offers us a fascinating comparative analysis of the complex and multifaceted relationship between the armed forces and the political establishment in postcolonial India and Pakistan. It highlights the historical evolution of the army in the post-1947 South Asian context to map out two conflicting trajectories of democracy. An overtly indifferent and apolitical army contributes to the establishment of democratic form of government in India, while a highly active and interventionist army establishes its dominance as a legitimate political player in Pakistan. No serious scholar of comparative democracy can ignore this important and path-breaking study'—Hilal Ahmed, associate professor, Centre for the Study of Developing Societies (CSDS)

'Contemporary developments in the Indian subcontinent make the issue of civil–military relations a timely and complex question. This volume provides a vital historical analysis that is engaging as well as informed and incisive. The resulting overview not only helps the reader understand the past but also points to lessons that might be drawn from it with respect to future trends and debates around institutional development and democracy promotion, in South Asia as well as elsewhere. The volume is a vital read not least because in a world where instantaneous judgements often predominate, it is important to have studies of crucial issues that take the long view'—Ian Talbot, emeritus professor of Modern South Asian History, University of Southampton

POLES APART

The Military and Democracy in India and Pakistan

ADITYA SONDHI

PENGUIN
VIKING
An imprint of Penguin Random House

VIKING

Viking is an imprint of the Penguin Random House group of companies whose addresses can be found at global.penguinrandomhouse.com

Published by Penguin Random House India Pvt. Ltd
4th Floor, Capital Tower 1, MG Road,
Gurugram 122 002, Haryana, India

First published in Viking by Penguin Random House India 2024

10 9 8 7 6 5 4 3 2 1

ISBN 9780670098446

Typeset in Minion Pro by MAP Systems, Bengaluru, India
Printed at Replika Press Pvt. Ltd, India

www.penguin.co.in

For Dr Iqbal Ahmed—schoolmaster, confidant and friend

Contents

Author's Note

This book is the outcome of research done for my PhD thesis 'The Interface between the Army and Democracy: India and Pakistan Compared (1947–2008)' submitted to the University of Mysore in 2013, which earned me my doctorate. It has undergone revisions and updates over the years, to make it more current and readable. As the title of the thesis suggests, my research was confined to 2008. But for the purpose of this book, I have added a short chapter on the post-2008 developments. This phase of approximately fifteen years has been less eventful in the context of the study. A chapter on Bangladesh has been added too.

Author's Note

[illegible]

Introduction
The Context

Any study in comparative politics necessarily entails comparisons of the political systems of different states, and a comparison of the 'similarities and differences between political phenomena across countries'.[1] The emphasis in such a study is on a comparison of *institutional* practices between states, and the effects of such institutions on political processes and results. The role of institutions, therefore, is central in comparative politics and is used liberally. Some scholars call this 'new institutionalism'.[2]

While questions have been raised previously about the viability of the comparative method in political science, arguing that nation states are far too unique and complex to be compared—each having their own *Gestalt,* or unique profile[3]—even sceptics, such as the American political scientist Harry H. Eckstein have, as far back as 1963, recognized that comparative politics is a theory in transition.[4] The relevance of comparative politics has increased with the corresponding growth of similar institutions across most nation states in the world. The British political scientist and economist Mark Pennington distinguishes these political institutions as 'hard' and 'soft'[5]—the former being conventional political participants, such as the bureaucracy, political parties, the judiciary or the electoral process, and the latter comprising culture, traditions, belief systems and the like.

In the study of political systems prevailing in different nation states, the reference to hard institutions is apposite. In the context of democracy, one could say that a comparative study of the electoral practices and processes of two or more nation states would provide a preliminary assessment of the health of democracy in the respective states. But, as the Indian political scientist Zoya Hasan observes, the understanding of democracy on the basis of the holding of regular elections is but a 'minimalist', Western–liberal definition of democracy.[6]

Democracy is far more complex, more so in Asia and Africa, where it is relatively newer, taking into its fold the interplay of various ideologies, institutions and experiments. The participatory notion of democracy is not merely confined to the elementary electoral process whereby a popular government is voted into power, but extends to the constant representation of the people's will, interests and grievances in the body politic, coupled with the constant accountability of the ruling government. Such continued representation and accountability are achieved through the creation of strong secular institutions that function under a constitutional umbrella with autonomy. For instance, a strong and bipartisan media enables such representation and accountability during the interregnum between two elections.

Institutionalized democracy is viewed as a basic method of expressing pluralism, of which electoral democracy is an indicator.[7] However, as political theorist Alan T. Wood observes, democracy is complex, being, '[but] a continuum that ranges from full-scale tyranny [to] partial and hybrid democracies of various kinds, to full democracy on the other end of the spectrum . . . No one has reached the end of the spectrum [as] democracy is not a destination but a process which requires constant renewal.'[8]

Therefore, the thresholds and forms of democracy practised in two nation states would perennially differ, but the reasons for the difference (or success) would often depend on *similar* institutions.

The role of the military and the corresponding civil–military relations are crucial to the study of democracy in any political system. The history of democracy itself betrays the role of military intervention in its subversion. The genesis of democracy can be found in the recognition of adult (albeit, male and white) suffrage in the United States of America in the early nineteenth century, receiving its first major global setback due to the militarism of Mussolini between 1922 and the commencement of the Second World War in 1939. By the end of the Second World War, the world saw an increase in the number of countries 'practising' democracy from twenty-nine to thirty-six.[9]

The traditional role of the military in matters of defence and territorial integrity has undergone a sea change, with the armies of the world today being involved in transnational, humanitarian and 'civilian' endeavours, such as peacekeeping, dispersal of unlawful assemblies, rescue operations and creation of infrastructure such as roads, bridges and the like. At times, this close involvement with matters of civilian policy could lead to the 'militarization of politics' and the 'politicization of military',[10] both of which could affect civil–military relations. Military intervention in politics is no new phenomenon, with over 50 per cent member states of the United Nations (as of 1987 and not very different as on date) having been under military rule at some stage, with Latin America and Asia dominating the number of attempted coups—both successful and aborted.[11]

The Pakistani scientist Ayesha Siddiqa describes six forms of civil–military relations which are (a) civil–military partnership, where democracy is stable and marked by the presence of strong civil society and civilian institutions, and the military is professional and 'hands off' on matters other than purely of defence; (b) authoritarian political party–military partnership, typically found in communist states where a strong single party governs with the military as an instrument of policy; (c) ruler military, where the military sees itself as an alternative to civilian power and imposes itself as the 'legitimate' power centre with long-term authoritarianism (d) arbitrator military, that assumes power periodically to resolve the (self-perceived) imbalances in national politics, stabilizes matters over a short- to midterm and returns to military functions after a transition in power, (e) parent–guardian military and (f) warlord type, in which the top brass of the military consolidates its political power through constitutional reform, often aided by the civilian government, and leads to the military's influence and investment in the economy.[12]

A few instances of such types of governments are catalogued below:[13]

Civil–Military Relations	**Partner**	**Dominant**	**Hegemonic**
Civil–military partnership	USA, France, UK, South Africa, India, Brazil, Israel		
Authoritarian political party–military partnership	China, Iran, Cuba, Sri Lanka		
Ruler military		Chile, Haiti, Burma, Argentina	

Arbitrator military		*Pakistan (pre-1977)*, Turkey (pre-1961), Indonesia (pre-1966), Thailand, Vietnam, Cambodia, Bangladesh	
Parent–guardian military			*Pakistan (post-1977)*, Turkey (post-1961), Indonesia (post-1966)
Warlord		Nigeria, Ethiopia, Sierra Leone, Angola, Somalia, Sudan	

(Italics supplied to denote Pakistan's standing)

It is only in the first typology, i.e., civil–military partnership that democracy thrives in theory *and* practice. Here, the participation and interests of the military in the economy (or the involvement of the military in business—defined by Siddiqa as 'Milbus') are insignificant and subordinate to civilian power, which is a critical factor in limiting the amount of control that the military exerts on the political system.[14]

An activist army is the antithesis of democracy. The army is disentitled to any legitimate right to governance and does not lawfully reflect people's representation in politics. However, a responsible army plays a vital role in the creation of an environment of stability and sovereignty which could *enable* the evolution of democratic practices and institutions. This is particularly true of 'young' democracies. Moreover, an army that abstains from any forays into the civilian domain permits the people and civilian institutions to determine the fate of the democracy, be it by fresh elections or any other constitutional means. Here, it acts as a relevant, albeit 'soft', institution.

However, experience has shown that civil–military relations are complex and often the military exceeds its mandate and intrudes into the political space. The reasons for military intervention in politics are manifold and diverse. In a democratic system, when public trust in the government declines, electoral turnout is low, institutions such as the executive and the judiciary are weak (or corrupt or both), political parties are several and polarized, and stability is lacking, the military often steps in to ostensibly stem the tide in such situations.[15]

The Bangladeshi political scientist Emajuddin Ahamed attributes the reasons for successful military intervention in politics to three major factors: (a) organizational superiority (b) corporate and national interests and (c) performance failures of the civilian leadership.[16] These appear to be particularly true in the South-Asian context, and Pakistan proves the case in point.

The British academic Martin Edmonds, in his seminal work *Armed Services and Society*, also attributes 'prestige of the nation' and 'war—civil or external' as causes for military intervention in civil societies, which may be direct or indirect.[17] Social and political realities obtaining in the nation at the prevalent time often determine the mode of military intervention. The American sociologist Morris Janowitz, in his essay 'Armed

Forces and Society: A World Perspective', outlines the varying role of the military in civil matters depending upon the existence of authoritarian–personal systems of military control, dominant civilian mass party system, existing democratic competitive systems, civil–military coalitions and military oligarchies.[18] The role that the military plays is often dependent on the legitimacy provided to it by the civilian polity.

The *political* success or otherwise of a military regime, again, depends on a multitude of factors. Often, a charismatic leader could singularly dominate the stage, as was the case with Kemal Ataturk—a military officer who is regarded as a nation-builder in Turkey and who transformed into a widely acceptable civilian leader. The study of the correlation between the military and democracy therefore needs to transcend the mere interference of the military in civilian rule. It should take into its fold the quantum of 'militarism'—the dominant military influences on the political, socio-economic and foreign policies of the state.[19] This intertwining of political narratives and ambitions in the working of apolitical institutions, such as the army, could drive these bodies to get politicized and, worse still, involved in the politics of the day. This is what Samuel P. Huntington broadly defines as 'praetorianism'.[20] Huntington, in his other notable work *The Soldier and the State*, refers to the 'tragic necessity' in the relationship between the professional aspirations of the military and civilian control, and that often professional success in the military breaches this barrier, breeding 'its own downfall by stimulating political involvement'.[21]

As a contrast to such praetorianism, where there exists civilian control of military institutions coupled with the isolation of the military from politics, such a nation state often witnesses the development of an apolitical military and, correspondingly, the conspicuous growth of civilian institutions.[22] This contrast is particularly true of young democracies such as Pakistan, where democratic institutions are lopsided and dictatorship camouflages itself as being 'democratic', thereby paving the way for the military to legitimize its involvement in governance. Such regimes are totalitarian or authoritarian, though the populace is often accepting of this flawed democracy as being 'good enough' for want or awareness of better options.[23]

It is against this backdrop that this work seeks to investigate the interface between the army and democracy in India and Pakistan. The history of India's army, as we understand it today, can be traced back to 1607 when the military personnel of the East India Company (EIC) arrived under the command of Captain Hawkins on the *HMS Hector* to commence their mercantile operations. With this began the fourfold phase of the growth of the armies,[24] as under:

1607–1708: The army of the EIC
1709–1894: The Presidency Armies of Bengal, Madras and Bombay
1895–1920: The United Indian Army (formed by the unification of the Presidency Armies)
1920–47: The Indian Army leading up to Independence (with the addition of the Indian Territorial Force and the Auxiliary Force [India])

Circa 1879, the Indian Army comprised 6602 British officers, over 1,00,000 Indian soldiers, over 60,000 British soldiers and *no* Indian officers. Lord Curzon, and his ilk, firmly believed that Indians lacked military acumen and there was a general opposition to the creation of an Indian officer corps.[25] However, the stellar performance of the Indian troops in the First World War persuaded the British to permit Indians to become King's Commissioned Officers (KCOs), leading to the admission of Indians to the prestigious Royal Military College (RMC), Sandhurst, and the formation of the Prince of

Wales Royal Indian Military College (RIMC), Dehradun, in 1922 and the Indian Military Academy (IMA), Dehradun, in 1932.[26] The initial batch admitted to RIMC included India's future chief of army staff (COAS) General K.S. Thimayya and Air Marshal Asghar Khan of the Pakistan Air Force (PAF).[27] The selection process preferred boys with British-style public school education and affluent backgrounds and, as the American political scientist Stephen P. Cohen observes, boys from 'politically inert' families.[28] The British Army officer corps itself was largely fed by boys from elite public schools such as Rugby, Eton, Harrow and St Paul's.

It is at the IMA that future Indian Army officers were bred in the culture of hard-boiled professionalism to become 'officers and gentlemen'. Scholar Apurba Kundu pointedly refers to the course of instruction for cadets at the IMA as having the objective of '[instilling] in him [the cadet] a high sense of duty and of honour, and a realization of *the responsibilities of a servant of the State*.'[29] (Emphasis supplied.) The 'Chetwode Credo' of the IMA—drawn from the inaugural speech of the Commander-in-Chief Sir Philip Chetwode—begins with the words, 'The safety, honour and welfare of *your country* come first, always and every time.'[30] (Emphasis supplied.)

These instructions point to the obligation of an officer to remain loyal to the State and to the country, and not necessarily to the government in power. However, the spirit of training is intrinsically that an officer remains loyal to the legitimate government in power and does not himself/herself determine the vexed issues of the best interests of the country. Equally, the emphasis on the safety and welfare of the men under the command of an officer was critical in the development of an ethos of regimental honour, which prevailed over any selfish interests that officers may have countenanced. As General Sinha puts it, 'The men who came forward to [the British Indian] Army looked upon fighting as their profession and they fought for their honour. *They did not have any other cause to serve.* And the British fostered the regimental spirit in them . . . Even in the changed circumstances today, the regimental ethos of the combat units of the Indian Army is all important.'[31] (Emphasis supplied.)

The real coming of age of the Indian KCOs was during the Second World War, where Indian officers performed admirably, earning not only decoration but also the admiration and trust of the British leadership. The aftermath of war witnessed the rapid promotions of officers such as Cariappa, Thimayya, Thorat, Chaudhari and Rajendra Sinhji, who would assume the command of the Indian Army in various capacities in the coming years.

The rapid political developments in the 1940s made it clear that the exit of the British regime was certain. What, however, was uncertain was whether independent India would be one state or two, with serious demands being made for the formation of Pakistan. While the British leadership hoped that the Indian Army—which was its red-lettered creation—remained unified,[32] the Indian political will was otherwise. Jawaharlal Nehru rejected the option of having an undivided army.[33] By June 1947, it was announced by Lord Mountbatten that power would be transferred to *two* independent Dominions of India and Pakistan on 15 August 1947 and General Claude Auchinleck would carry out the painstaking task of the division of the armed forces. Interestingly, Brigadier Cariappa (as he then was)—the senior-most Indian officer in the army at the time—is reported to have met Lord Ismay on 25 April 1947 and suggested that instead of the armies being split, it would be better to have a common army take over (civilian) power, with either Jinnah or Nehru at the helm as commander-in-chief. Ismay's response was, that

> . . . the proposal was not only wholly impracticable, but highly dangerous, that throughout history rule of an army

> had always proved tyrannical and incompetent and that the army must always be servants and not masters. [That] the Indian army, by remaining united and refusing to take sides, could wield tremendous influence for good . . . *but they (the army) must always be subservient to civil power.*[34] (Emphasis supplied.)

Later, General Cariappa, as COAS, would reiterate Ismay's sentiment of avoiding involvement in politics by calling politics in the army a 'poison' and asking his troops to 'keep off it' as the army was meant to serve the government of the day and not to get mixed up with party politics.[35]

Apart from the official Indian Army that now had commissioned officers and had served the British regime, the 1940s witnessed the emergence of 'national armies' in India, the most prominent being Subhas Chandra Bose's Indian National Army (INA)[36], which was established with a political and nationalist agenda of ousting the British and seeking swaraj. However, when the question of integrating these troops into the Indian Army arose on the eve of Independence (as many of them were former soldiers of the Indian Army), senior officers such as Thimayya, Thorat and others strongly opposed their reinstatement as their induction would lead to the politicization of the forces.[37] Nehru agreed with them stating that he did 'not want politics to enter the army'[38] as INA personnel would carry with them Bose's 'aggressive political legacy'.[39]

General Auchinleck's terms of reference as chairman of the Armed Forces Reconstitution Committee, as adopted by the Partition Council set up in June 1947, were pressed into service. This included a preliminary bifurcation on a communal basis.[40] The division was made on a 70:30 ratio favouring India, though the communal division suggested by the Council proved troublesome as the regiments were ethnically diverse, there being *no* all-Muslim units[41] with regiments being formed functionally—Infantry, Artillery, Cavalry, etc. The regiments could be subdivided on an ethnic basis—Sikhs, Rajputs, Gorkhas, Kumaon, etc. or on a regional basis—Madras Engineering Group, Bengal Lancers, Jammu and Kashmir, etc. Post the division, the Pakistan Army turned out to be ethnically more homogeneous, being largely drawn from (West) Punjab (over 75 per cent) and the North-West Frontier Province (NWFP) (20 per cent).[42] The reorganization also found rapid promotions being made of officers to fill the higher commands, though Pakistan suffered from a shortage of quality officers at the higher echelons[43] and British officers continued to command both armies in the early phase after Partition. General F.R.R. Bucher and General Sir Douglas Gracey were appointed commanders-in-chief of the Indian and Pakistani armies, respectively.

On the civilian front, at this stage India had a surfeit of strong and popular leaders in Gandhi, Nehru, Sardar Patel, Ambedkar and others, as well as a strong, mass-based national party in the Indian National Congress (INC). These leaders were committed to constitutional governance, and the Constitution of India (that would come to be adopted within a brief period of two-and-a-half years of Independence, in January 1950) would, in its Preamble, pledge to provide a democratic form of government. Kundu rightly points out that India is perhaps the only 'third world' state to have enjoyed a combination of a professional officer corps, stable democratic rule at Independence and armed forces containing a representative mix of personnel.[44] The absence of even one of these ingredients could be detrimental to the survival of democracy.

Pakistan, on the other hand, had no nationwide political party that was disciplined, organized and popular. The Muslim League, headed by Quaid-e-Azam (Great Leader) Mohammed Ali Jinnah, was dominated and supported by wealthy feudal landlords from the Punjab. The peasants who supported the Muslim League prior to Partition largely belonged to the state of Uttar Pradesh and stayed back in India after Partition, unable perhaps to assure themselves of a safe financial future in the new land.[45] While reasons to migrate or stay were complex and subjective, the middle class (often Punjabi, Urdu or Bengali speaking) migrated in greater numbers than the poorer or richer classes, largely on account of the financial stability at stake.[46] Scholar and author Robert W. Stern comments that the absence of large feudal landlords in the pre-Independence polity of India was perhaps the single greatest factor that assured a successful future for parliamentary democracy in the country.[47] Even the leadership of Jinnah, though charismatic and inspirational, was marked by the absence of corresponding party structures, other leaders of substance and a robust constitutional framework, all of which are critical for the success of democracy in a nascent state.

Jinnah proclaimed that: 'The new state [Pakistan] would be *a modern democratic state* with sovereignty resting in the people and the members of the new state having equal rights of citizenship regardless of their religion, caste, or creed.'[48] (Emphasis supplied.)

He had, on the eve of the birth of Pakistan, further declared, 'You are free to go to your temples, you are free to go to your mosques or to any other place of worship in this State of Pakistan. You may belong to any religion or caste or creed—that has nothing to do with the business of the State.'[49]

However, the interim Constitution of Pakistan, further which was an adaptation of the Government of India Act, 1935, was conspicuously bereft of any secular or democratic provisions, with powers vesting almost entirely in the governor general. The task of framing the final Constitution of Pakistan, bestowed upon the Constituent Assembly, would take a significantly long time (almost ten years) to result in the first

Constitution of 1956, by which time, the army had already taken centre stage. Jinnah was idealistic in expecting that pending finalization of the Constitution (which he hoped would be done within eighteen to twenty-four months), the wheels would turn on the basis of the provisional Constitution, which he viewed as one 'based on fundamental principles of democracy, not bureaucracy or autocracy or dictatorship'.[50]

Jinnah passed away in 1948 and the developments in a short period thereafter were sufficient to put paid to his hopes. It must equally be stated that Jinnah's Pakistan was primarily a homeland for undivided India's Muslims based on his understanding of Islam, which he explained '. . . did not advocate a democracy which would allow the majority of non-Muslims to decide the fate of Muslims.'[51] Hence, the ethos of his democratic imagination was rickety. Zoya Hasan describes this as the 'democratic deficit in the Muslim world'.[52] The general incompatibility of doctrinal religiosity with democratic practices is critical, as secularism acts as the crucial regulator of the descent of democracy to authoritarianism.[53]

The British economist and former Labour politician Lord Meghnad Desai attributes the survival of democracy in India, among other reasons, to the availability of Western-educated lawyers in the politics of the time, while the Pakistani lawyer–politician Aitzaz Ahsan attributes the absence of democracy in Pakistan to the inheritance of a strong military culture and infrastructure at its birth. Both agree that the role of secular institutions, such as the judiciary, in the evolution of democracy is vital.[54] The American researcher scholar and academic Philip Oldenburg sees both countries as 'fraternal twins', where the appetite for democracy in India was whetted early and continued in a self-replicating fashion from election to election.[55]

In both countries, the role of the army is unique and decisive. While it is seen as the illegitimate power centre in Pakistan and the cause of many of her troubles, the political 'inaction' of the Indian Army remains undervalued in its contribution to the growth of democratic space. Is there a nexus between the 'non-event' of a coup and the growth of democracy? Have there been instances where civil–military relations in India broke down to the extent of 'justifying' a military coup? If so, what factors precluded such a reaction? Correspondingly, what factors led to Pakistan being subjected to military rule for significant parts of its history? How damaging was this to its democratic trajectory? What led to the army's foray into politics and its continuance there?

This book seeks to examine these and related questions as to the interface between armies and the growth of democracy in India and Pakistan, from 1947 to the present day, with a chapter on Bangladesh. It looks at episodes in times of war and peace alike, when relations between the army and the civilian government were seriously strained. And the diametrically opposite reactions of the armies in two countries, that were once one.

[illegible] in the Indian Army [illegible] in the world of [illegible] between the [illegible] and the growth of democracy [illegible] civil [illegible] in India [illegible] [illegible] appointment [illegible] India [illegible] being [illegible] [illegible] the question of [illegible] [illegible]

This book [illegible] to examine these and related questions [illegible] relations between armies and [illegible] in India and Pakistan from 1947 to the present day, with a [illegible] on Bangladesh [illegible] [illegible]

India: The Enablement

1

Kashmir (1947–48)

'The Indian Army continued by choice to remain away from politics and socially distant from the political class, which continued to ignore the importance of the army despite its praiseworthy role during the near civil war conditions during the partition of India and the war in Kashmir.'

—Major General L.S. Lehl (Retired), cited in
Major General Ian Cardozo (Retired) (Ed.),
The Indian Army: A Brief History

The conception of India as the 'Hindu other' and the demand for Kashmir were integral to the idea of Pakistan as a conglomeration of Muslim-dominated states in undivided India.[1] India, on the other hand, was not obsessed with Pakistan being a largely Muslim state or, for that matter, the large presence of minorities in its citizenry. Indeed, some states and territories were minority-dominated, for instance, Punjab (Sikhs), Kashmir (Muslims) and states in the North-east that would come to be created over the years (Christians). India also believed that if Maharaja Hari Singh of Kashmir and the state's most popular political leader, Sheikh Abdullah, joined the Union, it would demonstrate 'the hollowness of the two-nation theory'.[2]

During the transfer of power and the consequent merger of princely states into the Dominion (later Republic) of India, the 'troublesome' states were Junagadh, Hyderabad and Kashmir—for the resistance offered by their princely rulers to the idea of integration with India.[3] Jinnah was hopeful of the last three fully integrating into Pakistan and 'riding in triumph into Kashmir',[4] but to his dismay, all three chose (with varying degrees of reluctance and stratagem) to be part of India. The military option in Junagadh and Hyderabad was very much on the table. Though used moderately in Hyderabad, it was carried out under camouflage as 'police action'.[5] In Kashmir, the Indian Army was directly called in to intervene on account of the stalemate.

Sardar Patel had, while overseeing the unification of 560 princely states with the speed of a 'soft whirlwind',[6] informed Maharaja Hari Singh in June 1947 that independence was not an option and that his state would necessarily need to accede to India or Pakistan. When the state faced infiltration from Pakistani intruders, Krishna Menon offered Indian military assistance to a desperate Maharaja only if it acceded to the Indian Union.[7] This led to its accession to India in October 1947. The resultant introduction of the Indian Army to counter Pakistani insurgents and forces led to the first military conflict between the two nations.

These operations merit some elaboration. Vide a 'top secret' document dated 20 August 1947, which was accidentally opened by Major (later Major General) O.S. Kalkat as the brigade major of a brigade in Bannu, Pakistan, the Pakistani plan for the capture of Kashmir by force was discovered.[8] Code-named Operation Gulmarg, the plan was to be implemented through a collaboration of Pakistani troops, Lashkar extremists and tribals from the NWFP. When Major Kalkat managed to escape to India and disclose the plan to Defence Minister Baldev Singh and senior army officers, he was thought to be 'hallucinating'.[9]

However, once the gravity of the incursion was understood, the attacks from bases in Pakistan were clearly construed as an act of invasion on what was now Indian territory. Though Pakistan denied its hand in the happenings in Jammu and Kashmir, independent observers were convinced of its complicity.[10]

Major K.C. Praval, author of the influential work *The Indian Army after Independence,* confirms that it was known 'early enough' that Major General Akbar Khan, who was at the time director of Weapons and Equipment at Pakistan's Army Headquarters and functioned under the nom de plume 'General Tariq', 'had organized the invasion'.[11] The Indian troops reacted swiftly. On hearing of the landing of these troops at Srinagar, Jinnah was furious and 'ordered' General Sir Douglas Gracey (who was at the time acting as Pakistan's commander-in-chief in the temporary absence of General Messervy) to send regular troops into Kashmir. This could not be done sans the orders of the Supreme Commander, Field Marshal Sir Auchinleck, who curtly informed Jinnah that on account of Jammu and Kashmir's accession to India, any intervention by Pakistani troops would amount to an invasion and 'would involve automatically and immediately the withdrawal of every British officer serving with the newly formed Pakistan Army'.[12] As the Pakistan Army was heavily reliant on British officers, Jinnah recalled his orders,[13] and a confrontation was temporarily averted.

On the resumption of hostilities, the Indian Army undertook 'Operation Rescue', spearheaded by Colonel (later Field Marshal) Sam Manekshaw and Air Commodore (later Air Marshal) H.C. Dewan. After continuous combat for several months in a typically war-like scenario, the Indian troops were able to push back the Pakistani army and infiltrators in May 1948,[14] leading to a premature ceasefire at India's instance under the auspices of the United Nations.

The Government of India, through the Ministry of Defence, released an official version of the 1948 Operations titled *Operations in Jammu & Kashmir 1947–48* as late as 1987. The version concluded with an expectedly fair-weather observation: 'Thus in the very first military campaign forced on India after her Independence and Partition, her totally unprepared armed forces and many civilians gave an account of themselves of which any nation may feel proud. Her good old sword (sic), the world saw, was still not rusted. And this ancient land of sages was also the land of heroes.'[15] The unsaid part remains—that an unfavourable outcome in Kashmir at the time could have jeopardized the geopolitical stability of the region and embarrassed India considerably. This is particularly relevant as there was 'no preparation beforehand' by the army for such a task.[16]

Being an official work, the book glosses over the efficacy of the ceasefire that was struck at a time when the Indian forces were bordering on settling the larger Kashmir dispute. Lieutenant General S.K. Sinha (Retired) describes the episode as 'one of the finest hours of the Indian Army' though it remains 'a point of debate that the war could have ended more favourably, if a cease-fire had not been imposed for another few months'.[17] Many veterans still maintain that this would have put to naught the Kashmir issue, though it is simplistic to believe that Pakistan would have steered clear of precipitating the matter (politically or otherwise) in the future.

In *Without Baggage: A Personal Account of the Jammu and Kashmir Operations 1947–49*, a book written soon after the skirmish but published only after author Lieutenant General Vas's retirement in 1987, the author predicts fairly accurately that 'the enemy' [Pakistan] would continue to engage India in low-scale combat and 'undiplomatic means, short of war'. He does not resist a comment on the politics of the issue, and bemoans that the army must assume the 'difficult and thankless' task of advising the government on matters of fighting a 'defensive war' as those who ought to be future statesmen are rarely prepared in a democracy where leaders are elected and changed periodically.[18] This betrays a glimpse of how the civilian leadership is viewed by its military counterparts—with a sense of despondency. On the other hand, the army in Pakistan would, in the same period (1948–87), assume a prolific political avatar, as is discussed separately.

The fact remains that as early as 1948, the two armies had a face-off in what was a full-blown and lengthy, though localized, war. The unexpected attack on Kashmir in 1948 required the interim government in India at the time (remember, the first general election was held only in 1951–52) to call up the army for a military solution. By then, the Kashmir issue had already bubbled up to the United Nations and India had committed, reluctantly, to holding a plebiscite in Kashmir, a decision that caused Prime Minister Nehru considerable heartburn[19] and has continued to keep the Kashmir issue boiling internationally.

In Pakistan, the Muslim League, as a fledgling political party, had already betrayed its dependence on the army in politically sensitive operations, which would have telling consequences on the impact of the military in Pakistan's early political trajectory. The Indian leadership under Nehru at the time was described as being an '*ahimsic* mould', bitten by the 'bug of world peace' and driven by 'Hindu morality'.[20] Air Marshal Nehra points to the close affinity between the British political leadership and the military—an institution the British nurtured, in contrast with the Indian leadership, soon after Independence, which viewed the army as an imperialistic remnant that was sidelined from its inception.[21]

The consequences of the role played by the respective armies on the future of democracy in India and Pakistan were evident as early as 1948, and played out in diametrically contrasting ways, as the subsequent chapters will disclose.

Both countries at the time were vulnerable to military coups as civilian structures of governance were yet to be firmly installed, and the introduction of the army to the limelight could easily have encouraged political adventurism on its part, as Pakistan showed in this early decade.

2

The Nehru–Menon–Kaul Axis

'The King [George IV] gave the officers dispensation from drinking to his health or standing for the National Anthem . . . as their loyalty could never be in doubt.'

—Lieutenant Colonel R.J. Dickinson, *Officers' Mess: Life and Customs in the Regiments*

It has been said that 'distrust of the soldiers and even fear of a coup has never been far from the minds of the politicians in India', lacking the confidence of Western political scientists in 'the invulnerability and vitality of [its] civilian order'.[1] India's first Prime Minister, Jawaharlal Nehru, brought to the office a strong dislike for the armed forces. He wrote disparagingly of the soldier,

> . . . bred in a different atmosphere, where authority reigns and criticism is not tolerated. So he [the soldier] resents the advice of others, and, when he errs, errs thoroughly and persists in error. For him the chin is more important than the mind or brain . . . stiffening to attention, drops his humanity and, acting as an automation, shoots and kills inoffensive and harmless persons who have done him no ill.[2]

He viewed the army as a remnant of the Raj and largely disregarded the military as an institution of worth at the political high table. Defence budgets were mediocre as he and his advisers saw defence spending as detrimental to both economic growth and civilian dominance.[3] The increasing tensions with China and the 1958 coup by Ayub Khan in Pakistan, however, prompted Nehru to appoint V.K. Krishna Menon as his minister of defence to improve military self-reliance, particularly through indigenous production.[4] The economic cost of militarization after Independence was preferred over the 'political cost if the standing army had been disbanded'[5]—the idea of disbanding a standing army being not entirely outside the realm of consideration at the time, though was a remote possibility at best.

On Nehru's attitude towards the army, Cohen comments, 'Nehru not only disliked the armed forces, *he distrusted them*. One of Menon's tasks was to help control the generals.'[6] (Emphasis supplied.) Ironically, the leadership was more focused on controlling its own military, rather than developing a robust military doctrine and infrastructure.

It has been suggested that the civilian leadership, headed by Nehru, was so uncomfortable with a popular and opinionated army leadership that it packed off General (later Field Marshal) Cariappa to New Zealand as the high commissioner on his retirement in 1953, rather than providing him with a gubernatorial posting in one of the states in India.[7] The fact that the general's appointment to New Zealand had anything to do with his growing 'political' posture is refuted in his biography by his son, Air Marshal K.C. 'Nanda' Cariappa.[8] Field Marshal Cariappa only assumed an overt political avatar much later when he fought an election from the North-East Mumbai Lok Sabha constituency, as an independent in 1971, and lost.[9]

The popularity of General K.S. Thimayya, who was COAS between 1957 and 1961, also caused considerable disquiet to the civilian leadership[10], leading to an explosive showdown between the general and the civilian establishment. Prior to his appointment as defence minister, Krishna Menon led most of India's delegations to the UN and was closely involved with the Ministry of External Affairs. Krishna Menon was an old friend of Nehru's and his proximity to the prime minister initially augured well for the forces. However, a strong personality clash and a difference of opinion saw Menon at loggerheads with General Thimayya.[11]

A winner of the Distinguished Service Order for leading his battalion in operations in Burma during the Second World War, with a prolific military record, including an enviable record at the helm of the UN Peacekeeping Force to Cyprus and as the head of the Korean Neutral Nations Repatriation Commission, General Thimayya was the only Indian to have commanded a brigade before Independence. He commanded the Indian brigade that formed part of the British Commonwealth Occupation Force in Japan. Thimayya had once asked Motilal Nehru whether he should resign his army commission and join the nationalist movement. (This was an indication that the military was otherwise detached from the independence struggle.) The latter advised him clairvoyantly to stay on in the army on the ground that free India 'would need officers like him'.[12]

However, Thimayya and Menon differed sharply on the threat perception vis-à-vis China, with the former regarding the threat as being clear and present, while the defence minister shrugged it off and confined his focus to Pakistan. Initially, the two men established a good working relationship. To his credit, Menon took prompt decisions; new ordnance plants came up and he authorized many new barracking and housing schemes. Like Nehru, Menon had leftist leanings and had faith in China's good intentions.[13] Writing of this period, Air Commodore Jasjit Singh observes that Menon had 'a deep-rooted, almost ideological, belief that China would never go to war with India [and] the Minister reduced the senior military leadership to simply being bystanders'.[14] Prime Minister Nehru too, innocently believed that the Chinese would never go to war. Events like the building of the Aksai Chin Road and the arrest of Indian personnel did not raise any alarms either.

While the Chinese were building the infrastructure that would enable them to launch their forces from the Himalayas, the Indian Army (4 Infantry Division) was too busy building residential accommodation for itself at Ambala. The divisional commander at the time was Major General B.M. Kaul, who had personally overseen the project. More on him, presently.

Curiously, in 1958, India also permitted a Chinese military delegation, led by Marshal Ye Jianying, to undertake a close inspection of India's defence installations. Under General Kaul's auspices, 4 Division made a demonstration at Ambala for the Chinese.[15] Ironically, this was the Division that suffered enormous casualties in the 1962 War at the hands of the Chinese troops.

The short-sightedness of the defence minister apart, the last straw that broke the proverbial camel's back was Menon's inexplicable decision to promote General Kaul to the rank of lieutenant general, thereby superseding officers senior to him.[16] Kaul was a Kashmiri and closely known to Nehru, a fact that Menon obviously took cognizance of. Kaul received many other assignments from Nehru which were not a part of his military duty, including a role in the arrest of Sheikh Abdullah in 1953. Not only did this bring him closer to the political leadership, it also *brought political influence closer to the army*.

The 'accepted practice' was for a committee of senior officers, presided over by the COAS, to recommend names to the government, based on a detailed assessment of the officers who qualified for promotion; 'it was also the usual practice for the Government to accept them'.[17] Accordingly, General Thimayya recommended the names of major generals P.S. Gyani, P.P. Kumaramangalam and B.M. Kaul (in that order) for promotion to the two available posts of lieutenant general. However, the Cabinet, acting on the defence minister's advice, promoted generals Kumaramangalam and Kaul.

On promotion, Kaul was appointed quartermaster general at Army Headquarters, and would meet the prime minister in the evenings, when the latter was in a relaxed mood.[18] General Thimayya knew of Kaul's minimal combat experience, because of his being an Army Service Corps (ASC) officer. Besides, the promotion was seen as an affront to the COAS's position. Unable to withstand such overreach, on 31 August 1959, General Thimayya tendered his resignation to Prime Minister Nehru, stating among other things how 'impossible it was for (him) and the other two Chiefs of Staff' to carry out their responsibilities 'under the present Defence Minister'.[19] The text of the resignation letter read:

> You will remember a few days ago I mentioned to you how impossible it was for me and the other two Chiefs of Staff to carry out our responsibilities under the present Defence Minister and that we sought your advice. Since then you have conveyed our feelings to the Minister of Defence and he quite rightly feels that my talking to you directly is an act of disloyalty to him. Under these circumstances you will understand how impossible it is for me to carry out my duties as Chief of the Army Staff under Mr. Krishna Menon.

> I, therefore, have no alternative but to submit my resignation from my present appointment and that you will permit me to proceed on long leave pending retirement. The interest of the Army and my loyalty to the country forces me to take this step after 33 years of service to the Indian Army both in war and peace.[20]

General Thimayya's resignation left the nation astonished and provoked strong reactions, largely against the defence minister. Indian historian Ramachandra Guha recounts, that '[even] the normally pro-government *Hindustan Times* said that Krishna Menon must go, not Thimayya' and that the minister had reduced the armed forces to 'a state of near-demoralization by trying to create, at the highest level, a cell of officers who would be personally loyal to him'.[21]

Sensing the gravity of the situation, Nehru persuaded General Thimayya to withdraw his resignation, offering the olive branch of consulting him on important matters such as promotions. Convinced that Nehru sincerely meant to investigate the matter and take action to confine Menon's conduct to the proper scope of a minister, Thimayya withdrew his resignation. However, this proved to be a smokescreen, with Nehru criticizing Thimayya in Parliament once the latter had withdrawn his resignation in good faith.[22]

This was a humiliation of the COAS and army alike. The officers, of course, were now further demoralized that their favourite 'Timmy' (as General Thimayya was fondly known) was 'misled' into recalling his resignation and more so that the civilian government now completely called the shots. Notwithstanding this development, the army refrained from any overt action to protest its position, much less question the civilian leadership's right and legitimacy to hold its own.

Indian historian Srinath Raghavan argues that the reasons for Thimayya's resignation 'went rather deeper', and puts it down to Menon's resistance to taking the threat from China seriously and even dissuading Nehru from meeting Ayub Khan on a stopover in India in September 1959 to explore possible 'joint defence arrangements' to tackle the growing threat from China.[23] Incredible as it may seem, Ayub did indeed make such a proposal, as reported in the *Statesman* of 2 September 1959.[24]

Thimayya's resignation brought to the fore the seriousness of the threat from China. Despite Nehru's misconceived slogan of 'Hindi Chini Bhai Bhai', China had established posts and built a tarred road up to and beyond Indian borders. The Opposition and the media asked for Menon's resignation. Home Minister Govind Ballabh Pant advised the prime minister to change Menon's portfolio. Some even accused Menon of being a 'Communist supporter'.[25] However, for reasons unexplained, Nehru remained faithful to Menon, a decision that was to affect Indian history and military reputation alike.

Praval comments on Menon's influence thus:

> Till the border clashes of 1959, the Defence portfolio did not have much political importance. The country's pacifist approach and the low priority given to the development of its armed forces were responsible for this. Politicians who counted looked for portfolios like Home, Finance and Industry. Barring one or two exceptions, the Defence Ministers till 1957 were weak or indifferent men and senior officers of the armed forces often got the impression that their demands for better equipment fell through owing to the inability of the Defence Minister to pull his weight. All this changed with the arrival of Menon.[26]

Menon's dealings with his senior military officers bred divisions and undermined the discipline and morale of the officer cadre. General Kaul relates in his autobiography how his own seniors sometimes asked him to put in a word in the right quarters when they wanted something done for themselves.[27] This set the tone for increasing political interference in military promotions that is today a major aberration in the autonomy of the Indian armed forces.[28]

When the time came for Thimayya to retire, in accordance with custom, he recommended that Lieutenant General S.P.P. Thorat should be his successor. The government disregarded Thimayya's recommendation and named P.N. Thapar as COAS. Indian military historian Arjun Subramaniam explains that 'the Nehru–Menon combine were said to be uncomfortable with the prospect of an aggressive Maratha taking charge of the Indian Army and influencing their China strategy. They instead appointed a milder and more acceptable General P.N. Thapar, who was not considered much of a strategist.'[29] The government was impervious to receiving hard advice on China and, with Thorat passed over, the coast was clear. Of course, this would have serious ramifications in the war to come in 1962, and also lead to the conception of a new brand of officer—the 'pliant general'.[30]

Menon himself was rather eccentric but strikingly intelligent and egoistic, described as 'acerbic and vitriolic', indulging in 'unnecessary rudeness'.[31] He was known to encourage officers he liked to be in direct contact with him 'ignoring the (Service) Chiefs'[32], which was bound to undermine discipline and politicize the military. Menon's biographer T.J.S. George describes him as a defence minister who had been successful in 'short-circuiting' the bureaucratic channels and was a minister who was 'accessible to all'.[33] George interestingly also states that General Thimayya was 'close to Menon' prior to the Kaul episode, and reiterated that he (General Thimayya) had '*no doubt about civilian authority over [the] military*'.[34] (Emphasis supplied.)

Another perspective on hand is that 'the appointment of the army chief had always been driven by political considerations (and) Thimayya himself had been chosen because of his acceptability to the political leadership.[35] Jairam Ramesh, in his biography of Krishna Menon, reinforces this dimension:

> Thimayya was third in order of seniority. Yet, given his track record, his public persona both within the army and outside and his equation with Nehru, he was appointed the army chief. Krishna Menon would undoubtedly have been consulted but having known Thimayya earlier, he would have registered no objections to the seniority principle being overlooked. Four years later he would invoke this very principle while selecting Thimayya's successor. The combination of Krishna Menon and Thimayya was expected to infuse new life and dynamism into the Ministry of Defence, which till then had had a somnolent reputation. Nobody could have expected or guessed that within two years the two would be at each other's throats.[36]

The differences, it was clear, were over the perceived threats from Pakistan and China, and at a personal level, driven by a personality clash among friends-turned-foes. The prime minister's proximity to *both* the individuals perhaps complicated the situation even further. Added to this personal dimension, was the fact that 'Thimayya was acutely aware of the prime minister's deep distrust of the military' and was bothered by its constant neglect.[37] Journalist and writer Shiv Kunal Verma notes that although publicly Nehru was seen to be fond of his top general, 'however, behind his back . . . *he viewed Thimayya as a rival who could challenge his position as the undisputed head of the Indian Union.*'[38] (Emphasis supplied.)

In fact, a 'spy system' seemed to be operating within the army, with certain officers 'clandestinely sending reports to (General) Kaul about the activities of their seniors' who were not seen as being close to the General.[39] One victim of this 'espionage' was Major General (later Field Marshal) Sam Manekshaw, then the commandant of the Defence Service Staff College at Wellington. Manekshaw—a Military Cross winner for exemplary bravery in Burma, 1942, and an officer with significant combat experience (having suffered nine bullet wounds in his intestine and survived)—did not shy away from criticizing Kaul for his 'political' approach, especially his unholy nexus with Menon.[40] At the time when his promotion to the rank of lieutenant general had been announced, and when Kaul was chief of general staff (CGS), the latter, directly, initiated and conducted an inquiry against Manekshaw, based on reports from insiders.

The charge, among others, was that Manekshaw had hung portraits of British viceroys, governors-general and commanders-in-chief in his office, and was thereby more loyal to England than to the Union of India. The 'intelligence report' on General Manekshaw was produced by the chief of the Intelligence Bureau B.N. Mullik 'at the behest of' Lieutenant General Kaul, though Mullick did not depose at the inquiry and General Kaul ultimately resigned 'in disgrace'.[41]

The facts were that these pictures had come from the Defence Services Staff College, Quetta, as India's share of the assets of that institution and on Manekshaw's taking over as instructor, he found them dumped in a warehouse and resolved to hang them on his office walls. The portraits included stalwarts such as Clive, Warren Hastings, (Field Marshal) Kitchener and others who had been closely involved in the administration of India. Nehru, the COAS and other dignitaries had since visited the Staff College (at Wellington) and had never objected to these pictures.[42]

Eventually, as expected, Manekshaw was exonerated, but only after an ill-advised and much publicized foray by the defence minister into the affairs of the army. In fact, Lieutenant General Daulet Singh (later killed in a helicopter crash in Poonch in 1963) recommended disciplinary action against those who had made false allegations, but no such action was pursued.

It is also anecdotal that Field Marshal Manekshaw, as divisional commander, was once asked by Menon what he thought of General Thimayya, his COAS. Manekshaw retorted that he was not allowed to 'think' of his senior, to which Menon aggressively responded, 'Stop your British way of thinking. I can get rid of him.' Manekshaw replied, 'You can get rid of him, but then I will have another Chief, and I won't be allowed to think about him. I think it is very wrong asking me, a major general, about General Thimayya. Tomorrow you will be asking my brigadier what he thinks of me. It is surely not the right thing for the Army's discipline.'[43]

Perhaps the fact that the British military tradition of professional soldiering was thriving at the highest ranks of the Indian Army ensured minimal politicization of the institution, notwithstanding aberrations such as the Menon–Kaul episode under discussion.

Ultimately, despite overwhelming provocation and despite General Thimayya being (initially) as close to Prime Minister Nehru as Lieutenant General Kaul was to Defence Minister Krishna Menon, any discussion of a coup by the Indian Army as an institution was liable to be 'dismissed as unfounded'[44] as the political leadership was otherwise strong and credible, and the army was itself apolitical and professional. Hypothetically, the 'coup', if any, could have been initiated by Menon and Kaul, both of whom, some felt, saw themselves as worthy successors to Nehru.[45] American journalist Welles Hangen conjured up a possible scenario where 'military rule could be imposed on India while Kaul stayed discreetly in the background' as 'a Nasser to Thapar's Naguib or some other venerable façade' within which arrangement he could 'rationalize the demise of Indian democracy as skillfully as he does his relationship with (Krishna) Menon.'[46] Hangen caustically adds that General Kaul's performance 'would certainly have more drive and polish than does the faltering Indian democracy in the second half of a cyclonic century of change . . . He could be the idol of lovers of order.'[47]

Though Hangen's theory may seem simplistic in hindsight, at the given point in time (1960–61), it could not be completely discarded. At this stage, Indian democracy was still finding its feet and the judiciary was yet to impose itself as the ultimate protector of democracy, which is part of the basic structure of the Constitution. The irony of the discourse is that while the top brass of the military leadership, under General Thimayya, was averse to any political adventurism, the civilian leadership itself was propping up individual officers such as Kaul and trying to undermine the army. It was however clear that, *as an institution,* the army would not let itself be dragged into any narrative around military rule.

As discussed previously, though Nehru was critical in Parliament of Thimayya's resignation after having persuaded him to withdraw the same, the debacle in the ensuing 1962 China War (discussed in the next chapter) made the civilian leadership value the priceless advice of generals such as Thimayya and Cariappa, both of whom discouraged any confrontation with China. The government rued having paid heed to the divergent views of Defence Minister Krishna Menon. Menon himself was the ultimate casualty of the 1962 War—resigning his post and fading into oblivion. Significantly, on account of ill-advised civilian decision-making, the Indian Army suffered not only an enormous loss of its officers and soldiers, but also loss of face. This would paradoxically help it reclaim its position at the political high table, without assuming a political avatar, unlike its counterpart in Pakistan which had already done so.

3

War with China

> *'India could not retreat militarily because it could not retreat politically.'*
>
> —Stephen P. Cohen, *India: Emerging Power*

Lieutenant General M.L. Chibber in his book *Military Leadership to Prevent Military Coup* notes that the politicization of the officer corps by the 'subjective control' of army promotions by the government is the 'first step to Praetorianism' and that the 1962 debacle paradoxically saved India from this catastrophe.[1]

The complacency induced by the belief held by the political leadership that for all the aggressive posturing, the Chinese would never go to war over the border dispute, proved to be fatal. Indeed, in 1960, General Thimayya went to Italy to study its alpine troops and tactics and, on his return, recommended the raising of some light and mobile divisions for the defence of the Northern/Sino borders. The proposal was rejected by the government as 'unwarranted'.[2]

Ironically, even Lieutenant General Kaul was in favour of a proactive reaction to the Chinese but his views were shot down by Nehru. The reason, according to author and scholar Lorne J. Kavic, seemed to be,

> [that] the Government's assessment was that the Chinese were not as strong as they were made out to be; that they had their internal problems and if India dealt with them strongly, she would have the better of them. It was considered that all the scare [sic] the Army high command were making was a military miscalculation.[3]

Krishna Menon, who was fixated with anti-Pakistan and anti-West sentiments, admonished the army top brass with a grossly misjudged prophecy, stating 'Pakistan is our only enemy. The Western Powers are trying their tricks to make India fight China but China will not attack us.'[4] By then, the Indian and Chinese troops at Ladakh had already clashed. Incidentally, when Field Marshal Cariappa, as Commander-in-Chief (as the COAS was then called), had previously suggested positioning troops along the McMahon line as the Chinese might have set their sights on this region, Nehru is reported to have flared up, thumped the table hard and said, '*It is not the business of the Commander-in-Chief to tell the Prime Minister who is going to attack us where.* In fact the Chinese will defend our Eastern frontier . . . You mind only Kashmir and Pakistan.'[5] (Emphasis supplied.)

Such admonition of sound military advice from the commander-in-chief reflected the awkward civil–military relationship at the time. Ironically, Mao was open to brainstorming with his top brass—both civil and military—on methodologies for the imminent war with India.[6]

Even Sardar Patel (then deputy prime minister), as far back as 1950, had described China as being 'unfriendly' and its policy 'expansionist' and that the invasion of Tibet would bring the Chinese Army to 'the gates of India and throw into the melting pot all past frontier settlements with Tibet'.[7] The response, in keeping with the fetish for reducing defence spending (and possibly Chinese appeasement) was the retrenchment of about 50,000 soldiers in 1951![8]

Senior officers like Lieutenant General Daulet Singh, General Officer Commanding-in-Chief (GOC-i-C) Western Command, also advised against provoking a clash with the Chinese due to the lack of preparedness as hostilities would be inevitable if the sensitive Aksai Chin Road (vital for the Chinese) was threatened.[9] He, instead, recommended the strengthening of troops in Ladakh to a division of four brigades to match the Chinese, but was overruled. In late August 1959, there was a clash at Longju, along the McMahon Line, and later in October at Kongka Pass in Ladakh, with allegations of trespass from both sides.[10] Nine Indian soldiers died in the attack on Kongka, but the attack did not serve as an alarm call.

As a shock to the smug leadership in Delhi, on 8 September 1962, the forward posts of the Assam Rifles at Che Dong sent a frantic radio signal, intimating that about 600 Chinese soldiers had descended on the post and surrounded it. Menon sent for Lieutenant General L.P. 'Bogey' Sen, Army Commander of the Eastern Command, the next day as Prime Minister Nehru was away in London at the time, and directed that the Chinese be evicted, if necessary, by force, from the Indian territory they had trespassed on.[11] However, by then, the Chinese were already on Thag La in strength, with regular People's Liberation Army troops.

The lack of preparation or foresight was obvious from Brigadier (later Major General) D.K. 'Monty' Palit's statement, as director of Military Operations at Army Headquarters a month earlier in August 1962, that for the next few years there was no question of any combat in a war-like sense with the Chinese '*as they were incapable of mounting a serious offensive till the completion of their rail-link with Lhasa some time in 1964*'.[12] (Emphasis supplied.) This was despite Lieutenant General Kaul's premonition that the Chinese would attack India in late 1962, a fact apparently not disclosed to his colleagues at Army HQ.[13]

The situation brought to the fore the peculiar dilemma of uniformed subordination to uninformed civilian dictates. For the fallacies of the government at the time, the senior army officers who were away from action did not acquit themselves honourably enough, failing to consult the field commanders before assuring the government of instant military responses, which were horribly weighed against the Indian Army.[14]

Only in November 1961 did Prime Minister Nehru come up with what is described as the 'forward policy', which, in spirit, was still defensive. It provided (verbatim):

> a. So far as Ladakh is concerned, we are to patrol as far as possible from our present positions towards the international border. This will be done with a view to establishing our posts which should prevent the Chinese from advancing further and also dominating any posts which they may have already established in our territory. *This must be done without getting involved in a clash with the Chinese, unless this becomes necessary in self-defence.*
>
> b. As regards UP and other northern areas (NEFA) there are not the same difficulties as in Ladakh. We should, as far as practicable, go forward and be in occupation of the whole frontier. Where there are any gaps, they must be covered by patrolling or by posts.
>
> c. *In view of the numerous operational and administrative difficulties*, efforts should be made to position major concentration of forces along our borders in places conveniently *situated behind the forward posts* from where they could be maintained logistically and from where they can restore a border situation at short notice.[15] (Emphasis supplied.)

The implementation of this policy also left a lot to be desired. For instance, Lieutenant General Umrao Singh protested to Lieutenant General Sen about 7 Brigade being hustled into the impossible venture of evicting the Chinese from Thag La, more so, as the troops were short of rations and resources such as clothing for cold weather, tents, etc. Expectedly, he was overruled and ordered on 15 September 1962 'to capture, as soon as possible after arrival on the Namka Chu, the Chinese position 900 metres North-East of Che Dong, contain the Chinese South of Thag La and, if possible, establish two posts atop the Thag La Ridge'[16]—which were at a height of over 5250 metres. Nehru and Menon were both abroad at the time and COAS General Thapar's request to the Deputy Defence Minister K. Raghuramaiah to reconsider the decision also fell on deaf ears.[17] Though the COAS had not earlier raised any demur, the Indian public was getting increasingly restless for retaliation.

To break the impasse, the government directed 4 Corps to undertake the operation to evict the Chinese; in lieu of Lieutenant General Umrao Singh, Lieutenant General Kaul was chosen as his replacement. The eviction was to be carried out from Namka Chu, beyond the McMahon Line and strictly not in Indian territory! Carried on the back of a porter, Kaul made the climb only to discover for himself the gravity of Operation Leghorn, though it was never recommended that the same be called off.[18] Soon after, Kaul relinquished command in order to return to Delhi and give a first-hand account to the government; meanwhile, the status quo continued. The political leadership remained adamant that critical but highly treacherous positions such as Tsangle, at the intersection of Bhutan, Tibet and India be maintained in order to display a show of strength, though the army commanders (including Kaul) advised against such a suicidal task.

The plot got more absurd when Lieutenant General Kaul took ill but continued to exercise command over 4 Corps from his bed at home. According to precedent, when a commander becomes a casualty and is evacuated, as Kaul was, the next officer in seniority assumes control. However, as Praval pithily puts it, '. . . in the Army of 1962, a person with Kaul's connections could get away with anything'.[19] Kaul himself, towards the end, even sought foreign (American) military intervention to rescue the situation, causing his DMO, Army HQ Brigadier Palit, to comment that Kaul sounded 'so desperate so as to be demented' and the COAS to conclude that Kaul had 'finally lost his mind'.[20]

At Tsangle, the Chinese took merely three hours to demolish the resistance and in those few hours, 282 Indian soldiers were killed and the rest captured.[21] Moreover, in the 1962 campaign generally, many soldiers perished due to starvation and hypothermia, due to the lack of resources.

However, the troops fought gallantly in the face of severe adversity—in terms of the lack of resources, the extreme weather, a dominant opponent and the lack of strategy of offence on its part. The loss was not only of men, but a demolition of the morale of the army, brought about in no small measure by the collective failure of the civilian leadership as also certain senior officers. But markedly, there was no trace of a protest, much less a revolt, by the troops against the leadership of the time, despite 'just' cause and the acute sympathies of the Indian public. Of course, the abject failings were not those of the civilian leadership alone.

In response to the debacle, on 24 October, the highly regarded Lieutenant General Harbakhsh Singh took over 4 Corps, and Major General A.S. Pathania replaced Lieutenant General Niranjan Prasad. Menon himself was subjected to severe criticism for the disaster and Jawaharlal Nehru relieved him of the defence portfolio, and retained it himself.

The anticlimax came about unexpectedly, on 20 November 1962, when the Chinese announced a unilateral ceasefire, effective from the midnight of 21 November. A combination of international pressure, the knowledge that extending the war in the approaching winter was going to be self-defeating and the satisfaction of having scored a victory over India apparently prompted this decision. As per the announcement, the Chinese troops agreed to withdraw on 1 December, though they remained in parts of Ladakh even thereafter. Unexpected as it was, the Indian media knew of the ceasefire before the Cabinet did![22] Shiv Kunal Verma, in his book *1962: The War That Wasn't*, points to the fact that the 'inexplicable and absurd' delay in New Delhi finding out about the ceasefire also left the troops high and dry. The Chinese field commanders issued orders to 'maximize Indian casualties' and avoid taking prisoners of war (POWs), thereby having 'annihilated surviving Indian troops'.[23] The author also accuses the then Prime Minister Nehru of the 'virtual destruction of his own military' and 'downgrading' the military in the paradigm of civil–military relations.[24]

On the 1962 debacle, Lieutenant General S.K. Sinha (Retired) comments:

> In this war, regrettably, both our political and military leadership failed totally and the nation suffered a traumatic defeat. Our faith in the infallibility of our foreign policy, the impregnability of the Himalayas and the invincibility of our Army was violently shaken to its roots. Yet it should not be forgotten that in places like Rezengla in Ladakh, our soldiers fought to the last man, last round, in keeping with the highest traditions of valour and sacrifice. Major Shaitan Singh and his gallant soldiers with their supreme sacrifice carved a special place for themselves in the annals of India's military history. It is also not fully known that *only about 5 per cent of the Army was involved in operations against the Chinese*. The bulk of the Army remained deployed near

> the border with Pakistan or inland in the country. Had the Chinese tried to continue the fight in the winter across their Himalayan line of communication, on the plains of Assam, matters may have been very different. It was an awareness of this military reality that prompted the Chinese to declare a unilateral cease-fire.[25] (Emphasis supplied.)

No doubt, there was tremendous gallantry on display, especially among the lower ranks of the army. However, the withdrawal of the Chinese appears to be more on account of international pressure rather than any deterrence of larger Indian troops being deployed along the border. The very fact that most of the troops were positioned along the Pakistan border and only 5 per cent were used to face the Chinese cried out for some soul-searching on the part of the leadership of the time.

The 1962 War had an instant impact on the top brass of the political and military leadership. Besides the 'sacking' of Menon, who was asked to resign and replaced as defence minister in due course by Y.B. Chavan, the COAS General P.N. Thapar also resigned, citing ill health, and was replaced by General J.N. Chaudhari. The omnipresent Lieutenant General Kaul retired prematurely, as did Lieutenant General Pathania. A formal inquiry was ordered under the auspices of Lieutenant General T.B. Henderson Brooks, though the contents of the inquiry remain classified till today across various governments.[26] The Henderson Brooks–Bhagat Committee (comprising Lieutenant General Brooks and Major General P.S. Bhagat) inexplicably failed to summon the most crucial 'witness' to the event—Lieutenant General B.M. Kaul, purportedly on the ground that he was senior to Lieutenant General Brooks, though it was stated that he was shielded by 'orders from above'.[27]

Though the committee was manned by army officers, Shiv Kunal Verma records that the report 'became a clever ploy for the government to deflect the blame *from itself onto the army*.'[28] The new defence minister, Y.B. Chavan (who had replaced Krishna Menon), let it be known that the government 'did not wish to institute an inquiry into high-level policies and decisions' and was to confine itself 'to analysing IV Corps' operations only', and that the failure was owing to the 'military commanders and to the tactical mishandling of troops on the ground'.[29] This was the stated position of the government despite the report neither reviewing (civilian) policy failures nor being made public. Yet, the army took it on the chin.

Notwithstanding this 'whitewash', the greater casualty, as Guha comments, was Nehru's reputation. In failing to protect the nation's territory, 'the border war was Nehru's most consequential failure in fifteen years as Prime Minister'.[30] This was reinforced by the fact that Nehru was instrumental in developing the self-defeating Indo–China policy that ultimately cost hundreds of lives and, more importantly, the stature of the armed forces.

The exponent of Panchsheel and the author of the slogan 'Hindi Chini Bhai Bhai' had paid little or no attention to cartographical warfare by China. On the other hand, the Indian government went out of its way to appease the Chinese. For instance, during the British regime, the Government of India had recognized only the suzerainty of China over Tibet. The new stated position referred to Tibet as a 'region of China'.[31] Academic Sisir Gupta sees this phase as an exception to the Chinese, otherwise seen as 'fanatic ideologues and brutal automatons' that has kept the Indian Army 'puzzled and impressed'.[32]

Major General 'Monty' Palit also attributes the failure of 1962 to a 'mood of combative smugness' on the part of the political leadership after the takeover of Goa in 1961 through Operation Vijay, so much so that Home Minister Lal Bahadur Shastri asserted in February 1962 that: 'If the Chinese will not vacate the areas occupied by her, India will have to repeat what she did in Goa. She will certainly drive out the Chinese forces.'[33] Vide Operation Vijay, the Indian armed forces had forced the Portuguese out of Goa, Daman and Diu when the colonists failed to vacate peacefully. However, it is intriguing, firstly, as to how the Portuguese managed to rule Goa for a full fourteen years after India's independence and secondly, as General Vassalo e Silva, the last Portuguese governor general of Goa, Daman and Diu, queried whether the Indian government would have fathomed the venture had the Chinese attacked India a little *before* Operation Vijay![34]

The fait accompli was a crushing defeat to India's forces in 1962 and also to its morale. The reasons for the defeat were a combination of lacunae in intelligence, leadership, operations and strategy. However, a singular cause appears to be the refusal on the part of the political leadership to allow the army to fully deploy its strategy and forces in the defence of the nation, and part acquiescence thereof by the army itself.[35] Nehru's biographer Sarvepalli Gopal records that he confessed to 'have been lacking' and having 'approached those things (the military's demand to import arms and equipment) in a somewhat amateurish way'.[36]

Notwithstanding this fiasco, the Indian leadership continued to nurture a constant, misguided fear of a military coup. Nehru had earlier turned down Lord Mountbatten's suggestion regarding the creation of the post of the chief of defence staff (CDS) and appoint General Thimayya to the post. Even after the Sino–Indian fiasco, Nehru's phobia remained constant; he wrote to Bertrand Russell in December 1962 that he was concerned by 'the danger of military mentality spreading in India and the power of the Army increasing'.[37] Prime Minister Nehru even 'firmly believed' that the army top brass was 'conjuring up the Chinese bogey' to get their demands through.[38] History proved him wrong. Some commented that besides the mind block against the army, the policy of 'austere non-alignment' brought upon India the 1962 War.[39]

The democratic government of the day did not suffer any real threat of a coup from the military leadership as the military top brass did not see it as a sufficient motive for forsaking its professional, apolitical avatar, and more so because the military top brass *itself* had a great deal to share in the blame.[40] Besides, the political leadership addressed the grievances of the military leadership with necessary transfers and replacements at both the political and military levels, and made strenuous efforts to reform civil–military relations.[41]

The army's role was recognized as being pivotal to the defence of the nation and the loss to China proved to be a turning point in the strengthening of the military in India, in matters that directly concerned the military.

It is to be mentioned that India and China clashed again in 1967, at the Himalayan passes Cho La and Nathu La, in the wake of the unrest in Sikkim for separation. This proved to be an unsung but telling victory for the Indian forces. Probal Dasgupta is one of the few to have covered this episode in his work *Watershed 1967: India's Forgotten Victory over China*. He comments:

> News of victories at Nathu La and Cho La flickered briefly on the front pages of mainstream Indian newspapers in 1967 but soon became mere passing mentions in the media. Over time, they would be forgotten. After the battles, a deflated Peking tacitly cooperated with New Delhi to hush up the news. But why did Delhi choose to downplay the battles? Perhaps

because the battles of 1967 were too closely tied to memories of the horrific defeat of 1962. Highlighting the victories of 1967 could bring into focus and remind people once again of the military indecisiveness and political ineptness displayed in 1962.[42]

4

War with Pakistan (1965)

'It had, indeed, been a war of missed opportunities, and to no purpose, political or military.'

—Major General Lachhman Singh Lehl, PVSM, VrC,
Missed Opportunities: Indo–Pak War 1965

Australian journalist and scholar Neville Maxwell analyses the post-1962 debacle as resulting in a change in the 'political position' of the Indian Army, with reduced interference by the civilian leadership of 'chastened politicians', who now knew 'their place', rather than 'cavalierly' showing the soldiers theirs.[1]

The fear of a military coup, however, seemed to endure even after the 1962 debacle. Lieutenant General Harbakhsh Singh attributes his being posted as general officer commanding-in-chief of the Western Command in 1964, instead of the expected posting at the Eastern Command, to the fact that the government was anxious about COAS General Chaudhari and Lieutenant General Sam Manekshaw (as he was then) planning a coup against it.[2] The government introduced 'counter-coup planning' and roped in the Intelligence Bureau (IB) to respond to this perceived 'crisis'. On the demise of Jawaharlal Nehru on 27 May 1964, when General Chaudhari ordered extra troops into the national capital, New Delhi, as a security measure to manage the swelling crowds of mourners, he was asked to show cause by Defence Minister Y.B. Chavan at the instance of the IB Chief—B.N. Mullik, who suspected a probable military manoeuvre.[3] Such was the trust deficit at the time.

The civilian leadership would have to rapidly fall back on its army to combat Pakistan in 1965. To better understand the preparedness for the 1965 operations, it is relevant to dwell a little further on the casualties of the 1962 showdown with China. The Chinese inflicted a total of 9743 casualties: 1423 killed, 3078 wounded, 1655 missing (believed killed) and 3587 prisoners captured, with a high casualty rate of 40 per cent.[4] Major General Palit candidly states:

> [A]ll of us—the PM, the government, the Army HQ and the Generals in the field—all must shoulder the blame for the operational trap into which we led ourselves. Our forces could *not* have stopped the Chinese . . . and should not have been sent there for that purpose.[5]

Against this backdrop, Major K.C. Praval closely analyses the political and other causes for the defeat. These causes deserve to be reproduced here in full:

1. 'The professional soldier after 1947 got *increasingly isolated* from the process of decision-making on defence matters. The situation had deteriorated to such an extent that written orders to the Chief of the Army Staff for evicting the Chinese from the border were handed over to him *signed by a mere joint secretary* in the Ministry of Defence.
2. 'Both in protocol and in terms of promotions, civil servants had improved their position considerably since 1947. The Army, for one reason or another, had been given step-motherly treatment in these spheres. Consequently, there was

a feeling amongst Army officers of *being denigrated* which led to lack of élan amongst them and to lowering of morale.

3. 'An officer who lacked the essential background and training was first elevated to the post of Chief of the General Staff at Army Headquarters merely on account of his political connection and then given command of a corps to fight the Chinese in NEFA. Because of the *political patronage*, Lieutenant General Kaul had become a law unto himself and ignored his military superiors.
4. 'The Government based its assessment of the intentions of a foreign power on the *personal whims* and beliefs of certain individuals instead of acting on the advice of successive Army Chiefs.
5. 'There was *no correlation* of the country's foreign policy with its defence capability. The Army was ordered to assert the country's claims without first ensuring that in the event of China asserting her counterclaims, it would have the capacity for adequate riposte. When Lieutenant General Daulet Singh recommended that the 'forward policy' be suspended in Ladakh till the Army had acquired this capability, he was told to carry on regardless of such considerations.
6. 'There was *political interference* in the tactical handling of the situation, for example the insistence on holding the indefensible positions on the Namka Chu and the post at Tsangle.
7. 'There was abject *failure of higher command* in the field in NEFA. Troops were continuously being reshuffled, no one was taking any decision in time, and when one was forthcoming it was entirely out of tune with the realities of the ground situation. Sound tactical decisions were replaced by gross interference at the sub-unit level.'[6] (Emphasis supplied.)

The disturbing development was the increasing politicization of the army, especially in the matter of promotions, as also bizarrely in operations. While this surely led to India's loss to China, the system corrected itself to the extent that Defence Minister Menon and Lieutenant General Kaul were ousted, as detailed earlier. But perceptibly, there was no semblance of a military resistance to civilian interference, and the political influence was itself not deep-rooted enough to change the ethos of the army.

Indeed, the shock of defeat to China aroused a powerful reaction and a new spirit of leadership, and collaboration between the government and the army. The loss to China led to India building a closer relationship with the United States, who obviously wanted to contain communist China, and aid the rapid growth of India's military assets and strategy. Defence spending and development increased radically and contributed to the development of indigenous industries such as Hindustan Aeronautics Limited, Bharat Electricals Limited, Bharat Earth Movers Limited and others.

Noticing the build-up of infrastructure, Pakistan's Foreign Minister Zulfikar Ali Bhutto advised President Ayub Khan that it was better to move against India before it grew too powerful.[7] At such time, the supply of modern military arms and Patton tanks (ironically, also from the USA) gave Pakistan a narrow edge over India.[8] Kashmir was always a fixation with every government in Pakistan. It chose to make a foray into the Rann of Kutch, a 23,000 square kilometre salt pan of a desert, with large parts of it being disputed territory, as a precursor to a strategic, localized attack in Jammu and Kashmir. This was done with the hope that the Pakistani 'irregular' troops would be supported by a local uprising against the Indian government. The Kutch suited Pakistan due to its proximity to Sind. Preparations for the incursion had been going on for some time. Conscription was introduced in Pakistan-occupied Kashmir for young men up to the age of twenty-five and a special paramilitary force of 1,50,000 'Mujahidins', or crusaders, was created for the purpose of supporting the army.[9] For reasons best known to it, the Pakistani leadership believed that the response to its attack would be confined to Kashmir alone.

When Pakistan chose to make its clandestine intrusion into Kutch in early-1965, followed by the foray into Kashmir with the support of tribal radicals, India's response was not localized and she reacted strongly across her Western border. India's troops marched into Lahore, provoking a full-fledged war. Even initially, when the early intrusions were noticed in Bhuj, Indian formations quickly took their place and Prime Minister Lal Bahadur Shastri informed the Lok Sabha in April 1965 (and the world at large) that the conflict could spread.[10] This temporarily caused a pullback, ordered by President Ayub Khan, only for infiltration to resume on a larger scale in Kashmir in August 1965, using the Haji Pir pass to cross into areas close to Srinagar and Gulmarg. This was part of Operation Gibraltar.[11]

Pakistan counted on the support of local Kashmiris to its army but, in many cases, the locals gave away precious information regarding the guerrillas to the Indian troops, who reacted swiftly and strongly.[12] The Indian Army seized Haji Pir and other critical positions under the able leadership of senior officers such as generals Bhagat, Dayal and Harbakhsh Singh—all gallantry award winners. The combat spread to Chhamb in the Punjab, resulting in a counteroffensive by India, who attacked the towns of Phillora and Pagowal, with a view to cutting off Sialkot from Lahore.[13] Unlike the 1962 War, the defence ministry *supported the army* in its decision to respond firmly and retaliate as per the operational plans devised by the COAS General Chaudhari. This change in position was a watershed in positive civil–military relations in the country, at the very least, in operational matters.

The UN Security Council intervened with the commencement of hostilities and India responded positively, while Pakistan did not. Despite her aggressive retaliation, India refrained from expanding the war to East Pakistan. Pakistan continued to use the settlement of the Kashmir issue as a prerequisite to any declaration of ceasefire. However, when the Pakistani troops suffered heavy losses in Khem Karan and the Sialkot sector, President Ayub Khan did a volte-face and, on 15 September 1965, called for 'a purposeful cease-fire and an honourable settlement'.[14] Accordingly, on 20 September, the Security Council adopted a resolution demanding a ceasefire with effect from 1230 hours (IST) on 22 September and a subsequent withdrawal of all armed personnel to positions held before 5 August 1965.[15] The Tashkent peace pact ensued in January 1966, with an agreement to yield territories usurped by both sides. Prime Minister Shastri passed away rather suddenly in Tashkent after providing commendable civilian command, as compared to the 1962 War with China.

For the 'China deniers' who discount her role in the conflict, Mao's biographers Jung Chang and Jon Halliday confirm that China was ready to 'nuclearize' the dispute in 1965, if needed, and was happy to trigger a faux border conflict along the China border so as to get Indian troops fighting on both fronts.[16]

The 1965 War redeemed the prestige of the Indian Army to a great extent and considerably diminished the stature of President Ayub Khan. The Army Commander of the Western Command in the 1965 War, Lieutenant General Harbakhsh Singh, observes that the material gains of India's achievements were 'very modest', that India's losses were lesser than those of Pakistan, that the Indian soldier provided 'moral ascendancy' over an 'arrogant foe' and significantly that the 'slur' of the 1962 attack had been wiped out so that the army enjoyed a 'prestige rarely equalled before'.[17]

The Indian Army had acquitted itself admirably under trying circumstances, with ordinary equipment and preparation, and won several tactical battles.[18] Senior officers believed that if the forces 'had more time', they would have 'done even better'.[19]

The 1965 War provided occasion for the US and the UK to suspend military aid to both countries who, as beneficiaries of military intelligence and arms, were not expected to set these off against one another. This also pre-empted the ambitions of Pakistan to continue the war, as it heavily depended on military supplies from the West.

The war exposed India's poor border intelligence to a great extent, a weakness that would haunt India in Kargil in 1999,[20] and invite criticism for unsatisfactory weaponry and coordination between the services—the army and the air force. However, the next few years were used to consolidate and train the army for tougher battles ahead, and the army responded to the call of the nation, earning well-deserved success in 1971. All this while the attention of the army leadership remained fully focused on military matters, giving the civilian leadership no cause for any anxiety regarding interference in political decision-making or the process of democratic elections.

While the 1965 War cannot be claimed as an outright victory for the Indian Army,[21] the conquests made were also short-changed at a political level. Major General Lachhman Singh comments:

> The political object, the original motive of war, determines military objectives and continues to be the guiding factor at peace talks . . . It was felt by the Generals that India had the

> legal right to retain her liberated area in POK. The Indian delegation at Tashkent led by Mr. [Lal Bahadur] Shastri, . . . somehow accepted [the] status quo as on 5 August 1965 so that all the gains at Hajipur, Tithwal and Kargil in POK, won with a heavy loss of blood and sweat, were returned to Pakistan at the political level.[22]

Be that as it may, the army was now representative of a fighting force free from political intervention, when compared to the situation prevailing in 1962. Besides, the army was absorbed with military matters, and was altogether detached from matters political. This was crucial in laying down the foundation for the development of healthy civil–military relations and consequently of democratic practices and processes in a young Republic of India, which was not even twenty years old.

5

War with Pakistan (1971)

'. . . the tasks set for the Western Command were accomplished and the officers and men justified the trust reposed in them.'

—Lieutenant General K.P. Candeth,
The Western Front: The Indo–Pakistan War 1971

Since Independence, Indian democracy had advanced considerably leading up to the general election in 1971. Up until the split in 1969, the Congress was 'the only party with [a] national following' though, after the split, the Congress, under Indira Gandhi, began the 'delinking' of 'national and state political arenas', leading to greater autonomy of local politics.[1] The dominance of the Congress alliance was confirmed by the rousing mandate it received in the 1971 elections. It must be added that though democracy in India was yet to transcend the social needs of its people, it had been able to attain a 'deepening legitimacy' and detach itself 'from the institutional infirmities that surrounded it' on account of nascent democratic processes.[2]

What dominated India's attention after the 1971 elections was the plight of East Pakistan, which continued to be alienated and treated as a 'colony'.[3] India, however, deployed a wait-and-watch policy. This was in no small measure at the instance of the COAS General (later Field Marshal) Sam Manekshaw who candidly told Prime Minister Indira Gandhi that it would be imprudent to send his men into battle before the monsoons had ended[4] and sought time till the end of the year to regroup his forces (then deployed in various sectors). It was also felt that if India could hold back until the winter, it would be impossible for the Chinese army to get over the Himalayas and come to Pakistan's aid, which was also a perceived threat. The general offered his resignation in lieu of his advice, which the political leadership abided by in sharp contrast with the developments of 1962. Nine years and two wars later, the trust deficit between the military and civilian establishments had markedly reduced, though it is still debated as to whether it was the general's advice that tilted the scales.

Manekshaw often recounted his version in a 'flavoursome and well-polished' style for it to have assumed a 'halfway mythological character'.[5] He is reported to have told US Army Chief General William Westmoreland that the Indian military had 'sobered its hawkish civilian politicians, who were eager to strike in East Pakistan'.[6] Jairam Ramesh cites Chandrashekhar Dasgupta to describe Manekshaw as a 'raconteur', and credits P.N. Haksar with being the 'mastermind' of the decision to defer the attack.[7] The grandstanding could be ignored, keeping in mind the larger success of the operation and the general respect that pervaded the leadership of the military and civilian sides.

Tactically, India opposed the 'secret trial'[8] of Sheikh Mujib and sought international intervention. When US President Nixon wanted to give the military government in West Pakistan two years to tackle the situation in the East, Indira Gandhi argued that 'the situation was explosive and could not be defused until Mujibur (Rehman) was released and a dialogue started with the already elected leaders of East Pakistan'.[9] She added that '. . . India would be forced to retaliate if Pakistan continued its provocations across [India's] border'.[10]

At this point, India's armed forces were looking formidable from the restructuring carried out over the years. Leading West German analyst Dieter Braun observed that the difference in outlook between 1962 and 1971 was that under Nehru, India pursued a 'globally oriented foreign policy with an eye on the power blocs of East and West and usually at a careful distance from them', but under Indira Gandhi, 'the consolidation and protection of its dominating position in *its own sub-region*, along with the elimination of Pakistan's long-standing claim to the greatest possible parity with India, in particular, had become the primary goal.'[11] (Emphasis supplied.) Axiomatically, the military perspective assumed far greater importance for New Delhi.

Indira Gandhi was undoubtedly more proactive in military matters than her father and this led to the Indian Forces crushing the Pakistan Army, the resulting liberation of the Bengali people and the creation of Bangladesh. Unlike 1965, when neither side could claim absolute success, the 1971 showdown confirmed India's military and strategic supremacy, helped in no small measure by the Pakistani leadership's incoherent military strategy.

While there was comparatively less fighting on India's western border with Pakistan, the role played by the Indian Navy made a telling difference. This was the first time that the navy was involved in a war on this scale, revealing India's supremacy over land and sea. Admiral Nanda, Chief of Naval Staff (CNS) at the time, is categorical that the 1971 War led to a reassessment of the role 'hitherto assigned to the navy', and that it (the navy) could no longer be treated as a 'coastal adjunct to the other two services'.[12] The Indian Navy not only sank *PNS Ghazi*, which was gunning for India's (only) aircraft carrier *INS Vikrant*, but emerged as a force to reckon with 'in the classic traditions', destroying enemy bases ashore and strangling 'him' (sic) with 'effective blockade' at first, and then 'contraband control'.[13]

Cohen observes that the war revealed a characteristic of Indian strategic policy—'a reluctance to commit significant orders or policies to paper'. He is categorical that even though the Indian defeat of the Pakistan Army seemed to be well planned, in fact no orders were actually issued for the capture of the capital of East Pakistan, Dhaka, and that as was later revealed 'a senior Indian general took it upon himself to make the decision'.[14]

At one level, this discloses a pronounced lack of clarity in matters of military direction, leading to the then Chief of Staff, Eastern Army Command Lieutenant General J.F.R. Jacob to argue for the creation of a Chiefs of Staff Committee or a National Security Council[15] as a redressal. Nevertheless, it was apparent that by 1971, the civilian leadership had an unspoken faith in the decision-making of the military leadership.

The 1971 War will also be obliquely remembered for the presence of the US aircraft carrier *USS Enterprise,* which had potential nuclear capabilities and was positioned south of Sri Lanka in the Bay of Bengal. Though she stayed clear of the action, the symbolism of the gesture was enormous and clearly indicative of an American 'countermeasure' to India's military advance against Pakistan.[16] Seen as being hostile to India, Cohen comments, 'Its [USS Enterprise] dramatic appearance on the strategic scene influenced an entire generation of Indian civilians and shaped Indian naval and nuclear strategy thereafter.'[17] On the part of the Indian Navy, the officers were instructed to 'stand firm' and, if confronted with American naval officers in the high seas, to merely exchange identities and invite them over for a drink![18]

The victory in 1971 heralded a new status for the Indian armed forces, with a high degree of popularity among Indians at large. The war saw India capture as many as 90,368 prisoners of war,[19] in one of the most dramatic surrenders of power since the Second World War. Equally, the political leadership was lauded for its firm handling of the situation, especially the role played by Indira Gandhi. There was one peeve though—the fact that the prime minister was 'outmanoeuvred strategically' by Zulfikar Ali Bhutto in excluding the Kashmir issue from the Simla Agreement that occurred after the war, causing India to miss the opportunity to resolve the matter 'once and for all'.[20] The forces and the civilian government generally enjoyed a healthy symbiotic relationship, perhaps though, only in wartime.

The 1971 operations also brought to the fore an operational synergy among all three services—the army, navy and air force—although the then chief of the air staff Air Chief Marshal P.C. Lal made an impassioned plea for the creation of a Chief of Defence Staff to sit above all three Service Chiefs and ensure better cooperation and collaboration among all three services and to reduce friction and one-upmanship.[21]

Returning to the marked improvement in civil–military relations leading up to the success of the 1971 operations, Major-General Kotera Bhimaya (Retired) rightly observes that: 'Often, the military's conception of national interest is not uniform' and 'if in democracy, popular sovereignty resides with the people who have elected the government to power, then it is incumbent for the military to obey the government in power, however transient; as it is the duly elected government in power that can best define what the interests of the state are.'[22] While courts, media and civil society may differ with this perspective, it rings true when it comes to the military in the course of its professional functions.

Bhimaya elaborates, '[I]n cases of policy differences between the military brass and the government in power, often these are resolved in the best interest of the nation, as was done when Manekshaw refused to commit the Indian army prematurely in March–April, 1971.' In this context, he adds that 'it is important to remember that Manekshaw disagreed with the timing of the army operations; he *never questioned* Indira Gandhi's policy of liberating Bangladesh.' For him, here lies 'the subtle but important nuance that can make a difference between civilian control and military intervention.'[23] (Emphasis supplied.)

The stoic submission to civilian control by the Indian Army seemingly marked the development of civil–military relations, whereby the civilian leadership was free to pursue its priorities, bereft of any intervention on the part of the armed forces. The 1971 operations accentuated the collaboration between the army and the government in a matter of grave national importance (and, indeed, of international ramifications). Even senior army commanders were forthcoming in their admission that the Bangladesh War represented tremendous civilian leadership[24] under a 'pragmatic, determined and courageous' prime minister and an 'able administrator [with] an excellent grasp of military strategy' in Defence Minister Jagjivan Ram.[25]

6

Emergency

'A soldier owes allegiance to the Constitution but when he sees that Constitution being systematically destroyed, should he remain a silent spectator?'

—Lieutenant General S.K. Sinha (Retired), PVSM, *A Soldier Recalls*

In the years immediately preceding the Emergency, the role played by the Indian Supreme Court, in interpreting the Constitution as being supreme,[1] and all actions of the Legislature or the Executive being subject to judicial review, led to a new democratic order where Parliament was not absolute and the balance of power was getting increasingly adjusted. This led commentators to observe that '[T]he failure of diverse and divided opposition parties to provide an effective check on an increasingly autonomous and powerful executive had opened the way for the Supreme Court to play an opposition-like role'.[2]

That the lack of a strong political opposition did not tempt the military to indulge in political adventurism of any sort, even after a resounding victory in 1971, is something to note. American historian of the Indian Constitution Granville Austin observes that the 'forces of unity outside the Constitution' had begun to strengthen in India, and after the success of the 1965 and 1971 wars, the army had become a 'symbol of nationalism'.[3] Indeed, the politically passive role played by it facilitated democracy and enabled an environment where key institutions such as the judiciary could evolve into strong pillars of Indian constitutionalism. The *non-event* of a military coup has proved significant in this regard. However, the Emergency marked a dark period when the promise of democracy was betrayed.

'Power in a democracy resides with the people' was paradoxically something Prime Minister Indira Gandhi said in 1967.[4] Eight years later, in 1975, she stifled Indian democracy by imposing 'Constitutional Emergency', which went untested in the courts, as there was no direct challenge to its imposition. At such a time, fundamental rights and liberties were suspended and the State's rule was draconian and absolute. The challenge facing the army was whether it would support the unilateral dictates of Indira Gandhi or question the legitimacy of the decisions made under her stewardship.[5] This is a perennial predicament that could face the military in any democracy—is the army's loyalty to the government or to the nation? Are the two indistinguishable in a democracy? Military officers 'often identify themselves as servants of the State and not the Government' and seek to resolve the conflict between one's loyalty to the nation and to 'any transient in the seat of power'.[6] The Emergency brought this conflict to the fore.

The period leading up to 1975 witnessed economic crises such as crop failures and drought, an unprecedented increase in the price of imported oil and a slump in industrial production. Inflation was at a mammoth 23 per cent in 1973 and increased to 24 per cent in mid-1974.[7] Meanwhile, Indira Gandhi's popularity was waning, with a corresponding increase in the popularity of the Opposition, led by freedom fighter Jayaprakash Narayan (or 'JP' as he was known). Strikes, bandhs, riots and protests were omnipresent and the breakdown of stable governance was apparent. P.N. Dhar argues that the chasm between the democratic ideals envisioned in the Indian Constitution and the political practices and upheavals in the years leading up to 1975 (specifically, 1969 onwards) had gradually contributed to the breakdown of the rule of law, resulting in the decline of democracy.[8]

Indira Gandhi's own election was set aside by Justice Sinha of the Allahabad High Court on grounds of corrupt electoral practices, and stayed partially by the Supreme Court, permitting her to attend Parliament but not vote thereat[9]—a humiliation for any prime minister. Finding herself cornered, Indira Gandhi prevailed upon loyalist President Fakhruddin Ali Ahmed to declare Emergency by invoking Article 352 of the Constitution of India.[10] Cohen describes the declaration of Emergency as Indira Gandhi's 'euphemism for a personalized dictatorship'.[11]

The army was required to participate in this quasi-dictatorship. However, the civilian government itself did not fully trust the army at this delicate time, as it needed a more pliable force, and therefore had already constituted a 'force' comprising the Border Security Force (BSF), the Research and Analysis Wing (R&AW) and the foot soldiers of the Youth Congress.[12] This 'second army' as Selbourne described it, 'both frees the regulars from the task, always unpopular with the troops, of acting in support of the civil authority' and thereby freed the Congress of its dependence on the army in the launch of its repressive actions.[13] This astutely kept the army less excessively involved in the implementation of the Emergency which, in turn, might have mitigated the chances of any resistance.

Just before the imposition of the Emergency and earlier, JP had pleaded publicly for the police and the army to refrain from obeying orders that were 'illegal and immoral' and save the Constitution from being hijacked.[14] Ironically, Indira Gandhi was advised by West Bengal Chief Minister and legal expert

Siddhartha Shankar Ray to *use* JP's call for non-cooperation, especially by the army and police, as an act of incitement of internal rebellion to justify the imposition of Emergency, on grounds of threat to India's internal security, as no other grounds of threat to external security or otherwise existed![15]

Some factions of the Congress leadership perceived JP's growing stature and the mounting agitation all over India as a ploy by the (American) Central Intelligence Agency (CIA) to destabilize the country, for which the recommended solution was the imposition of Emergency.[16] Indira Gandhi's confidante and chief of R&AW, Rameshwar Nath Kao, in fact advised her *against* the imposition of Emergency but was overruled.[17]

Indira Gandhi did not stop short of meddling even in matters of judicial promotions, superseding three judges of the Supreme Court—justices Hegde, Shelat and Grover—in appointing Justice Ray as the chief justice of India (CJI) and later superseding Justice H.R. Khanna[18] by appointing Justice Beg as CJI. This led to the resignation of the aggrieved judges[19] and as chief justice of the Bombay High Court Justice M.C. Chagla described it, the 'emasculation of the judiciary'.[20] The media was gagged, the Press Council was abolished[21] and as T.J.S. George quips in blunt terms, 'journalism, like politics, was overtaken by a new tribe of gifted operators who thrived on the debris of forsaken principles'.[22]

Even at such a time when the legitimacy of the civilian government was at its lowest ebb and the involvement of the military in civilian functions was deemed 'legitimate',[23] the army did not transcend to a state of revolt, and instead paved the way for a return to democracy in due course. The army was not directly involved in the high-handed detention of opposition political leaders and journalists and this, by itself, pre-empted any form of revolt or reaction. Defence Minister Bansi Lal claimed publicly that there was no politics in the army that was 'united and one' and that the army was not used in the Emergency to maintain law and order or break up strikes, which was done by the paramilitary alone.[24] This is corroborated by the fact that the closest army base to New Delhi was as far as 150 miles away in Ambala, while the BSF had ready and free access to the national capital.[25] This perhaps also betrayed the distrust that New Delhi had towards the army.

It must be acknowledged that there was some amount of unease among the ranks of the army at being privy to the implementation of the Emergency, with many officers viewing the imposition as being a perversion of democracy which could justify a coup,[26] especially in the wake of the emergence of the 'extra-constitutional source of power' of coteries of power, headed by Sanjay Gandhi.[27] However, the army, being subjected to a single, centralized source of power in Indira Gandhi—who was the de facto power centre for the federal and state governments—made the option of obeying the command largely unavoidable. The legality of such a decision would be best left to the judiciary to determine, as in such circumstances the military could have a 'considerable presumption of validity of the opinion of the statesman.'[28] The ethos of the army precluded any intervention in matters of civilian governance, except to the extent constitutionally required and permitted. The absence of a (peacetime) precedent in India was arguably also a factor in this regard.

It is revealing that when Indira Gandhi privately sought the opinion of all three service chiefs as to whether they would support her in the declaration of Emergency, all of them are stated to have refused, as did the army commanders of the critical Eastern and Western Commands.[29] The distrust of the political leadership in the army was apparent from the fact that along with keeping opposition leaders in jail under scathing Emergency powers, even senior army commanders (including, reportedly, Field

Marshal Sam Manekshaw) were alleged to have been kept under house arrest for a certain period of time.[30] However, neither of Field Marshal Manekshaw's biographers corroborates this fact.[31] Indeed, neither biography makes any detailed reference to the Emergency period, by which time the field marshal had retired as COAS. Major General Shubhi Sood does, however, make a reference to Indira Gandhi frankly telling Field Marshal Manekshaw in 1969 that she feared his taking over the country and that she was oft advised that he was her biggest threat.[32]

The related development was the increasing frequency with which the government manoeuvred senior military appointments, and some officers curried favour by appearing to be 'pro-government'. General T.N. Raina was appointed COAS superseding other senior officers. However, General Raina as COAS did not play into the hands of his appointing authorities, and bluntly refused to permit the prime minister 'to use the army to further her ends'.[33] Though General Raina showed 'no special attachment' for Indira Gandhi, Defence Minister Bansi Lal felt 'that Raina had strong links' with her and she, thus, did not 'unduly meddle' with the army.[34]

The debate whether the government was legitimate, or otherwise, was made redundant by the declaration of general elections in March 1977. The Opposition routed the incumbent prime minister and her party, and Morarji Desai took over the reins of the newly elected government. This overwhelming ouster of the ruling Congress government pre-empted any volatile situation involving the use of the armed forces for the suppression of the newly elected political leadership, and chances are that in such a situation, the army would have abstained from any 'improper action' and would instead have leaned in favour of the clear mandate of the people. Such circumstances, in neighbouring Pakistan, would have been tailor-made for a military coup.

The Emergency raised doubts about the success and survival of democracy in India, despite the incidental sense of discipline and order. Quoting a reporter from *Time* who visited India in October 1975, Guha recounts:

> The Prime Minister has won widespread support for seizing a rare opportunity to ram through a score of social reforms. These days India is engrossed in a frenzied campaign to encourage discipline, punctuality, cleanliness [and] courtesy.[35]

Expectedly, India received a fair deal of criticism for subverting democracy and violating human rights. The *Sunday Morning Herald* caustically commented that India had 'relapsed into traditional Asian autocracy' and 'the blame must be shared between 'Empress Indira' and her father [Nehru], who had fostered heavy industrialization and nationalized bureaucracies upon the Indian entrepreneur, Soviet style, in the name of 'socialism'.[36] Austin points out that by the introduction of the powers of preventive detention under the Defence of India Act (DIA), 1915, in matters of 'internal emergency', and related detentions under the Maintenance of Internal Security Act (MISA), 1971, Indira Gandhi had 'snuffed out democracy' with 'the sweep of her hand'.[37] The press too succumbed, but for a few honourable exceptions such as Ramnath Goenka of the *Indian Express*, and 'quickly . . . accepted its lowly fate'.[38] Indira Gandhi's speech-writer at the time—H.Y. Sharada Prasad, a fine bureaucrat himself—observes that by the hasty and ill-advised imposition of Emergency, the one thing that Indira Gandhi achieved was that no other prime minister would ever be tempted to resort to this option.[39] That seems prophetic today.

As for the army, the professional ethos of the senior officers, the fact that the Emergency was not extra-constitutional (certainly not declared as such by a Court of Law), the 'distancing' by the civilian leadership and the gravity of such an unprecedented step precluded the military from taking any controversial positions at the time.

Kundu comments that the absence of political interference in military matters, keeping the military away from sensitive political endeavours and the fact that the military top brass would not be comfortable with the austerity that could come with the introduction of JP's leftist rule were also factors that influenced the army to stay at an arm's length from the political developments of the time.[40]

In Bhimaya's view, Indian political parties 'were mature enough not to politicize the armed forces personnel, and even power-hungry leaders such as Indira Gandhi never employed [the] armed forces against political opponents [as was done by Prime Minister Zulifkar Ali Bhutto of Pakistan in 1977]'.[41]

On the political front, the Emergency spelt Indira Gandhi's downfall in the elections of 1977. Though Desai's Janata Party assumed power with a sweeping majority, it did so only to make way for the return of the Congress party in 1980. Democracy in India was in full swing. The 'Khalistan Movement' in Punjab was, however, reaching the boiling point.

7

Operation Blue Star

'[T]he capture of Bhindranwale . . . was a task well within the capability of the police and paramilitary forces; Army involvement in such tasks should be avoided.'

—General K.V. Krishna Rao, *In the Service of the Nation*

In order to better understand Operation Blue Star, it is necessary to provide some historical context. Contrary to the earlier position on the region's demands, the government in 1966 supported the division of Punjab into the states of Haryana, Himachal Pradesh and a largely reduced Punjab, purportedly on a linguistic basis, as per the States Reorganisation Act of 1956 (though religious considerations were apparent, with 56 per cent of the population in the Punjab being Sikhs).[1]

When the 1973 Anandpur Sahib Resolution of the Akali Dal—the prominent political party in the state—articulated its demands for Chandigarh as the exclusive capital of Punjab and matters relating to land distribution among the three states, the government turned a blind eye to the demand. This saw the Akali Dal defeat the Congress in the 1977 elections. By such time, though Indira Gandhi was out of power after the Emergency, the former Chief Minister of the Punjab (and later the first Sikh President of India), Giani Zail Singh, advised the setting up of a new political challenger to undermine the Akali Dal's increasing popularity.[2]

Sanjay Gandhi spearheaded the search for this 'trump-card' and came up with Jarnail Singh Bhindranwale, a young orthodox religious leader with strong fundamentalist leanings and a strong following among the Sikhs. He (Bhindranwale) received the tacit support of the Congress party and, in 1980, campaigned actively for the Congress in three constituencies.[3]

Bhindranwale's ambitions, however, quickly got the better of him, and he declared his 'independence' and then demanded the creation of a sovereign Sikh state called 'Khalistan'. His organization turned into assassins, murdering critics such as the respected editor Lala Jagat Narain. This led to Bhindranwale's arrest. Ironically, his arrest gave him unprecedented publicity, and no sooner was he released at the instance of Home Minister Zail Singh, than his men resumed their unruly activities.[4] Political opponents, and particularly Hindu leaders and temples were targeted, to drive a wedge between the two communities and trigger an exodus of Hindus from the state.[5] Then, Bhindranwale and his followers moved into the holy Golden Temple in Amritsar from where their nefarious activities were safely carried out, attracting global media attention. For the government, the chickens had come home to roost.[6]

For over a year, the central government remained a silent spectator to the carnage, hoping that the Akali Dal would 'break up'[7], ignoring the fact that that this was not a local problem. It was, indeed, a national emergency of enormous magnitude, with international focus (and of far greater gravitas than when Emergency was *actually* imposed.) However, when it was no longer open to wait and watch, negotiations commenced, but swiftly failed. Meanwhile, New Delhi undertook an act of tokenism to appease the Sikh population by ensuring the appointment of Zail Singh as the President of India.[8]

The failure to contain the Bhindranwale menace resulted in knee-jerk reactions by the government whereby *all* Sikhs were viewed suspiciously and a large number of baseless arrests were made, which rightly infuriated the Sikh populace.[9] Indira Gandhi once again attempted to negotiate, this time with the Akali Dal, through Captain Amarinder Singh (later chief minister of Punjab) and reached a tentative agreement on the issues of Chandigarh and the sharing of river waters.[10] This agreement was dumped when the affected states—Haryana and Rajasthan—strongly opposed the pact.

Bhindranwale openly scorned the government and continued his unrestrained terror. In a daring episode, on 25 April 1983, the chief of the Amritsar Police, A.S. Atwal (a Sikh officer), was shot dead while leaving the precincts of the Golden Temple, as he was opposed to the idea of 'Khalistan'.[11] The government had not yet sanctioned police action against Bhindranwale, who moved his headquarters from the periphery into the heart of the temple—the sacred Akal Takht. In view of the growing terror and violence against innocent Hindus, Indira Gandhi dismissed Chief Minister Darbara Singh and inevitably imposed President's rule, but the slaughter continued unabated.

For the first time, contingency military plans under the auspices of Rajiv Gandhi and his close supporters furtively began to be devised to smoke out Bhindranwale and his men from the Golden Temple, though the government was hesitant to invoke this drastic option.[12] Unaware of these plans, Home Minister P.C. Sethi made a statement in Parliament that force would not be used in the Golden Temple.[13]

Negotiations with Bhindranwale were thorny as he insisted on the unconditional implementation of the Anandpur Sahib Resolution demands. Simultaneously, Akali Dal leader Harchand Singh Longowal declared an impasse on the movement of grain out of Punjab, which was a key supplier of grain to the rest of the nation. The deadlock made intervention by force inevitable and on 5 June 1984, at 10.30 p.m., the 350 Infantry Brigade and attached troops of the Indian Army, commanded by Major General (later Lieutenant General) Kuldip Singh Brar, descended on Amritsar. Curfew was imposed, foreign media persons were evicted, communications terminated and borders frozen.

The professional nature of the Indian Army was evident as the siege of the hallowed Golden Temple was commanded by General Brar, himself a Sikh officer, who recalls how his Sikh soldiers volunteered to be the *first* to go into the temple premises to execute this most delicate operation against their 'own people'.[14] Interestingly, Bhindranwale's key strategists in the siege were retired army officers—Major General Shabeg Singh and Major General J.S. Bhullar.[15]

General Brar was a Jat Sikh, whose ancestral village was a few miles from Bhindranwale's. He was someone who knew Shabeg Singh intimately from the army.[16] Brar confesses to having a high regard for Shabeg as a soldier, as he had served as Brar's instructor at the IMA, Dehradun, and later had seen combat together in the 1971 operations.[17] Brar was briefed by two lieutenant generals—K. Sundarji (who would later become COAS) and R.S. Dyal, a Sikh.

The official mandate to the forces was to use 'minimum force', to inflict 'as little damage as possible' and not to violate the holy sanctum sanctorum 'Harmandir Sahib', containing the holy book of the Sikhs, the Guru Granth Sahib.[18] Earlier, the prime minister had expressly indicated that the army would not be sent into the Golden Temple at all.[19] P.C. Alexander, Indira Gandhi's principal secretary at the time, states unequivocally that even the military operations authorized by her in May 1984 were only to seize and fish out the terrorists, an order which was changed (very reluctantly) by the prime minister in June 1984—ostensibly at the instance of COAS General Vaidya, in consultation with Lieutenant General Sundarji—to 'the usage of commando operations inside the Golden Temple'.[20] General Sundarji, in turn, blamed the intelligence for poor information on the extent of infiltration.[21]

From his refuge in the temple, Bhindranwale learnt of the developing military presence through his competent spies and insolently claimed, 'If the authorities enter this temple, we will teach them such a lesson that the throne of Indira will crumble. We will slice them into small pieces . . . They will chew iron lentils . . . Let them come.'[22]

The 'look out sentries' of the army found 'armed militants' in the precincts.[23] On 5 June, the Indian Army ordered the civilians to leave the temple and, as a final warning, called upon the extremists to surrender. None of the extremists paid heed, forcing the army commandos to enter the fray. They were received with heavy downward gunfire from the temple terrace, using automatic weapons and causing large fatalities among the soldiers.

The redoubtable response caused the army to use tanks and artillery to gain access to the temple complex. This naturally damaged the sacred construction and more significantly hurt the sentiments of the Sikhs, for whom this was an unpardonable incursion. The precious library of the Golden Temple, containing handwritten manuscripts by Sikh Gurus, was largely extinguished in combat firing and the Harmandir Sahib and Akal Takht were riddled with bullets. President Zail Singh—who was otherwise kept in the dark about the operation[24] proclaimed:

> [T]his [the Golden Temple] was the place built by the fifth Guru, an apostle of peace, as a symbol of love and unity of mankind. This was the temple of God . . . the shrine built on a lower level than the surrounding land in a spirit of humility. It has doors on all four sides proclaiming its accessibility

> to people of all faiths and creeds. It had taken an *act of desecration* to destroy Bhindranwale.[25]

Late on the night of 6 June, the army finally entered the shrine and found Bhindranwale's dead body along with several of his men. This put an end to the encounter, with several hundred commandos and civilians killed in the process. Lieutenant General J.S. Aurora, the Sikh general who commanded the army in the 1971 operations, pithily said, 'The army was used to finish a problem created by the government. *This is the kind of action that is going to ruin the army.*'[26] (Emphasis supplied.)

However, despite the severely provocative nature of the assignment, the army acquitted itself as a dispassionate and efficient institution. Kirpal Dhillon, who was director general of police (DGP) Punjab, at the time, makes an important observation. He notes that in times such as Operation Blue Star, the army functions as per the manual of military aid to civil authority, as there is no express provision for martial law under the Indian Constitution. This would require orders to emanate from the local district magistrate. However, the army was accustomed to being beyond civilian scrutiny in matters of its operations—what the author puts down to a 'colonial hangover'—and chose to operate dehors such protocol.[27] For instance, detenus were not presented before the local magistrate within the twenty-four-hour period prescribed, and this often required the DGP to fly to Amritsar, along with the security adviser, to 'fix the many legal infirmities'.[28]

All said, Operation Blue Star was a(nother) potentially breaking point when the army was involved in a delicate internal assignment. This task was particularly delicate as Sikh soldiers and officers, who are regarded as among the finest in the force, were largely opposed to the correctness of the decision and, moreover, to the idea of killing their fellow citizens.

Though the troops immediately under General Brar readily took on the mantle, thousands of Sikh jawans across the country mutinied in a rare contamination of their otherwise spotless track record.[29] On 7 June 1984, about 500 soldiers of the 9th Battalion of the Sikh Regiment in Ganganagar, Rajasthan, mutinied, followed by mutinies among the Sikh jawans in Bihar, Jammu and Rajasthan.[30] These uprisings were swiftly brought under control by the army (itself) and significantly no Sikh *officer* participated in the revolt.[31] The mutiny caused some concern among commentators at the time as to the role that the Sikh soldiers[32] would play in case of a future war with Pakistan or in the Punjab anti-terrorism operations.[33] In retrospect, however, this mutiny stands out as an ad hoc instance of overt protest by the forces in independent India.

Intriguingly, the casualty of Operation Blue Star was Lieutenant General S.K. Sinha, a *non-Sikh* officer, who strongly opposed Operation Blue Star and was passed over by the civilian government. General A.S. Vaidya was appointed as the COAS, leading to General Sinha's resignation from office.

While General Sinha points to the acquiescence of COAS General K.V. Krishna Rao in his supersession (despite the allegations against General Vaidya's fitness),[34] General Rao clarifies:

> [T]he Prime Minister called me . . . to ask who should take over from me. As it was not usual for an incumbent chief to be consulted, I expressed surprise. [On making] a thorough analysis . . . it was clear that Lieutenant General Vaidya should be the next chief, according to professional performance of the officers concerned. She [the PM] would no doubt have

> consulted the Defence Minister also . . . *as far as I know there were no political considerations and the selection was purely based on merit* . . . Lieutenant General Vaidya was absolutely fit being in medical category Aye-One.[35] (Emphasis supplied.)

Such supersession of senior officers to the post of chief of staff (whether politically motivated or not) are to be found in the other services as well, with one such instance being the appointment of Air Chief Marshal O.P. Mehra over Air Marshal Shivdev Singh, though the latter was Defence Minister Jagjivan Ram's 'choice'.[36]

Prime Minister Indira Gandhi paid the price for Operation Blue Star; she was assassinated by her Sikh bodyguards—Satwant Singh and Beant Singh—on the morning of 31 October 1984 at her official residence. The vicious anti-Sikh violence that followed her assassination did not affect the role of the army in patrolling the streets, enforcing law and order, during the crucial interregnum when a new prime minister (Rajiv Gandhi) was to be appointed. General Vaidya was himself assassinated in 1986 in Pune by Sikh militants in retaliation for his role in Operation Blue Star. There was no strong-arm reaction from the army to its chief being taken down soon after his retirement, though there was civil unrest in Pune and Mumbai.

The groundswell of resentment against the leadership had begun to increase exponentially among segments of the Sikh population across the nation after Blue Star. When Defence Minister (later President of India)—R. Venkataraman—insisted that the prime minister transfer her security from the police to the army, she refused, affirming that 'she was the leader of a democratic, not a military government'.[37] She even overruled IB Chief R.N. Kao's prescient order to remove all Sikh officers from her personal security.[38] This decision cost her life. After her assassination, the Special Protection Group (SPG) was raised on the lines of the US Secret Service to provide protection to prime ministers (and later, to ex-prime ministers) and to function directly under the Prime Minister's Office.[39]

The reaction to Indira Gandhi's assassination was a brutal, surgical and mindless genocide of innocent Sikhs in the New Delhi region. While mobs butchered harmless Sikh citizens, the administration and the police looked the other way, or tacitly condoned the violence.[40] The violence stopped only once army tanks drove into the city of New Delhi, as late as 3 November. As for the army, not only did it professionally discharge its assignment at the Golden Temple, it also came out later to stem the massacre of innocent Sikhs by bloodthirsty mobs at a time when killings were taking place under the nose of the police officials.[41]

The mindset of the soldier in Operation Blue Star is summed up by General Brar, when he states:

> [F]rom the highest in command to the last man in uniform . . . we answered the call of duty as disciplined, loyal and dedicated members of the armed forces of India . . . I have never felt prouder in my life than to see, for myself, the stuff of which the Indian soldier is made.[42]

It is to be noticed that due to the awkwardness of deploying the army in an internal operation that has religious sensitivities, and perhaps due to the mutiny by the Sikh jawans, the army has scarcely been used in politically sensitive domestic operations, except in a deterrent and at times, belated peacekeeping mould such as the post-Babri Masjid demolition in 1992 or the Gujarat riots of 2002; more often than not, the paramilitary outfits were pressed into service[43]. The exception to this principle is the deployment of the army in direct operations in states covered by the Armed Forces (Special Powers) Act, 1958.[44]

Soon after the revolt among the Sikh soldiers during Operation Blue Star, the Indian government enabled the creation of the National Guards[45] (later the National Security Guard) that functions directly under the Ministry of Home Affairs. This is reminiscent of the creation of the BSF, the Central Industrial Security Force and other such organizations that would underplay the importance of the army and would lead to the creation of a separate paramilitary force that is hydra-headed and bereft of direct military command and control. This may be explained as the government's effort towards reining in military operations in 'peacetime' and does betray a certain discomfort in leaving complete autonomy with the military in such operations.

8

IPKF in Sri Lanka and Admiral Bhagwat's Dismissal

'For if the Trumpet give an uncertain sound,
Who shall prepare himself to the battle?'

—The First Epistle of Paul to the Corinthians, Chapter 14, Verse 8, cited by Field Marshal Sam Manekshaw, MC, in Foreword to Lieutenant General Depinder Singh, PVSM, VSM, *Indian Peacekeeping Force in Sri Lanka*

While Operation Blue Star was a questionable deployment of the army in an internal operation, its deployment in an external operation in Sri Lanka became equally contentious. Sri Lanka, in the mid-1980s, was witnessing the spirited emergence of Tamil militancy under the Liberation Tigers of Tamil Eelam (LTTE, earlier known as the Tamil New Tigers), led by Velupillai Prabhakaran.[1] While the Sri Lankan government commenced its 'civil war' against the LTTE, launching Operation Liberation in 1983, the Indian government involved itself through Operation Pawan to support the Sri Lankan regime.[2] The Indo–Sri Lanka

Accord (ISLA) led, in 1987, to the 54 Infantry Division of the Indian Army being sent to Sri Lanka in the avatar of the Indian Peace Keeping Force (IPKF). The 'peace-keeping' mandate itself was amorphous and driven more by political compulsions than by military strategy.

The political mindset of the Indian leadership under Prime Minister Rajiv Gandhi can be gathered from writings on the eve of the 1987 IPKF foray. Authors V.K. Murthi and Gautam Sharma note:

> India has accepted the stand of the Sri Lankan government that the [LTTE] issue is *an internal problem*. However, India cannot stand and stare while Tamil exodus takes place . . . India has therefore intervened *to settle the issue*. He [Rajiv Gandhi] has to dispel the fears in Sri Lankan minds that India is at the back of the terrorists.[3] (Emphasis supplied.)

Though many senior army officers opposed such (muddled) intervention mainly due to the lack of experience in unconventional jungle warfare (and intelligence agencies underestimated the power of the Tamil rebels), General K. Sundarji, COAS at the time, did not oppose the utilization of the IPKF in Operation Pawan.[4] The general was criticized for having 'shoved' the army into an unwilling war—the divisional commander of 54 Infantry Division that was sent to Sri Lanka, Lieutenant General S.C. Sardeshpande, attributes the 'clumsy' response of the army to the lack of 'inspired leadership' at the higher levels, and '[t]he bluster of the GOC [General Officer Commanding] IPKF, the tentativeness and uncertainty of the Army Commander above him and the Army Chief's loquaciousness which did little to change the systemic incongruities and tackle the hidden rot, in all those two years and more of our military venture'.[5]

The GOC IPKF—Lieutenant General Depinder Singh, on his part, concedes that '. . . a situation was created where the Army was *forced into an operation for which it was not fully ready*, mentally or structurally.'[6] (Emphasis supplied.) He adds tellingly that even when the army was in a position to declare a ceasefire, it was overruled by the Indian leadership, displaying 'gross political and diplomatic ineptitude'.[7] This reflects poorly on the civil-military relations at wartime. Major General Ashok Krishna concludes that the strengths of the LTTE were underestimated as 'peanuts' and forces were inducted 'piecemeal' and in a 'hurried manner'.[8]

For the apparent military and political failings, the jawans and junior/middle-level officers of the Indian Army faithfully played their part in fighting a long-drawn battle in hostile, alien terrain with a fuzzy mandate of 'peacekeeping'. The political casualty again, as was the case post Operation Blue Star, was Rajiv Gandhi, who was assassinated by an LTTE suicide bomber in Sriperumbudur in Tamil Nadu, on 21 May 1991.

Operation Pawan has been pithily branded 'India's Vietnam'[9] and a 'March of Folly'[10] for the tremendous political constraints placed on the ability of the IPKF to have fought an all-out battle, unfettered by the caveats imposed by the powers in New Delhi. While the officers of the IPKF are reported to have complained about 'interference from the Indian High Commission in Colombo', equally, they are alleged to have been 'more interested in meeting the Tigers' increasing demands' rather than for a 'shooting war against them'.[11] A clear dichotomy in command and objectives was evident.

General Sardeshpande poignantly states that while a soldier does not hesitate to undertake an assignment such as Operation Pawan, '[A]s a human being and a citizen, he has the right to expect a thorough thought [sic: to be] given to such enterprise by the powers that be . . . to ensure that [there] is no doubt, reservation or conflict in their mind as to the aim of undertaking . . .'[12]

Indian troops were denied even this basic expectation by the political/military leadership, reminiscent of similar gaffes in the past. The military in India was now accustomed to being used for matters of political expediency and played along in obedience.

The case of Admiral Bhagwat

In December 1998, CNS Admiral Vishnu Bhagwat was summarily removed from office, for having lost the pleasure of the President of India under Article 310 of the Constitution of India. Admiral Sushil Kumar was appointed in his place as CNS. This was the first and only instance of a serving chief being removed while in office. The reasons for this eventuality were his strong objections to the promotion of Vice Admiral Harinder Singh to the post of deputy CNS, which the cabinet approved but the CNS refused to accept.[13] According to Anit Mukherjee, the CNS was perceived as a 'divisive figure', whose actions were seen by the government in a one-of-a-kind 'white non-paper' as a 'challenge to civilian control . . . and democracy' and an attempt to function 'beyond parliamentary/cabinet control'.[14]

Admiral Bhagwat goes as far as to refer to the situation resulting from his dismissal from service as a 'politico-military coup'. 'How is it,' he asks, 'that the new incumbent [Admiral] Sushil Kumar was flown in a R&AW aircraft in *a politico-military coup*, defying the authority of CNS in moving out of his command's territorial limits, directly under the illegal orders of the [Defence] Minister?'[15] (Emphasis supplied.)

He proceeds to make a statement on the larger issues at hand:

> The Cabinet system of Government does not permit a politico–military coup, nor can such a coup be legalized or sanctified, as the Cabinet is accountable to the Parliament. Is it that the Parliament does not understand? How was Parliament totally bypassed? The armed forces demoralized and politicized and the ACC permitted to make such a spectacle of themselves? . . . [T]his was a Government that was not particularly successful in managing the parliamentary system. It did not care at working according to the norms and practices of a parliamentary democracy and the rule of law.[16]

Former Cabinet Secretary B.G. Deshmukh recalls having to remind General Sundarji that in 'a democracy . . . the army functions under a civilian democratic government' when the general was alleged to have been making derogatory remarks about the political class in general.[17]

All said, the government acted strongly in removing its CNS and, some would say, the dismissal occurred in a high-handed *manner*. This was essentially an executive decision, and Parliament and the media were not closely involved as one would have expected.[18] Admiral Bhagwat however resorted to purely constitutional remedies against this perceived 'coup' and challenged his dismissal in the Supreme Court of India, albeit unsuccessfully.[19] His book *Betrayal of the Defence Forces: The Inside Truth* pulls no punches and castigates the government of the day for its suppression of military honour and tradition. Of course, it comes from a place of personal betrayal, and is to be read against that backdrop. Today his removal has remained a footnote in the discussion on civil–military relations in India when potentially it could have rewritten the text.

9

Kargil (1999), Operation Parakram and Mumbai 26/11

'Intelligence agencies can employ many means of surveillance, but nobody expects a RAW or IB man to be leaping from peak to peak at 16,000 feet while soldiers are snug in base camps below.'

—Brian Cloughley, *A History of the Pakistan Army: Wars and Insurrections*

In 1999, crucial peaks in the Batalik sector had come to be occupied by Pakistani soldiers with a view to seizing the vital National Highway that connects Srinagar to Leh. This would cripple the defence of Jammu and Kashmir by cutting off supplies to the troops. The Kargil conflict, however, has to be understood in the larger context of the friction between India and Pakistan over Kashmir. The first Indo–Pak War of 1947–48 was fought in and over Kashmir,[1] while the 1965 War again commenced due to intrusions by Pakistani troops in Kashmir.[2] Besides these, there have consistently been low-intensity conflicts in Kashmir with the active or tacit support of the Pakistan Army. The nuclearization of both countries has also kept the pressure on the armies to maintain eyeball-to-eyeball contact at the borders out of caution.

Ever since India's occupation of the critical Saltoro Ridge in Siachen in 1984, which caused grave embarrassment to the Pakistani leadership, there was increasing pressure on Pakistan to retaliate. Having failed to evict the Indian troops from Saltoro by direct assault in 1987, Pakistan came up with a plan to apply 'indirect pressure' on India in the 'un-held areas' in the Kargil sector, which would draw the Indian troops towards Kargil and open up the Siachen sector.[3] Though these plans were under deliberation from 1987, it was only in 1999 that they took concrete shape under the stewardship of General Pervez Musharraf.[4]

The Saltoro range is a 12,000 feet-high, 110-kilometre-long frontline that divides the Siachen glacier from Baltistan in Pakistan, while the mountain ridge on the opposite side separates it from China.[5] The strategic position of the range is therefore critical; both India and Pakistan have historically tried to conquer Saltoro. While proxy attempts have been made for years through military-mountaineering expeditions, the Indian military had intelligence of a botched Pakistani attempt at an armed occupation of Saltoro in 1983.[6] In response, the Indian Army chose Colonel Narendra 'Bull' Kumar—a mountaineer *par excellence*—to make a symbolic expedition into Saltoro followed by military occupation in 1984, which has continued as a long-term occupation by the Indian troops.[7] The Siachen conflict has seen intermittent attempts at negotiated settlement as well as spurts of high-intensity combat, causing loss of troops and assets. Prof. Stephen P. Cohen described Pakistan's Kargil intrusion of 1999 as 'a response to what Rawalpindi perceived as an Indian grab of the glacier in 1984'.[8]

Indeed, senior officers believed that in the wake of increasing nuclearization, 'conventional engagement' between India and Pakistan was unlikely.[9] The actual foray by the Pakistani troops caused a 'considerable degree of surprise and consequent shock'[10] to the Indian military leadership, which had hitherto underestimated Pakistan and the need to develop HUMINT (human intelligence).[11]

As far as the operation is concerned, the army was able to recapture key positions in Khalubar, Batalik and other infringed positions in Kargil and drive back the Pakistani troops and infiltrators. Its 1/11 Gorkha Rifles (commanded by Colonel Lalit Rai) and other units such as 22 Grenadiers, J&K Light Infantry, Ladakh Scouts, 1 Naga, 8 Mountain Div and 17 Jat acquitted themselves with rare distinction.[12]

It is another matter that the Kargil Review Committee (KRC) report indicted both civil and military intelligence for failing to detect the infiltration that took place several months earlier.[13] General V.P. Malik (Retired), the then COAS, acknowledges that the 'failure to anticipate military action of this nature on the border by the Pakistan Army reflected a major deficiency in our system of collecting, reporting, collating and assessing intelligence.'[14]

Besides, the political (and military) leadership in New Delhi took unusually long to acknowledge the presence of Pakistani troops and treated most field intelligence 'with contempt'.[15]

The KRC report recorded that 'there is no institutionalized mechanism for coordination . . . between intelligence agencies and consumers [sic] at different levels' and goes on to recommend that the 'role and place' of the JIC in the national intelligence framework 'should be evaluated' and that, '[T]he entire gamut of national security management and apex decision making and . . . the interface between the Ministry of Defence of Armed Forces' Headquarters should be comprehensively studied and reorganized.'[16]

A judgment of the Armed Forces Tribunal in Brigadier Devinder Singh's case[17] indicts the army top brass for preparing an Annual Confidential Report (ACR) of the petitioner (the brigadier) that was 'not objective or unbiased'[18] and consequently directed the respondents to not only correct the ACR of the officer *but also to put the records of the Kargil War* 'in correct perspective'[19] to the extent that they did not reflect the accuracy of the operations. This latter portion of the order was reversed by the Supreme Court in appeal.[20] That a senior officer needed to seek legal recourse to 'correct' the records of the Kargil operations (notably, referred to as a 'war' in the judgment) and seek his due, seems unfortunate. It is equally commendable that the travesties of Kargil (or other operations) were redressed lawfully by officers, sans any showdown with the establishment. This despite the fact that the Indian Army suffered over 1714 reported casualties, including as many as 499 deaths of officers, junior commissioned officers and soldiers;[21] many of these deaths could have been avoided with better intelligence and strategy.

On the contrary, the aftermath of Kargil witnessed mass uprisings against the Pakistan government for suppression of facts regarding the deployment of troops in the operations, especially in the North-Eastern areas,[22] and the rapid return of the military to power under General Musharraf. The contrast between the roles played by the respective armies could not be more acute than in the Kargil aftermath, as the sections relating to Pakistan discuss in detail.

Operation Parakram and Mumbai 26/11

Two years after Kargil, the Indian Parliament suffered an audacious terror attack by terrorists belonging to Pakistan-sponsored groups—Lashkar-e-Taiba and Jaish-e-Mohammed, where nine persons were killed, including six from Delhi Police. This led to the commissioning of Operation Parakram, which entailed a full-scale mobilization of the Indian Army to test and display its preparedness for war, and to present an aggressive posture to Pakistan.[23] The COAS at the time, General S. Padmanabhan, concedes that the operation was, '[A direct] response from the Government [of India] against Pakistan, which was clearly perceived as the source of this terrorist action [Parliament attack], as indeed most terrorism afflicting India.'[24]

The operation was expected to deter cross-border terrorism but was called off in October 2002. While the general does not expand further on its success or the reasons for its abrupt withdrawal, authors have described it as a 'knee-jerk reaction' to the terrorist attack on the Indian Parliament in December 2001 (and the earlier 11 September attacks in New York) during which operation the troops suffered over 130 fatalities (in laying mines along the border and related activities) and a dent to their morale.[25]

Operation Parakram raised questions as to the control dichotomy in matters related to the deployment of (para) military forces, with the Rashtriya Rifles being required to operate alongside the BSF, despite their being a specialized wing of the army to fight counter-insurgency.[26] The anomaly is caused by bringing several paramilitary forces under the command of the home ministry, rather than the defence ministry, as was seen in the context of the Mumbai attacks of 26 November 2008, which held the entire city to siege and caused the death of 179 persons and injured 296 (including twenty-six and twenty-two foreigners, respectively).[27] Defying naval, R&AW, Coast Guard and IB intelligence, these terrorists were able to sail into Indian waters from the Arabian Sea, dock at the Gateway of India in Mumbai and run amok in the city for two days, snuffing out lives in prominent landmarks of the city. The only terrorist who was taken alive was Mohammed Ajmal Kasab, who was sentenced to death by a Special Court in Mumbai and has since been executed.

In the wake of the 26 November attacks on Mumbai, while the nation seemed to unite in its vitriolic resentment of the political leadership, it also united in its appreciation of the role played by the special forces of the National Security Guard (NSG), comprising highly trained commandos from the Indian Army, commanded uncharacteristically by an IPS officer.[28] While the events and aftermath of '26/11' exposed a cumulative failure of action and coordination on the part of political, intelligence, police and other agencies, and caused heads to roll (including that of the then Union home minister), the striking facet of the entire episode was the precision of the special forces that led from the front. The anti-terror operations and the painstaking rescue mission that saved many civilian hostages also cost the NSG some of its best men.[29] Experts cried out for the 'operationalization of intelligence'.[30] Or as Mumbai's former Commissioner of Police Julio Ribeiro asserted, 'The need is operational independence *without political interference.*'[31] (Emphasis supplied.)

Those who were killed in this terror attack included senior police officers Hemant Karkare, who headed the elite Anti-Terrorism Squad (ATS), Ashok Kamte, a distinguished officer who is alleged to be the one who shot Kasab but was never so credited[32] and Vijay Salaskar, an 'encounter specialist'. They were all posthumously awarded the Ashoka Chakra, the highest gallantry award in India in peacetime.

Karkare's death, in particular, has been the subject matter of speculation, with former Mumbai Inspector General of Police (IGP) S.M. Mushrif propounding a theory that certain 'internal forces' were behind the CST Station–Cama Hospital attack in Mumbai. He argues that the said attack (alone, and not the rest of the 26/11 Mumbai episode) was stage-managed to eliminate Karkare, who had blown the lid off the Malegaon blasts case that occurred at a Muslim cemetery, next to a mosque, in 2006 and caused the death of forty persons, and was proceeding to expose the involvement of 'Hindutva' terror outfits.[33] Though there is no official response to Mushrif's charges available, the Bombay High Court in petitions filed by MLA Radhakant Yadav and Jyoti Bedekar asked the State of Maharashtra to respond to contents of the book.[34]

Intriguingly, the Malegaon blasts charge sheet implicated, among others, retired army officers Lieutenant Colonel Shrikanth Prasad Purohit, Major Ramesh Upadhyaya and Colonel Shailesh Raikar of the Bhonsala Military School, and quotes the intention of Colonel Purohit and some of his aides of wanting to 'create a separate Constitution and a separate national flag'.[35] A stray, but disturbing, reference to officers of the army being drawn into offences of such gravitas, though judgment in the trial is still awaited. Though Colonel Purohit was granted bail by the Supreme Court in 2017, the court rejected his request for discharge in 2023.

10

AFSPA

'General Padmanabhan in 2001 said that the army had done its job [in Kashmir], now it was up to the politicians to resolve the matter. Sadly, he was told that generals were not supposed to make political statements.'

—A.S. Dulat with Aditya Sinha, *Kashmir: The Vajpayee Years*

Under the Armed Forces (Special Powers) Act (AFSPA), 1957, power has been given to the Governor of the state or the central government to declare the whole or any part of such state as a 'disturbed area' if it is in such a disturbed or dangerous condition that the use of armed forces in aid of the civil power is considered necessary in their opinion. In the area declared as a 'disturbed area'[1] certain officers in the armed forces have been conferred with special powers, including powers to open fire, arrest without warrant and destroy arms dumps. Authorized officers can search any premises without warrant and after giving such due warning as considered necessary, fire or otherwise use force even to cause death, of any person acting in contravention of any law or order for the time being in force in the disturbed area prohibiting the assembly of five or more persons.[2] The law confers powers in excess of the general criminal law and provides immunity to officers acting under the Act from prosecution or civil suits, except with the previous sanction of the central government. Though AFSPA was enacted to deal with ethnic Naga revolts in India's North-east,[3] it has been extended to other parts of the country from time to time. It has been deployed in all seven states in the North-east, and in Punjab as a special enactment, and has been withdrawn in some states, such as Tripura, and relaxed in certain districts in other states such as Assam. In 1990, the central government declared the Kashmir valley a 'disturbed area' under AFSPA, and this is where the law has come under its closest scrutiny.

While the BSF headed the counter-insurgency in the early days in Srinagar, the Indian Army wielded 'absolute power' to the point of carrying out crackdowns known as CASO—Cordon and Search Operation—that would last a day or longer and lead to alleged militants being taken away to detention centres to be tortured and, in many cases, to become part of 'the disappeared'.[4] Sumantra Bose refers to admitted instances of 'alley deaths', where suspected militants would be taken to the next alley and shot dead.[5] The author also highlights the episodes of Kunan–Poshpora (1991) and Machil (2010).[6] In the former, about forty Kashmiri women aged fifteen to seventy were alleged to have been gang-raped, though the B.G. Verghese-led inquiry found these allegations to be a 'massive hoax orchestrated by militant groups . . . as an entry point for re-inscribing Kashmir on the international agenda'.[7] The latter refers to the 'fake encounters' in Machil where three civilians were gunned down after being branded Pakistani terrorists. The court-martial conducted by the army found five of its own (including the commanding officer) guilty of murder and sentenced them to life imprisonment. The Armed Forces Tribunal in appeal released them on bail.[8] Other dark episodes such as the alleged Mubina Gani rape case (1990) and Badar–Payein Handwara (2003) rape of a mother and minor daughter stand out for the absence of intent to bring such charges to trial and the perpetrators to justice.[9]

In a scathing criticism of the Indian soldier in the context of AFSPA, Arif Ayaz Parrey says:

> Coming from marginalized communities and classes, these soldiers have never had any measure of control over their immediate surroundings before being posted to the 'disturbed areas'. Thirsting for some power and control, the soldiers are tempted by the combined seductive power of the guns (provided by the state) and the impunity provided by laws promulgated by the state (like AFSPA), and the othering of the entire native community as the enemy lures them into the abuse of their newly found power.[10]

Though this criticism discounts the role of the commanding officers to whom the soldiers report, as also the levels of training they receive in comparison with police forces, the fact is that the Indian soldier, who is normally admired by civil society, becomes villainized in some sections when placed in an asymmetrical role under AFSPA. While the constitutionality of AFSPA was upheld in 1998 by a Constitution Bench of the Supreme Court of India in *Naga People's Movement of Human Rights* v. *Union of India*,[11] the effects of the law on the ground continued to have a serious political impact. In 2007, the Working Group on Confidence Building Measures within Jammu and Kashmir, constituted by the Manmohan Singh government, recommended a review of the provisions of AFSPA and 'if possible, in light of the improved situation, revoking them'.[12] This was keeping in mind the long-standing demands to repeal AFSPA, especially by the National Conference. General S. Padmanabhan—the corps commander in Srinagar from 1993 to 1995 and later COAS—had himself spoken about 'scaling down the military presence in Kashmir',[13] though other chiefs have largely resisted the abrogation of AFSPA. Radha Kumar, one of the interlocutors appointed for the state in 2010, is pointed in observing that 'AFSPA should be repealed and the Indian parliament should incorporate safeguards into the Army Act . . . as the use of the army in internal security required regulation.'[14]

Demands to withdraw the notifications issued under AFSPA were also made in Assam, in the wake of the report of the Gandhi Peace Foundation in 1980.[15] Assam witnessed the imposition of President's rule in 1990, when the Prafulla Kumar Mahanta government was dismissed, and Lieutenant General Ajai Singh was appointed the new Eastern army commander to deal with 'a law and order situation'[16] prevailing due to the ascendancy of the United Liberation Front of Asom (ULFA). Multiple petitions were also filed before the Gauhati High Court seeking release of detenus alleged to have been illegally detained by the security forces under AFSPA and the allied Assam Disturbed Areas Act, 1955, which came to be disposed with mixed degrees of success, with the army producing the detenus in court in some cases and failing to do so in others.[17] Sangeeta Barooah Pisharoty refers to reports of the People's Union for Democratic Rights and Asia Watch on 'army atrocities in Assam in May 1991',[18] echoing similar reports in other AFSPA applied states.

AFSPA represents a unique form of legislative plumbing where the army (comprised almost entirely of non-locals, in contrast to the local police force) is brought in to internal areas in the country during peacetime to act in 'aid of civil power', in what are not strictly military operations. Indian law per se does not recognize the idea of martial law though Article 34 makes an oblique reference to it.[19] Despite the absence of an express framework for the imposition of martial law, AFSPA permits military intervention over and above the role of the state police in certain states, at the discretion of the government. Much of the everyday exercise of individual rights of movement and expression come to be regulated by the military. In its working, there is a significant devolution of executive power to the military commanders on the ground, which is unlike any police operation in peacetime.[20] Anuradha Bhasin makes an interesting observation that alongside AFSPA, state legislation such as the Jammu and Kashmir Control of Building Operations Act, 1988, read with Section 3 of the J&K Development Act, 1970, which enable the deregulation of construction in declared 'strategic areas', can 'wreak havoc on private, state and forest land',[21] basis compensation that is often illusory or even denied.

Quite apart from the human rights violations that have come up in the context of AFSPA, the existence of such an enactment demonstrates a hybrid model, where the military exercises what are essentially functions of the security services of the states and enters obliquely into the realm of governance. The effect of such 'intrusions' into the democratic space has been significant in Pakistan, where the combination of legitimacy of operations, role in governance and landholding has driven the military into the heart of civilian democracy. In India, the application of AFSPA creates a lopsided scenario where some states find the application of quasi-martial law. The discretion on whether to impose AFSPA or not lies with the central government and, in that sense, the state governments stand subordinated to the decision of the Centre, and the *execution* of that decision by the army. The effect is felt not only in the federal relationship between the Centre and the states, but also in the democratic ethos of the states concerned.

There is a difference between rights violations in wartime[22] and 'peacetime', governed by domestic law and subject to judicial review by domestic courts. This is where the vesting of the armed forces with powers under AFSPA is unique in the context of its interface with democracy. The experiment has disclosed greater *scope* and possibly greater instances of human rights violations. It could be argued then that involving the armed forces in matters other than national security in the traditional sense could give rise to greater abuse of power. It is incumbent to point out that the armed forces are often called upon to carry out other operations in peacetime too, such as flood relief, rescue operations, disaster management, peace marches and the like, which are performed with professionalism and efficiency. Nevertheless, the armed forces are legitimized with an expanded role under the AFSPA. This expanded role was not envisaged in the original text of the Constitution and was made explicit by the insertion of Entry 2A to the Union List in Schedule 7, providing for the 'deployment of armed forces in any State in aid of civil power'.[23]

A.S. Dulat observes, 'Yet the AFSPA is linked to the bigger question of how much power the army is wielding, and the movement in Kashmir has provided the army with an opportunity to expand its presence in J&K . . . many Kashmiris feel the army has turned the entire Valley into a cantonment.'[24] After containing militancy in the 1990s, the army could well have returned to its customary role, yet it 'did not want to cede the power it wielded as head of the unified command, and insisted that only it could be in charge'.[25] Some might term this as political misuse of the conventional role of the army, reducing civilian political space and, vice versa, in terms of the army getting accustomed to its new role and power. This diminishes democracy once the tipping point is crossed, and the army begins to camouflage itself as the civilian administration. While upholding the constitutionality of AFSPA, the Supreme Court opined that the Act does not supplant or displace civil power but only provides for deployment.[26] This is technically a truism in terms of a reading of the law. However, the political power play and the overtones referred to above demonstrate that civil power is *willy-nilly* yielded to the military in real terms.

Lawyer and academic Surabhi Chopra, in her piece 'National Security Laws in India: The Unraveling of Constitutional Constraints'[27] alludes to the fact that under AFSPA,

> [T]he executive's decision to designate an area as unusually dangerous or volatile is unconstrained by threshold conditions or even guiding criteria. If the Indian government declared a part of India to be in a state of emergency under Article 356 of the Constitution, it would have to specify how long the emergency will last, and Parliament would review any declaration of emergency. By contrast, when an area is designated as 'disturbed' under AFSPA, this need not be reviewed by central or state legislatures. Such declarations can be, and have been, renewed by the executive repeatedly, effectively persisting for years at a stretch. As a result . . . laws like the AFSPA allow the Indian government to constrain rights in the way it could if it declared a constitutional emergency, while evading the constitutional checks that regulate a decision of such gravity.

She proceeds to make a more telling point.

> Spatially limited laws also have the potential to reinforce or validate racial and ethnic prejudice against those who live in 'disturbed' parts of the country. They can map easily on to regional or religious differences between the majority of the country where they do not apply and the areas where they do. When an area is designated as 'disturbed', this might more easily allow law enforcement authorities to perceive its residents with a broad brush, conflating the peaceful majority with the minority of people who have adopted violent means for political ends.[28]

This 'prejudice' has at times led to what are colloquially known as 'fake encounters', leading to orders by the Supreme Court of India to inquire into the extrajudicial killings in Manipur.[29] While such encounters are more commonly associated with the police, the army has found itself stigmatized by the allegations after the invocation of AFSPA. Such acts of commission do not tie in with the otherwise secular, apolitical and professional reputation of the army.

In conclusion, it can be said that the Indian Army has been drawn not just into politically sensitive operations such as Operation Blue Star or those of the IPKF and AFSPA, but equally so into politically sensitive *situations* such as the friction with Defence Minister Krishna Menon in 1959–61, the political ambivalence found at the time of the 1962 China War and the Emergency, among others. The political shortcomings in these and other scenarios discussed in the preceding chapters could well have triggered a more 'interventionist' approach by the military, but mercifully, the armed forces abstained from crossing any lines in the sand. The reasons for these are manifold, but in essence, one can conclude that the military in India respected constitutional space enough to let these situations work themselves out in a befitting manner.

Pakistan: The Usurpation

11

Martial Law (1953)

'The natural calamities could be efficiently handled by the military; the man-made *ones were another story.'*

—Stephen P. Cohen, *The Pakistan Army*

Stephen P. Cohen, in his seminal work *The Pakistan Army*, points to the fact that in South Asia, the relationship between the army and society is 'particularly complex', replete with important 'strategic and political consequences'. In understanding the role of the Pakistan Army and its own place in society one must, he opines, allude to its 'aid to civil power' role, which leads to understanding how the military originally acquired 'the confidence to intervene in Pakistani politics'.[1]

To fathom the extent of the army's intervention in active politics, it is helpful right away to list the various heads of state since the birth of Pakistan till date (the italicized names are those of army generals who assumed power through a coup):[2]

Name	Title	Period
Mohammed Ali Jinnah	Governor General	Aug 1947–Sept 1948
Khwaja Nazimuddin	Governor General	Sept 1948–Oct 1951
Ghulam Mohammed	Governor General	Oct 1951–Aug 1955
Iskander Mirza	Governor General /President	Aug 1955–Oct 1958
Mohammed Ayub Khan	Chief Martial Law Administrator/ President	Oct 1958–Mar 1969
Mohammed Yahya Khan	Chief Martial Law Administrator/ President	Mar 1969–Dec 1971
Zulfikar Ali Bhutto	Chief Martial Law Administrator/ President	Dec 1971–Aug 1973
Chaudhry Fazal Elahi	President	Aug 1973–Sept 1978
Mohammad Zia-ul-Haq	Chief Martial Law Administrator/ President	July 1977–Aug 1988
Ghulam Ishaq Khan	President	Aug 1988–July 1993
Farooq Leghari	President	Nov 1993–Dec 1997
Rafiq Tarar	President	Dec 1997–June 2001
Pervez Musharraf[3]	President	June 2001–Aug 2008
Asif Ali Zardari	President	Sept 2008–Sept 2013
Mamnoon Hussain	President	Sept 2013–Sept 2018
Arif Alvi	President	Sept 2018–

The table is revealing. Over thirty-one years out of the first sixty-one years of its existence comprise governments by military coups in Pakistan. This does not include periods of martial law separately in force and the role played by the army behind the scenes.

Jinnah had an ostensible vision of a constitutional government in Pakistan. Paradoxically, he himself was a singular source of power, being both the governor general and the president of the Muslim League as well as the head of the Constituent Assembly. He also believed that Islam 'does not advocate a democracy which would allow the majority of non-Muslims to decide the fate of the Muslims' and hence Muslims were, as 'a self-determining political community', justified in demanding a separate homeland to live 'according to their own spiritual, cultural, economic, social and political ideals'.[4] Notwithstanding the communal bent of his ideology, his concepts were based on constitutional methods, broadly in the presidential form and conspicuously silent as to democratic structures. His biographer, Rafiq Zakaria, however is categorical that Jinnah had a conception of Pakistan that was 'more democratic than India' but was let down by politicians, bureaucrats and army commanders who were 'hardly practising Muslims' and were instead 'products of Anglo–Saxon training' and 'viceregal systems'.[5] And, though he refused to be a life-President of the Muslim League, the fact remained that he was seen as the sole repository of public confidence, leading to the 'routinization of [his] charisma'.[6]

The concentration of power right from the inception in the Quaid-e-Azam appeared to stifle the initial establishment and growth of democratic institutions in Pakistan. Jinnah had a short term at the helm and passed away on 11 September 1948—barely thirteen months after the formation of Pakistan. Hence, it is difficult to conclude as to the efficacy and sincerity of his democratic objectives. He was succeeded by a benevolent lawyer—Liaquat Ali Khan—who, as prime minister, inherited a polity that was dominated by provincial powers and demands, and bereft of larger national character. The governor general was an East Pakistani—Khwaja Nizamuddin—an appointee of the prime minister.

Jinnah, in a speech delivered to an East Pakistani audience in Dhaka on 21 March 1948, had acknowledged the threat of provincialism by pleading that the vast territory of Pakistan did not belong 'to a Punjabi or Sindhi, or a Pathan, or a Bengali' and that the citizens would 'for God's sake give up this provincialism' if they wanted to build a nation for themselves.[7]

However, these demands proved to be wishful, as factional politics held the fray in Pakistan. Prime Minister Liaquat was immediately faced with provincial acrimony and violence in Punjab, with Chief Minister Nawab Iftikhar Hussain Khan Mamdot at loggerheads with a breakaway faction of the Muslim League, headed by Mumtaz Daultana and Sardar Shauqat Hayat Khan. This led to the imposition of Governor's rule in August 1949. Similarly, the North-West Frontier Province (NWFP) suffered riots, driven by the clash between the ruling Muslim League and the much-admired separatist leader—Khan Abdul Ghaffar Khan. In 1951, Sind too was brought under Governor's rule owing to acute political instability, and Balochistan, which was itself volatile, was ruled from the Centre to maintain a sense of order. Ironically, the only province that seemed to enjoy a sense of 'normalcy' was East Pakistan.[8]

Provincial leaders in Pakistan were essentially elitist, drawn from the Muslim League's pool of wealthy landlords and businessmen. A prominent member of the League, Chaudhary Muhammad Ali described them laconically as, '. . . landlords, the well-to-do lawyers, rich businessmen and the titled gentry . . . With some exceptions, they were not men noted for their total commitment to any cause. Their willingness to sacrifice their personal interests or comfort for the sake of the nation was often in doubt, and not unjustly.'[9]

This lack of 'nationalism' in the provincial leaders contrasts sharply with the civilian leadership in India at the time, where national leaders were those who had battled for independence and intended to lead India to greatness. In this background, the Pakistan Army, which was a hybrid of British and local officers, watched the disappointing civilian governance of Pakistan from a distance. Liaquat Ali Khan, a 'strong man . . . like Jinnah' with 'sensible' ideas for a Constitution, but without 'time to hone them and then lay them before parliament'[10] was himself oblivious of military matters. He was deeply impressed by the personality and acumen of Brigadier (as he then was) Ayub Khan and rapidly promoted him to the post of COAS, superseding other senior generals. Indeed, on taking over from General Gracey, Ayub was warned by Gracey of renegade officers in the Pakistan Army. Almost immediately on assuming office as the chief, Ayub Khan learnt from Prime Minister Liaquat of a conspiracy in the NWFP where a group of army officers were conspiring 'to overthrow the government and install a military-style nationalistic government'.[11]

Though the coup was repelled and the perpetrators punished with imprisonment, it is apparent that the army was disgruntled with the state of affairs almost immediately after the birth of Pakistan. Tellingly, it seemed willing to claim the right of (military) governance. The only antidote to such dissension would have been the development of strong constitutionalism. However, Prime Minister Liaquat was too preoccupied with the rumblings within the Muslim League to attend to such exalted matters, and delegated this paramount task of governance to the bureaucracy who scavenged political power and, along with the army, assumed a pivotal (and debilitating) role in the country's political progress.[12]

The political leadership itself was losing ground, with Liaquat facing stiff opposition and dissent from various quarters, resulting in his assassination at a political rally close to Rawalpindi on 16 October 1951. The investigating officer—Nawabzada Aitzazuddin—was mysteriously killed soon after in an air crash and, with him, were destroyed the records of the case.[13] Pakistan's political trajectory might have taken a different path had Jinnah and Liaquat not passed on in the early years. Had they been able to work with a constitution and developed systems to execute its ideals in the early decades, this 'partnership of highly devoted and talented leaders'[14] might have been able to stem the role of the army in politics and given democracy a chance in Pakistan.

During British rule, there was an enormous dependence on the bureaucracy to keep the wheels of the administration turning. In the absence of well-honed systems of democracy, the predominant position of the bureaucrat continued, more so in Pakistan, and the balance between the elected and non-elected institutions continued to be lopsided.[15] Political scientist Philip Oldenburg is pointed in his assessment of the difference in 'inheritance' between India and Pakistan at Independence—while India had a political apparatus stronger than that of its 'state' apparatus, Pakistan had a closer proximity to the civil service apparatus of the British. This resulted in a greater reliance on the bureaucracy, and the political leadership 'began to look feeble'.[16]

Following Liaquat's assassination, Governor General Khwaja Nazimuddin was sworn in as the new prime minister and the President of the Muslim League and notably, a bureaucrat—Ghulam Mohammad—the then Finance Secretary, was appointed governor general. Described as 'intelligent, ruthless and highly ambitious',[17] Ghulam Mohammad was to use the office of governor general to exercise political clout, whether or not the circumstances or precedent so justified. The absence of a strong political leadership in Pakistan at the time was exposed by this bureaucratic appointment.

Nazimuddin faced an expected and elevated state of unrest, particularly in Punjab, where religious riots had broken out on account of differences between the Ahrars and the Ahmadiyyas.[18] Punjab, even generally, suffered disquiet owing to the proposed constitution, which the Punjabis were keen on tailoring to suit their dominant status in Pakistan. Nazimuddin was unable to muster a political solution and, out of desperation, turned to the army for assistance and imposed martial law on 8 March 1953. This was the ominous toehold that the army was gifted by the civilian leadership itself.

The 1953 episode was vital to the army as '[I]t occurred near the central recruiting grounds, [and] the agitation began to affect the troops themselves, striking at the very heart of the army's cohesion, not least because the [civilian] disturbances involved sectarian religious differences.'[19]

Despite these peculiar challenges, the army swung into action under the command of Major General Muhammad Azam Khan, quickly restoring a sense of law and order by the use of force. The citizens viewed the army as a saviour of sorts, and the army itself took a dim view of the civilian leadership and assumed unto itself the powers of administration and quasi-governance. Significantly, the people of Pakistan saw the army as a legitimate source of power and having divested its powers to the army, the civilian leadership set a precedent that would return to haunt Pakistan for eternity.

Moreover, while the army grew in stature and jurisdiction, the governor general (who, as mentioned earlier, was a bureaucrat) dismissed Nazimuddin as prime minister in 1953 and replaced him with Muhammad Ali Bogra, an 'erstwhile rabble-rouser from East Pakistan'.[20] Such events confirmed that democracy in Pakistan was stillborn, as the Executive exercised absolute powers over the government in power—a usurpation that flies in the face of constitutional democracy. Of course, here was a government that was not yet *by the people* as elections were yet to be held.

Interestingly, Kotera Bhimaya, in his scholarly work *Civil–Military Relations: A Comparative Study of India and Pakistan*, comments that the bureaucracy in India was used by its early political leaders such as Nehru as 'a buffer between them (the political leadership) and the army', thereby creating a 'tradition of civilian supremacy'.[21] The key difference was that the executive in Pakistan enjoyed far greater latitude compared to India, where the democratically elected government that came into power in the 1952 elections called the shots. Pakistan was yet to even hold its first election at this point in time and hence there was greater scope for other institutions such as the bureaucracy and the army to grapple for absolute power.

The sanction for such overwhelming powers to be exercised by the military–executive axis in Pakistan was affirmed by Jinnah himself, while addressing senior army officers in 1948, when he stated that the oath taken by the officers affirming allegiance to the constitution of the Dominion of Pakistan *justified its interpretation by the army* and significantly, the fact that the army was duty-bound to act *only* upon the orders sanctioned by the executive authority, namely, *the Governor General*.[22]

This dichotomy with the source of power and the legitimacy of the civilian government proved to be a death knell for democratic processes in Pakistan. Shuja Nawaz succinctly describes this as the basis for the army to reserve 'the right to act as it saw fit in the interest of Pakistan and in *its own interest*'.[23] (Emphasis supplied.)

In essence, the lack of a healthy civilian government during the post-Jinnah era meant that power vested heavily in the bureaucracy, which was comparatively better organized and equipped to handle governance. As such, no single leader could make their mark in the first decade of Independence and multiple prime ministers shared centre stage during this period. The bureaucracy grappled for power with the political leadership, while instability and political violence (especially in the sensitive Karachi area) were rampant. Intriguingly, the task of enforcement of law and order fell on the army, which acquitted itself commendably and gained acceptance in the eyes of the general public as being a competent and disciplined institution. The political leadership itself, as recounted earlier, abdicated power to the army by imposing martial law in 1953, which greatly enhanced the role of the army and undermined the status of the political leadership.[24]

The delay in holding elections on account of pressure from the Mohajirs[25] for separate constituencies compounded the instability.[26] Prime Minister Bogra and his senior ministers unhesitatingly (and perhaps desperately) discussed sensitive political matters with mid-high level army officers and enabled their involvement in the politics of the time.[27] Hence, paradoxically, the experiment of democracy in the early years was sabotaged by the civilian government itself, which was not averse to yielding power to the army in order to protect its own position.

12

Ayub Khan's Coup

'*Keep out of politics . . . You must avoid taking any active part in party politics and propagation of any such views . . . we [the Army] are the servants of any party that the people put in power.*'

—General (later Field Marshal) Ayub Khan's Order of Day on taking over as the Chief of Pakistan Army in 1951, quoted in Shuja Nawaz, *Crossed Swords: Pakistan, Its Army, and the Wars Within*

Samuel Huntington observes that the causes which produce military intervention in politics lie not in the nature of the officers but 'in the structure of society [and] in particular, they lie *in the absence of effective political institutions in society*'.[1] (Emphasis supplied.)

According to the American scholar Allen McGrath, 28 October 1954 marks the destruction of Pakistan's democracy.[2] It was on this day that Governor General Ghulam Mohammad, after consultation with the chief justice of the Supreme Court, declared Emergency and dismissed the cabinet as well as the Constituent Assembly. He further ordered the police to prohibit the members of the Constituent Assembly from meeting in

Karachi, where they were going to vote on the draft constitution approved at the assembly's previous session.

McGrath notes, Pakistan had no shortage of talented politicians then, and they did not lack political and parliamentary experience. However, they were divided on the question of a constitution—especially opposed by the assembly's Bengali members from East Pakistan, some of whom joined with the West Pakistanis to argue that Pakistan was not ready for 'real' democracy and could only function as a virtual extension of the Raj. Stephen Cohen attributes this to a lack of confidence in their own political bases.[3]

The façade of the parliamentary system, as Talbot describes it,[4] continued for five years after the overthrow of Prime Minister Nazimuddin in 1953, but the power centre was made up of the ungainly mix of Governor General Iskandar Mirza, General Ayub Khan and the wily bureaucrat, Ghulam Mohammad, with three different prime ministers holding office during this period (apart from Bogra, who served until 1955). If the hitherto continuous involvement of the army in civilian matters 'persuaded' General Ayub Khan and his officers that 'they would be continually used and abused by civilians',[5] various other developments too laid the framework for a military coup in Pakistan.

Firstly, Ghulam Mohammad's decision to declare 'Emergency' and dissolve the Legislative Assembly, in order to prevent any vote on the new constitution, was legitimized a year later by the Federal Court,[6] thus leaving Pakistan in constitutional limbo: it was governed neither by the 1935 Government of India Act, nor by a new constitution. Further, General Ayub Khan had himself at the time (in 1954), while in a Dorchester Hotel in the UK, penned a document that foresaw a political system for Pakistan that had a supreme commander to head the joint staff who would also be an *ex officio* member of the cabinet.[7] This document contemplated a democracy to be worked 'in the spirit of the Quran' with the President as the Supreme Commander.[8] The document was silent as to the involvement of a general as the President.

During this period, the army and the bureaucracy grew in strength on account of the continuous bickering and horse-trading carried out by the provincial political leaders, who were yet to come up with an 'ethnic' constitution for Pakistan. Instead, the task of coming up with a new constitution was assigned to another bureaucrat, Chaudhary Mohammad Ali, and Major General Iskander Mirza—a former army man and later a civil servant—who was made part of the cabinet in 1956 and thereafter made President of Pakistan![9] The constitution came to be adopted in 1956, providing for a parliamentary form of government. Till such time, the administrative structures in Pakistan were broadly based on the Government of India Act, 1935, with the governor general and the (unelected) prime minister calling the shots. It is significant, as the succeeding sections will show, that the first direct general election in Pakistan could only take place in 1970, fourteen years after the coming into force of its constitution.[10] During this period, Pakistan saw scattered provincial elections (Punjab and NWFP in 1951, and Sind in 1953), military rule at the centre implemented *via* an unelected Chief Martial Law Administrator (or President) and, resultantly, a botched experiment with democracy.

The provincial governments in place also came to be replaced at will by the President. In March 1957, President Mirza invoked his plenary powers by declaring President's rule in the wake of the Muslim League coming together with the National Awami Party.[11] This alliance would have led to a solid political unit in West Pakistan and could have been a palpable threat to the Presidency (as well as to the concept of One Unit Scheme[12]). Soon after, in early 1958, East Pakistan's Governor Fazlul Haq was dismissed by Mirza and President's rule imposed, upon the dismissal of the cabinet of Ataur Rehman Khan. In June 1958, President's rule was again imposed in East Pakistan to enable a return to power of Ataur Rehman's cabinet when the National Awami Party withdrew support and brought down the ruling United Front. Perhaps the last nail in the coffin of democracy in Pakistan was when, in September 1958, deputy speaker of the Provincial Assembly—Shahed Ali—was beaten *to death* by fellow members of the Assembly for carrying a motion on behalf of the House that the absent Speaker was of 'unsound mind'.[13]

Shuja Nawaz quotes Ayesha Jalal to state: 'If developments in West Pakistan gave [President] Mirza good reason to want to banish the spectre of elections . . . the downfall of four ministries in East Pakistan within six months came as a welcome bonus.'[14] The proposed elections in February 1959 were hence a virtual non-starter, and democracy in Pakistan was a myth. The army, the bureaucracy and indeed the people of Pakistan had little faith in the politicians and were looking for other and better alternatives.

Be that as it may, General Ayub Khan was intrinsically involved in the developments at the time, being successful in obtaining a two-year extension to his term as commander-in-chief of the Pakistan Army (with effect from 1 January 1959) and being appointed by President Mirza as the chairman of Joint Chiefs of Staff, a newly created post. Simultaneously, his new-found stature was becoming an eyesore to the already insecure politicians, who began spreading rumours that Ayub Khan was a spy, selling secrets to India, and that his trip to the US in April 1958 was in fact a visit to collect his commission from agents of Jawaharlal Nehru.[15] This episode could equally be interpreted as being stage-managed by the Military Intelligence to spur Ayub Khan into coercive action, as there is no public record of any such statements being made by any political leader.

General Ayub Khan would, in October 1958, quite contrary to his earlier message in 1951, publicly state:

> A word for the disruptionists, political opportunists, black marketeers, and other such social vermin, sharks and leeches—*the soldiers* and the people are sick of the sight of you. So it will be good for you to turn [sic: turn over] a new leaf and begin to behave, *otherwise retribution will be swift and sure.*[16] (Emphasis supplied.)

Action, indeed, was to follow with even the US Ambassador James Langley conveying to the Pakistani leadership (i.e., Mirza) that though the US favoured democratic government over autocratic government, 'there may be exceptions which can be justified for limited periods'.[17]

It was against this background of political instability and internal chaos that on 7 October 1958, Pakistan's President Major General Iskander Mirza declared martial law and dismissed the central and provincial governments. (A day earlier, the army was called in to suppress a secessionist move in Balochistan when Mir Ahmad Yar Khan, the Khan of Kalat, lowered the Pakistani flag and began talks with Iran for a new political identity.) Further, political parties were abolished and Ayub Khan was appointed supreme commander of the armed forces and chief martial law administrator (CMLA). Mirza justified his actions based on all-pervasive corruption, the abhorrent struggle for power by the politicians, food and economic crises, and the exploitation of Pakistan's populace.[18]

In a letter to his son Humayun, circa 1958, General Mirza had confessed that, 'The country [Pakistan], to put it bluntly, is being ruined by politicians . . . the general state of the country is bad. Many think everything will be alright after general elections. I have my doubts, as people who will come to power will not come from the planets but from Pakistan.'[19]

It is critical to note that though Military Rule was bitterly opposed by a few Pakistani politicians, most found a role in the new system or dropped out of politics altogether, and the army was assisted by the civilian bureaucracy and the political elite in its 'supervisory' role. As Ishtiaq Ahmed observes, the peaceful transition 'from an inept, corrupt, faction-ridden, unrepresentative civilian government to military rule' through the medium of martial law, 'was widely supported by the larger society'.[20]

Cohen attributes the justification for the imposition of Military Rule at this time to three perceived and stated reasons: firstly, the alleged threat to Pakistan from India whereby India was portrayed as an ally of Moscow. Secondly, the conception that Pakistani armed forces had the best understanding of national defence, foreign affairs and security issues. Finally, the theory that regional peace was possible only if a military balance was achieved vis-à-vis India.[21]

Ayub Khan based his legitimacy of Military Rule in Pakistan on the above premise, often on Alberuni's framework of Hindu–Muslim differences:

> It was Brahmin chauvinism and arrogance that had forced us to seek a homeland of our own where we could order our life according to our own thinking and faith. They wanted us to remain as serfs, which was precisely the condition in which the Muslim minority in India lived today. There was the fundamental opposition between the ideologies of India and Pakistan. The whole Indian society was based on class (sic: caste) distinction, in which even the shadow of a low-caste man [is] enough to pollute a member of the high caste.[22]

Ayub opined that because of their hatred for Muslims, Indian leaders wanted to badger Pakistan into subservience and that Pakistan had to build a 'deterrent force with adequate offensive and defensive power; enough, at least, to neutralize the Indian Army'. He added, 'India can concentrate her forces against us without warning. We must, therefore, have a standing army ready to take the field at a moment's notice.'[23]

However, soon after Martial Rule, Ayub Khan started seriously considering a more active role for the army than just to combat the neighbouring nation. Even when he came up with the blueprint at Dorchester, referred to earlier, he noted that 'the army could not be unaffected by the conditions around it'[24] and would necessarily need to respond to the political woes that faced the country. Curiously, the army itself reflected the fissures of civilian society in Pakistan, being divided along sectarian lines, with the Punjabi-speaking sections seeking to dominate the Sindhi, Pushto, Bengali and Urdu-speaking rest. (Ayub himself was a Pathan, but spoke more Punjabi than Pushto, at least publicly.) More so, the divide between the 'insiders' and 'outsiders'[25] was even more pronounced, the latter comprising the migrants from India who were mainly Urdu-speaking Mohajirs from Uttar Pradesh and Hyderabad and generally regarded as elitist outsiders, due to their higher levels of education and standards of living.

Though Martial Law was purportedly a stopgap arrangement whereby the Mirza–Ayub combine would bring order to the political system in Pakistan before the proposed elections in February 1959, differences between the two men were far-reaching. Soon after the imposition of Martial Law, Iskander Mirza found himself eclipsed by Ayub Khan who, as the CMLA, was perceived as the de jure *and* de facto power centre. Having himself appointed Ayub as CMLA, President Mirza was now keen on nullifying the effect of the powers enjoyed by Ayub Khan, and even went to the extent of exploring the possible arrest of Ayub on his return from East Pakistan by the top brass of the forces in return for expedited promotions for the officers approached to undertake the operation.[26]

To President Mirza's chagrin, most of the army top brass were fiercely loyal to Ayub Khan and word of Mirza's plans soon reached Ayub (through Yahya Khan). Ayub Khan responded swiftly, with Lieutenant General Wajid Ali Khan Burki along with lieutenant generals Azam and Sheikh being deputed to visit President Mirza's residence on 27 October 1958 at 10 p.m. to 'extract' a resignation from him, which the latter tendered in his night robes![27]

Thus began the first full-blown stint of Martial Law, with an army general at the helm of affairs, having come to power bereft of the democratic process and setting the pattern for times to come. The eleven ministers (of whom three were army generals) under President Mirza took oaths afresh under the presidential cabinet of Ayub Khan, who was now the new President of Pakistan and retained with himself the ministries of Defence, Kashmir Affairs and the Cabinet Secretariat.

Ironically, the Ayub years were a break from the chaos and disorder that preceded his coup, with high levels of administrative efficiency. As Cohen states, the army 'set about disinfecting Pakistan, and the army public relations apparatus played down the coup aspect of Ayub's takeover, emphasizing its revolutionary and popular dimension' in keeping with Ayub's promise of the emergence of a 'sound, solid, and strong nation'.[28]

He also gave an unequivocal pledge that he would restore power to the people of Pakistan via a new political system that would provide suitable checks and balances on political parties and politicians.[29] Expectedly, there was no mention of democracy in his pledge.

Significantly, the public accepted the military leadership of Ayub and made little protest about the lack of democracy and even the judiciary upheld the takeover of power, with the Supreme Court of Pakistan refusing to set aside the action of Ayub Khan in perpetrating a coup that would otherwise be repugnant to constitutional democracy.[30] The doctrine of necessity was invoked to save the day. The military was thus supported by the weakness of key institutions—the electorate and the judiciary—in undermining the fundamental tenets of democracy and reinforcing the theory of Huntington with which this chapter began, i.e., the marked absence of political institutions leading to military intervention.

In the process, the 1956 constitution was repealed and repromulgated in its new avatar in 1962 with a presidency indirectly elected by 80,000 union councillors and the National Conference and Muslim League. In this arrangement, the generals ruled the roost, assisted by the bureaucracy, while civilian politicians were relegated to the background without much protest.

Ayub's economic policy paved the way for the military to align with the business community and further weaken the political leadership. Akin to the developments witnessed in Turkey (after the 1960 coup) and Thailand (martial law, 1959), this phase witnessed economic reform at the behest of the military leadership. The experiment in Pakistan resulted in the establishment of the Pakistan Industrial Development Corporation (PIDC), which would finance the industrial growth of the 1960s, often favouring those segments that supported the military regime. Other policy initiatives allowed new entrepreneurs to set up factories and mills, with businessmen coming from the ranks of Punjabi merchants, the feudal aristocracy, retired civil servants and even military officers.[31]

Resultantly, the Pakistan Army was now well and truly entrenched in Pakistani politics and governance. Though, over the years, 'periodic jugglery' would follow, the involvement of the army in politics, was a 'phenomenon . . . often prompted and welcomed by [the Pakistani] politicians'.[32]

13

War with India (1965)

'Indian Rulers were never reconciled to the establishment of an independent Pakistan . . . all their military preparations during the last eighteen years have been directed against us [Pakistan].'

—General Ayub Khan's radio address to his people on 6 September 1965, D-Day of India's retaliation against Pakistan, quoted in Gohar Ayub Khan, *Glimpses into the Corridors of* Power

Applying Edward Luttwak's definitions of coups,[1] Shuja Nawaz describes the Ayub episode of 1958 as a coup de main or putsch, being a coup carried out by players (Mirza and Ayub) who were themselves part of authority and not a traditional *coup d'état*, which emanates from forces outside the power structure.[2] The key factor in determining which constituent ultimately reigns, of course, was the army.

General Ayub Khan had himself reflected:

> . . . [as to] how, if the army got drawn into political life—and this seemed inevitable—it could withdraw itself from the situation. The outside world was going to interpret the action of the army in terms of *coup d'etat* . . . [which] would have

> a damaging effect on the image and reputation of Pakistan. A well-organized, trained, and disciplined army would find it extremely distasteful to be turned into an instrument for securing political power.[3]

. . . and then confessed, 'But as conditions were, *the army alone could act as the corrective force and restore normalcy.*'[4] (Emphasis supplied.)

The early part of the Ayub years witnessed an impetus to education and land reform, and increasing political alliances with sections of the hydra-headed Muslim League. Significantly, there was an increase in the size of the army to a quarter of a million, which was planned by the leadership to be an optimal size to counter that of India.[5] The force was also getting better equipped and, simultaneously, the results of the 1962 Sino–Indian War made the Pakistani leadership more sanguine about resolving the simmering Kashmir conflict by force.[6]

Against this backdrop—and largely at the instance of his Foreign Minister Zulfikar Ali Bhutto—General Ayub Khan (who had now *suo motu* become the first Field Marshal of the Pakistan Army) resolved to undertake a localized foray into Kashmir. This culminated (perhaps inadvertently) into war.[7] The objective was to bring India to the negotiating table and proceeded on the basis that the incursions would arouse a mass uprising from the local Kashmiris, who would support the Pakistani initiative. However, the Kashmiris did not respond as expected by Pakistan, nor did India take the aggression on the chin. Instead, she reacted strongly through her army and none of Pakistan's Western allies came to her rescue, while China paid mere lip service.[8]

It must be mentioned that there were ongoing skirmishes between the two troops along the Indo–Pak border in the Rann of Kutch area even in early 1965. However, these were low-intensity, low-publicity episodes as compared to 'Operation Gibraltar', undertaken by Pakistan in Kashmir. This was triggered also, purportedly, by the increasing military movement by India in the territory and the imprisonment of Sheikh Abdullah.[9] Pakistan, under Ayub Khan's orders, on (or about) 24 July 1965, directed the deployment of trained guerillas and army officers, who were to infiltrate the Valley and draw on local support in order to emancipate Kashmir.[10] However, the assumptions, firstly, that the dispute would remain local in nature and not spill over into a larger warlike scenario and, secondly, that the local Kashmiri populace would spontaneously support the movement were both seriously flawed.[11]

India responded strongly under the leadership of Prime Minister Shastri and decided to target Lahore. The meeting of 3 September 1965 between the prime minister, his defence minister and the army and air force chiefs[12] laid down the following objectives:

i. To defeat the Pakistani attempts to seize Kashmir by force and to make it abundantly clear that Pakistan would never be allowed to wrest Kashmir from India;
ii. To destroy the offensive power of Pakistan's armed forces;
iii. To occupy only the minimum Pakistan territory necessary to achieve these purposes, which would be vacated after the satisfactory conclusion of the war'.[13]

India's reaction stunned Pakistan, who suffered from lack of planning, coordination and morale at the higher levels of the military leadership. The plan of offence self-destructed and Pakistan basically had to switch to a defensive mode to save Lahore. There were several counter-attacks in areas like Khem Kharan in Indian Punjab and at Chawinda in Pakistan, the Pakistani troops appeared ill-prepared for a conflict of this magnitude.[14]

Ayub Khan realized the need to summarily put an end to the conflict as any continued combat would most certainly have resulted in a massive loss of men, money, territory and reputation. Having implicitly relied on the now dubious advice of Foreign Minister Bhutto and other army commanders and having failed to garner any international support of substance from the Chinese or the US (and having already expended hundreds of good soldiers and billions of rupees), Ayub Khan needed to offer an olive branch to India. Fortunately for President Ayub, the Indian prime minister himself was advised by the army top brass that ammunitions were running thin and a settlement was worth considering.[15]

On 23 September 1965, a ceasefire was declared, and subsequently the Tashkent Accord (infamous for Prime Minister Shastri's demise the night it was signed) followed in January 1966. The Accord was offered to the people of Pakistan as a smokescreen for the lapses of the leadership, the growing divide between Ayub and Bhutto and, in no small measure, the increasing divide between Punjabi-dominated West Pakistan and the Bengali-dominated East.[16] The key military and political centres of power were all in the West and controlled largely by Punjabis.

Cohen concludes that while in the 'dominant West Wing the 'idea' of Pakistan pertained to a martial people defending its Punjabi stronghold', Bengal and Bengalis seemed to only figure 'as an investment opportunity or source of foreign exchange'.[17]

The people of East Pakistan rightfully felt short-changed by the leadership in the West, who had neither consulted them in undertaking the adventure nor factored in their defence once India retaliated. This distrust between the two peoples would come back to haunt West Pakistan in 1971.

Cohen further analyses that the army officers, as a group, acquired an exaggerated view of the weakness of both India and her military, as a result of which the result of the 1965 War came as a shock, and some even came to believe that a conspiracy in Pakistan was responsible for the failure to achieve a clear-cut military victory.[18] The fact remains that the top brass of the Pakistan Army was perceived as being 'soft', capricious and politicized. This was, in a sense, symptomatic of Ayub Khan's regime, which was described by his ghostwriter/propaganda-meister Altaf Gauhar when he wrote:

> There was no recognition that the real cause [for the state of affairs] was the public apprehension of one-man rule, the domination of the centre over the provinces, the inequitable allocation of resources between East and West Pakistan, the extension of bureaucratic control over every walk of life, and the denial of fundamental human rights and freedoms.[19]

Field Marshal Ayub Khan was himself a casualty of the 1965 War. Suffering a rapid decline in health and status, in January 1968, he was unceremoniously subjected to a discreet coup d'état. Under General Yahya Khan's orders, his residence was sealed when he suffered a heart attack, though he continued as a titular head for another year or so.[20] By early 1969, the customary pressure to impose martial law was felt by the incumbent chief of the army—General Yahya Khan. In March 1969, Yahya Khan declared martial law (though not publicly) and, on 25 March, Ayub Khan had a taste of his own medicine when he was approached by the Army Chief with a 'request' to resign. Ayub Khan duly tendered his resignation and, in what is rightly described as 'an extra-constitutional step'[21] handed over the reins of power to General Yahya Khan rather than to the constitutionally mandated successor, viz. the Speaker of the National Assembly. General Yahya Khan now (on 26 March) publicly declared martial law and once more usurped the constitution from the people of Pakistan.

Ayub Khan retired to oblivion and died a few years later on 20 April 1974. Though regarded as being non-corrupt as an individual, Field Marshal Ayub's regime was conspicuous for the absence of any trace of democratic rule and set the sinister precedent of martial law that would dominate Pakistan's political landscape in the future.

14

Yahya Khan's Tenure

'The supreme irony . . . is that the constitution of Pakistan was to be suspended and altered by some of the officers in his [Jinnah's] audience, including Yahya Khan.'

—Stephen P. Cohen, *The Pakistan Army*

The unsuccessful adventure against India in 1965 and Field Marshal Ayub Khan's treatment of East Pakistan as 'militarily expendable' led to the events of March 1969, detailed earlier. In a quasi-'guardian coup'[1] the army chief, General Yahya Khan, removed Ayub Khan, imposed martial law, dissolved the national and provincial assemblies, and did away with the One Unit Scheme, which was intended to avoid lopsided provincial domination by West Pakistan. Though not as 'cerebral, principled or puritan' as Ayub Khan, General Yahya Khan seemed to be 'liked by more people than Ayub'.[2]

Yahya Khan was now the new CMLA and the President of Pakistan and made customary homilies to constitutionalism when, in his first speech to the nation, he said:

> My sole aim in imposing martial law is to protect life, liberty and the property of the people and put the administration on

> the rails . . . I wish to make it absolutely clear that I have no ambitions other than the creation of conditions conducive to the establishment of a *constitutional government* . . . [as] a prerequisite for sane and constructive political life and for *the smooth transfer of power to the representatives of the people,* elected freely and impartially on the basis of adult franchise.[3] (Emphasis supplied.)

The fait accompli was that even two decades after its formation, Pakistan was eons away from basic constitutional democracy and had entered its third phase of martial law. In fact, within a month of the making of the above speech, he alluded to having to rule the unfortunate country for another fourteen years![4]

The imposition of martial law meant that the skeleton of the 1962 constitution would apply, though fundamental rights would stand suspended and the regime would be immune from judicial review. These were the classic ingredients of autocracy. Additionally, General Yahya was himself an ad hoc administrator, with far lesser interest or expertise in civilian governance than even Ayub Khan, and the administration of the time was riddled with caprice and opacity.[5]

However, the army in Pakistan was no longer the apolitical institution that its Indian counterpart was, or that it was at the inception with the British traditions of being officers and gentlemen. The army was now politically sensitized, with an active involvement in governance and *ex officio* status in the form of the defence ministry and the CMLA. Significantly, the army was, by now, a key player in the economy of Pakistan, having vast interests in land, business and national assets, which interests were directly linked to the imposition and continuance of martial law—indicative of Ayesha Siddiqa's 'Milbus'.[6] As such, the focus of the army shifted, in many ways, from soldiering to matters of civilian administration, with selfish interests at heart.

Paradoxically, however, General Yahya Khan's tenure was to witness the most democratic elections thus far (1970), with a satisfactory electoral turnout, campaigning on public issues, general freedom of speech and an active media.[7] Yahya Khan had, upon assuming power in 1969, indicated timelines to hold an election to both the national and provincial assemblies in October 1970 and accordingly introduced measures such as the commencement of 'political activities' from January 1970, provincial autonomy and work on a new draft constitution. All the while, retaining with the President the power to amend, approve or reject the draft constitution to be submitted by the assembly. Hence, there existed a toxic cocktail of a few parts of constitutional governance and many parts of martial law.

However, true to his word, Yahya Khan laid the groundwork for the conduct of elections in 1970. The key concern of the regime in (West) Pakistan was the possible outcome of the elections in East Pakistan, especially with respect to the prospects of the explosive Awami League, headed by Sheikh Mujibur Rehman. Mujibur Rehman had emerged as a potential threat to the dominance of the West Wing, with a blueprint for the sharing of powers between the East and West wings, vide his 'Six Point Programme'.[8]

The anxiety relating to the increasing popularity of Sheikh Mujib and his proposed Six Point Programme is apparent from the secret report of the General Headquarters (GHQ), contained in their archives, which stated:

> Its [the Six Point Programme] modus operandi . . . stemmed from a callous and deep-rooted conspiracy to create regional hatred . . . The Six Points envisaged a weak centre and ultimately a weak Pakistan. Therefore, the Indian Government seized [t]his chance to exploit the situation to her advantage. The Indian propaganda media began voicing the grievances of the 'oppressed' people of 'Bangla Desh'.

> Their Propaganda organs [sic] openly infiltrated in East Pakistan. The local Hindu community came in the forefront in support of Bangla [Bengali] language and Six Points . . . Six Points became a movement, actively guided by foreign governments.[9]

The India bogey was evident.

Pre-poll assessments disclosed that neither the Awami League in the East nor the Pakistan People's Party (PPP) in the West would garner sufficient seats to form a government and, as such, Yahya Khan would, conveniently, continue to command a hung parliament of a shaky civilian government. Hence, the President was not averse to going ahead with the proposed elections.

Flooding in East Pakistan in October caused a postponement of elections to December, and ultimately, elections to the National Assembly were held on 7 December 1970. Voting took place in 300 general constituencies, of which 162 were in East Pakistan and 138 in West Pakistan. Another thirteen seats were reserved for women (seven in East Pakistan and six in the West), who were to be elected by members of the National Assembly. The results were publicly monitored through the print and electronic media about ten days later. To the shock of General Yahya Khan and his cohorts, the Awami League, which was expected to win no more than fifty to seventy seats out of 162 in the East, won an overwhelming 160 seats and all seven women's seats in East Pakistan. Zulfikar Ali Bhutto's PPP won only eighty-one seats and five women's seats, all in the West.[10] The Awami League hence had a majority *even* in the National Assembly, and won similar results in the provincial assembly elections. This potentially meant that Sheikh Mujib could now stake a claim to be prime minister.

Aghast at these developments, the anti-East Pakistan lobby in the West Wing, which included army generals, opted to support PPP's Zulfikar Ali Bhutto as their leader.

Yahya Khan himself was willing to consider the appointment of Mujibur Rehman as the prime minister but was advised against it by his military advisers and 'constitutional experts' on the ground that Sheikh Mujib may use his majority in the Assembly 'to secede from Pakistan or . . . reduce the army's power and influence.'[11] Bhutto himself refused to cooperate in commencing proceedings before the Assembly and the drafting of the new constitution (finding his party relegated to the Opposition) and Yahya used this alleged deadlock as a ruse to postpone the Assembly session. This was a brazen violation of the people's mandate in favour of the Awami League and evidence of the army vitiating democracy.

Ultimately, a great deal of closed-door negotiation took place in order to try and form a coalition of Bhutto and Mujibur Rehman, but when the latter refused to yield, it was resolved that emergency be declared in East Pakistan and the army (which was already positioned in the East Wing) be brought in to impose the will of the West. This came to be known as the nebulous 'Operation Searchlight'.[12]

The most scathing indictment of this arbitrary decision came from Major General Yaqub Khan, who was directed by General Yahya Khan to command the operation, and held the view that the only solution to the present crisis was 'a purely political one' which only the President could take by reaching Dhaka by 6 March. He is quoted in his telegram as saying,

> I am convinced that there is no military solution which can make sense in (sic) present situation. I am consequently unable to accept the responsibility for implementing a mission, namely military solution, which would mean civil war and large-scale killings of unarmed civilians and would achieve no sane aim.[13]

In March 1971, General Yaqub was promptly replaced by Lieutenant General Tikka Khan (who would be closely involved in the ensuing war with India) and precisely what Yaqub Khan dreaded—a sham military solution and a civil war that massacred thousands of innocent Bengalis and others—was to follow. Sheikh Mujib was arrested for treason and the result of the election of 1970 was, hence, never implemented.

The period leading up to the 1971 War with India was marked by USA's supply of strategic military equipment to Pakistan and General Yahya Khan's growing rapport with President Richard Nixon, who was 'pro-Pakistan and anti-India', and suffered an aversion to 'the clever and condescending Brahmin Kashmiri'[14]—Prime Minister Indira Gandhi. General Yahya Khan's sensitive decision to recall General Tikka Khan as the Governor of East Pakistan in August 1971 and replace him with a civilian—Dr A.M. Malik, a Bengali politician—was taken under instructions from visiting US Secretary Maurice Williams.[15]

The 1970 election will be remembered for the electorate's verdict on Mujibur Rehman's Six Point Programme in East Pakistan that could have resulted in regional autonomy. The election also saw the emergence of Zulfikar Ali Bhutto's PPP. However, the violent aftermath of the elections leading up to the unleashing of the army in East Pakistan to suppress the supporters of Mujibur Rehman and the resultant India–Pakistan War of 1971, which ended with the 'Surrender at Dacca' and the birth of Bangladesh, completely nullified the electoral process and ended up not only with disgrace to democracy but, more significantly, with the dissection of Pakistan. This dissection, many quarters believed, was inevitable due to obvious geographical reasons and the cultural and linguistic differences between the Bengali-speaking Muslims in East Pakistan and their Punjabi/Sindhi/Urdu-speaking counterparts in the West. However, the last word was still with the army and democracy was the obvious casualty.

15

War with India (1971)

'The defeat of Pakistan . . . in 1971 and the dismemberment of the country disgraced the Pakistan Army thoroughly. The army rule could continue no longer.'

—Golam W. Choudhury, *Pakistan: Transition from Military to Civilian Rule*

In 1971, Pakistan was a peculiar geographical state, with its two wings—the Punjabi-dominated West Pakistan and the Bengali-dominated East Pakistan—separated by 1200 miles of Indian territory, being governed from the West. The differences between the two wings were stark.

In her book *Reconciliation*, Benazir Bhutto, the late prime minister of Pakistan, admitted that:

> The majority province of East Pakistan was basically being treated as a colony by the minority West. From revenues of more than thirty-one billion rupees from East Pakistan's exports, the minority in West Pakistan had built roads, schools, universities and hospitals for themselves, but had developed little in the East. The army, the largest employer in our very poor country, drew 90 per cent of its forces from West Pakistan. 80 per cent of government jobs were filled by

> people from the West. There was racial and cultural conflict too. It was not difficult to distinguish between the generally smaller, darker Bengali-speaking East Pakistanis and their Urdu, Punjabi and Sindhi-speaking 'countrymen' in West Pakistan. Language, in fact, was a major cause of dispute between the two wings when Urdu—rather than, or in addition to, Bengali—was declared the sole official language of the state.[1]

The imminent movement for self-determination in East Pakistan emerged in the late 1960s, when Pakistan was already under army rule. This was led by Sheikh Mujibur Rehman, a visionary who belonged to the Awami League and was in favour of democratic rule. The 'democratization of East Pakistan' was, predictably, opposed by the army, which claimed it to be a step towards the division of Pakistan, but the very ethos of the army was anti-democracy. Significantly, a Bengali majority in the legislature was repugnant to the Punjabi–Pathan-dominated army and to political aspirants such as Zulfikar Ali Bhutto, who was from Sindh.[2]

Hence, General Yahya Khan and Zulfikar Ali Bhutto colluded to prevent Sheikh Mujibur Rehman from assuming power and, in response, the Awami League launched a massive civil disobedience movement in East Pakistan.[3] General Yahya was himself wet behind the ears when it came to political decision-making, especially when compared to the shrewd Bhutto, and underestimated the military operation in East Pakistan, treating it more as a domestic counter-insurgency operation and discounting the possibility of a full-scale war with neighbouring India. General Yahya Khan crushed political unrest by force, using the Pakistan Army for the purpose. The army did not acquit itself as the invigilator of civil rule—instead resorting to looting, rape and murder.

Katherine Frank describes the prevalent situation as one where 'any and everyone suspected of dissidence was hounded down and slaughtered, including students, university lecturers, writers, journalists, professionals and intellectuals.' While Mujib himself was arrested and flown to prison in West Pakistan, 'the East Bengali Police, the East Pakistan Rifles and the only Bengali regiment in the Pakistani army all mutinied' and East Pakistan declared itself independent. The Awami League leaders who had escaped to Calcutta (now Kolkata) set up a government in exile while 'back in what was still East Pakistan, the slaughter of Bengalis by West Pakistanis escalated into genocide'—in which an estimated three million people were killed by the end of the year.[4]

Soon, General Yahya Khan announced the in camera military trial of Sheikh Mujib in Pakistan by a special military court. The trial was pre-empted by international intervention, possibly at India's behest. For Pakistan, the fact that the exploits of 1965 had not been subjected to any critical review may have contributed to the disaster of 1971, and more so, the fact that the army continued to be involved in politics. After 1971, the authority of senior officers was not automatically taken for granted. Cohen remarks, 'The 1965–71 period came to be known as the 'sawdust years' during which military honour and professionalism slipped away from the Pakistan Army.'[5]

UN Secretary General U. Thant had pointed out in his Annual Report of 1971 that: 'The relations between the Governments of India and Pakistan are also major components of the [Bangladesh] problem . . . [which] is unfolding in the context of the longstanding and unresolved difficulties which gave rise to open warfare only six years ago [in 1965].'[6]

The people of Pakistan had been extremely wary of India's 'calculated wish to dismember Pakistan.'[7] Field Marshal Ayub Khan had written in his diary dated 12 November 1971,

'[P]eople are getting desperate of Yahya [Khan] and the future. They foresee Pakistan going under Indian domination in course of time . . . the Indian military threat is constant.'[8]

To the chagrin of Pakistan, India was able to gain significant victories in 1971, in both the Western and Eastern theatres, and Pakistan forever lost her Eastern Wing. A new nation state—Bangladesh—was formed after the historic ceasefire leading to Pakistan's surrender on 16 December 1971 in the presence of Lieutenant General Niazi and the GOC of the Indian troops, Lieutenant General J.S. Aurora.

Pakistan's defeat in 1971 resulted in the significant loss of territory, populace and 90,000 POWs to India. The more telling impact was to the 'notion' of Pakistan, which Cohen identifies as being threefold.[9] Firstly, with the loss of the Eastern wing, Punjab became the overwhelmingly dominant province, in terms of population, economy and the major feeding-zone to the army and bureaucracy. The omnipresent linguistic and sectarian influences in Pakistan made this a decisive factor. Next, the loss of East Pakistan severely affected Pakistan's cultural and social diversity—a body blow to any respectable nation. Finally, and significantly, the balance of power shifted away from moderate Islamists to the more radical Islamists, who dominated the Western wing, especially in NWFP and Balochistan.

As expected, the political casualty of the 1971 defeat was General Yahya Khan. Alleged to have taken to heavy drinking and out of sync with the requirements for leading an army, much less a nation, he was surrounded by a coterie of advisers who were themselves inefficient or otherwise motivated with a desire to remain in power at the cost of democracy.[10] Arshad Sami Khan however refutes the charge that Yahya was a compulsive alcoholic.[11] The CIA and the Indian Prime Minister Indira Gandhi alike foresaw the fall of Yahya Khan and his military regime. Indira Gandhi, in a declassified Intelligence Cable dated 12 December 1971, had observed,

> India will emerge from the war as the dominant power in South Asia and also the Indian Ocean. China will respect India and may even decide to improve relations with India. On the other hand, Pakistan will lose its economic power without which it will not be able to support a large military complex. *The current Pakistani leadership will not be able to survive the military defeat* . . . [I hope that] a new democratic Pakistan, based on autonomous republics, will emerge and that it will desire to have friendly relations with India.[12] (Emphasis supplied.)

In a scathing indictment of the Pakistani military leadership, Brigadier Zahir Alam Khan (Retired) published what has been described (by the publisher) as the 'first honest, no-holds barred autobiography of a soldier in the Pakistan Army'. His book *The Way It Was: Inside the Pakistan Army* comments elaborately on the operational, command and attitudinal failings of the army, leading to the fiasco of 1971. The surrender at Dhaka by Lieutenant General 'Tiger' Niazi on 16 December 1971 is described as the 'day of the 'jackal' [and] the shock of defeat was intense', with 'Niazi trying to hug Lieutenant General Aurora, getting pushed away and then signing the surrender and lowering the Pakistan flag . . . A jackal had masqueraded as a tiger.'[13] The brigadier pulls no punches in noting that 'on the night of 16/17 December, General Yahya announced that the war in West Pakistan would go on' but 'two days later, *to everyone's surprise* there was a ceasefire . . . everyone was stunned, we were defeated and lost half the country.'[14] (Emphasis supplied.)

Lieutenant General Niazi himself blamed the senior politico-military leadership for the loss in rather colourful terms:

> The entire blame for the political defeat was being passed on to the Eastern Command. How this was brought about militarily is a fascinating study of deception and double-cross imposed on the Eastern Command by Generals Yahya, Hamid, Gul Hassan, Tikka Khan and Farman, with both the Government and GHQ faithfully dancing to Bhutto's tune as he unfolded his diabolical plot for the dismemberment of the country.[15]

At one level, the West Pakistanis considered their eastern counterparts 'effete, given to literary and musical pursuits . . . [and] incapable of mounting a challenge to the country's military machine.'[16] But in reality, the Mukti Bahini, the Bengali resistance force, had fought along with the Indian troops and demonstrated 'that the Bengalis are a fighting martial race'.[17]

The consequent fall of the Pakistani leadership was inevitable. Though Yahya Khan had (a little before the ceasefire) sent his Foreign Minister Bhutto to the United Nations to submit a case in favour of his country, there was no meaningful support forthcoming. The Pakistan Army (more particularly the Brigade of 6 Armoured Division commanded by Brigadier F.B. Ali) had revolted against Yahya Khan in the wake of the loss to India and the loss of East Pakistan and threatened to attack the Presidency in Rawalpindi.[18] The US itself was keen on Yahya being replaced and under sustained pressure—ironically (again) from the army itself—Yahya Khan stepped down as President and CMLA and handed over both mantles to Zulfikar Ali Bhutto of the PPP.

Nawaz describes this episode as a putsch[19]—with the army itself being instrumental in the transfer of power from a military leader to a civilian leader. The proceedings before the Justice Hamoodur Rahman Commission threw up a stark analysis of the rot that had set into the system in Pakistan, as well as the pointed failures in not finding a political settlement with the Awami League in view of the electoral success enjoyed by it as well as the gross military failures in delaying the deployment of troops in the Western theatre. The report pithily concluded, 'The causes of the disaster vary from the running down of (sic) Army's professional efficiency *by years devoted [to] involvement in martial law duties at the cost of military training*, to inadequacy of resources, faulty policy formulation and unsound judgement and untimely decisions.'[20] (Emphasis supplied.)

However, the report was relegated to the back burner and, rather than dwell on the impact of the 1971 defeat and the political future of the nation, the Pakistani leadership was obsessed with vindicating the loss to India.[21] At no point did the leadership draw up a blueprint for building a robust democracy.

Cloughley succinctly sums up the prevailing position in these words: 'There was no longer a General ruling the country. But there was no democracy either.'[22]

16

The Bhutto Years

'Bhutto saw enemies where none existed. In his years of power, he treated his political opponents as dangerous subversives, and succeeded in making them so.'

—Salmaan Taseer, *Bhutto: A Political Biography*

The loss of East Pakistan raised serious questions regarding the status and existence of Pakistan, and the perceived threat from India. The army's involvement in civilian governance had not only undermined the democratic progress made in the country, but, more disconcertingly, resulted in the severance of East Pakistan. Bhutto, a fiercely ambitious and wily leader, capitalized on this situation. US-educated, a Sindhi with popularity even among the Punjabi constituencies and the founder of the PPP, Bhutto '. . . enjoyed more freedom than any other civilian leader before or since and set about implementing his own version of the idea and the state of Pakistan'.[1]

Following the humiliating resignation of Yahya induced by his fellow officers, it was the magnetism of Bhutto (and the relative downgrading of the army in public perception) that saw a civilian being anointed with power rather than another army general. During his regime, Bhutto served first as CMLA, then as President and finally as prime minister—the last under the new constitution adopted by Parliament in April 1973.

Bhutto assumed power in an environment where the morale of the country was at its nadir and the military was weak. This was an opportunity for bona fide civilian leadership to conclusively stamp its authority on the political canvas. Bhutto, however, was driven by the urge to aggrandize power and to impose his personal will on the system. He immediately dismissed key officials, including 1300 civil servants,[2] undertook large-scale financial and social reform, and significantly took on the institution that had brought him to power—the army. He was not averse to publicizing the defeat of the army in the 1971 War, criticizing its functioning and even dismissing senior officers based on his whims and fancies.

It was during his tenure that the War Inquiry Commission, headed by Chief Justice Hamoodur Rahman (referred to earlier), was constituted to look into the 1971 defeat to India. The report was a serious indictment of the role and conduct of the army, particularly its foray into civilian and business ventures and its lack of discipline.[3] However, the report gathered dust for over three decades and was not made public until 2002, by which time it was redundant as most of the key players had passed on and the army had regained control during the interregnum under General Zia and later under General Musharraf.

In order to undermine the dominance of the army, Bhutto constituted an alternative military force called the Federal Security Force (FSF),[4] which would exclude the army from internal security, and initiated a nuclear weapons project that sought to deny the army control of national nuclear assets.[5] He even had a showdown with the army chief—Lieutenant General Gul Hassan Khan, replacing him in dramatic and coup-like fashion with the popular Punjabi general—Lieutenant General Tikka Khan, who obeyed political commands, sometimes unscrupulous, unquestioningly. The FSF was also born of Bhutto's differences with General Gul Hassan, who refused to relieve his soldiers from border duty to take care of matters of internal security—an act that made Bhutto suspicious of his army.[6] All of this led the army to believe that Bhutto was a Frankenstein of their own making and made the army grossly distrustful of him.

Bhutto also 'eliminated' the civil service of Pakistan, replacing it with a District Management Group.[7] He proclaimed a vision of Pakistan as an Islamic *and* socialist state. Publicly, he wore a façade of being focused on the basic needs of the poor masses, which was more of a populist measure. He ruthlessly and violently crushed the political movement in Balochistan, a hotbed of separatism in Pakistan.

Bhutto evolved a unique brand of international relations, introducing 'bilateralism' as foreign policy, i.e., non-alignment without subordination to India, with special ties with the Islamic world.[8] The Simla Pact was signed with India in July 1972, resulting in the return of territory to and trade and commerce with Pakistan. The Pact subsequently secured the release of over 90,000 Pakistani POWs captured by India. Though going to Shimla was a 'forbidding experience' for Bhutto, considering his anti-India rhetoric coupled with his 'strong personal rivalry' with Indira Gandhi, he was able to extract a favourable settlement by arguing that his was '*the first democratically elected government . . . directly answerable to the people*' (emphasis supplied) and that in the absence of a favourable settlement, he would be overthrown by the army, leaving India to deal with a 'more intransigent' military dictator.[9]

Critically, he developed a robust equation with China, particularly in matters of defence supplies and support, which China was glad to pursue to gain a geopolitical advantage. It was on the advice of Bhutto, as foreign minister, that Ayub Khan had earlier developed relations with China and the Soviet Union. These were no minor accomplishments.

However, his autocratic approach saw him dismiss the provincial governments of NWFP and Balochistan and violently suppress any dissent, as was the case with the brutal beating of his erstwhile mentor—J.A. Rahim, for mild criticism of Bhutto's 'feudal' behaviour.[10] In his quest for dominance, in 1975, he took on the formidable National Awami Party (NAP) in Balochistan, and relied on the army to displace its leadership. Again, a civilian leader (as was the case with Liaquat Ali Khan) relied on the army to impose his autocratic ways on the people and thereby 'invited' the army back into the political fold.

Martial law suited Bhutto, as he believed it was 'required for the sole purpose of bringing basic reforms' and once this phase of reforms was over, 'the ground would be laid for the *full flowering of democracy*.'[11] (Emphasis supplied.)

This led to a growing awareness among the officers of the army of the actual functioning of the civilian leadership and the availability of an active platform for them in governance. The military leadership also saw Bhutto as a dictator and this led to widespread rumblings within the forces to overthrow him. Under the auspices of the military and a motley mix of the middle–upper class, well-educated mainstream Pakistanis, known as 'the London Group',[12] a chorus began for the removal of Bhutto and for the introduction of democracy, intriguingly, under a retired air force officer—Air Marshal Asghar Khan—though in his capacity as the leader of the opposition party, Tehrik-I-Istiqlal.[13] The lines between professional soldiering and politics seemed to be drawn in sand.

Air Marshal Asghar Khan describes his foray into mainstream politics thus:

> With the unfettered power that he now enjoyed, Bhutto began to behave more like a *wadera* [feudal lord] than a popularly elected leader in a democratic country . . . Having opposed Ayub Khan's authoritarian rule and having witnessed the

> disastrous consequences of Yahya Khan's stupidities, [sic] I could not sit back and accept a continuation of dictatorial rule. I therefore embarked on a campaign to criticize Zulfikar Ali Bhutto and his authoritarian policies.[14]

Bhutto responded strongly by setting up a military tribunal to try the delinquent officers. Bizarrely, as it would turn out, his choice of officer to head the tribunal was an officer whom he saw as pliable and subservient—Major General Muhammad Zia-ul-Haq, who would become Bhutto's *bête noire*. Zia was Jalandhar-born and perceived as a fitting, apolitical choice when the time came in 1976 for Bhutto to replace General Tikka Khan as the army chief. In doing so, Bhutto superseded several officers, including the veritably professional and apolitical soldier Lieutenant General M. Shariff.

For all his dictatorial actions, Bhutto also managed to push through a new constitution in 1973 that metamorphosed Pakistan from a presidential government into a highly centralized parliamentary government, with Bhutto at the helm as prime minister. Though he was viewed as being self-obsessed and someone who was 'appalled by the vehemence of the opposition against him',[15] he publicly received a good deal of sycophantic praise from all quarters, including a verbose General Zia, who played to Bhutto's weakness for eulogy. Even the media—PTV and the Pakistan Broadcasting Corporation—effusively praised and propagated the 'achievements' of Prime Minister Bhutto, emboldening him to actually announce elections in 1977.[16]

Despite a promise of a 'free and fair' election, Bhutto was insecure about his success and undertook massive electoral fraud in order to ensure his success. These acts included setting up proxy rivals and colluding with the Opposition to 'fix' results.[17] Though the legitimate opposition was charged up by these acts of commission and formed the Pakistan National Alliance (PNA), the PNA won merely thirty-six seats, as opposed to Bhutto's PPP which won 155 out of a total of 200 seats in the National Assembly.

Bhutto's overwhelming victory 'dumbfounded even PPP loyalists'[18] and vitiated the emerging spirit of competitive democracy in Pakistan. In the wake of these results, the Opposition took to the streets in a boisterous and spirited protest against the re-elected government. Bhutto responded with an iron fist, ordering the arrest of senior PNA leaders as well as imposing various curfews in the affected areas. However, the protestors only got more emboldened, mixing the protest with religious fervour by chanting Islamic verses and carrying the Holy Quran.[19] This had an effect on the police forces that hesitated to crack down on their own religious ilk.

Bhutto's own phobia was the Islamization of the army, which was impending with General Zia distributing copies of the Quran among the soldiers and curtly pointing out to Bhutto that 'Islam is not the private property of any individual'.[20] Once more, the army seemed to be at loggerheads with the civilian establishment.

Ultimately, Bhutto was left with no alternative but to call in the army and impose martial law in five major cities of Pakistan, which was done through an impromptu constitutional amendment. History repeated itself, in that the civilian leadership depended fatally on the military and paid the price for it. The army found its way back into the political mainstream, in the face of relations between Bhutto and his army chief General Zia having soured over their differing perception of Islam and civilian surveillance of army officers. Besides, the army was in direct contact with the people and felt the pulse of discontent in the aftermath of the dubious election. Even the international community at the time (read: the US) did not regard Pakistan as a genuine democracy and leant more towards India.

In this volatile situation, Bhutto used the army to his convenience by pushing it into matters of internal security and suppressing civilian protests in various parts, including Punjab. However, the Punjabi-dominated army was also politically aware and unlikely to tolerate such orders. In a swift, furtive reaction, Bhutto was placed under house arrest on 4 July 1977 under General Zia's orders and martial law was in full force once again.

For all his personal attributes and virtues, Bhutto's veritable dictatorship was manifest in the delegitimized parliamentary elections of 1977. Infamously, he had claimed, 'I will not go down in history as a rigger of elections.'[21] But not only did he manoeuvre the electoral results and undermine democracy, he underestimated the might of the army which he tried to use for his political convenience.

In his address to the nation on 20 December 1971, Bhutto had paradoxically said:

> I have been summoned by the nation as the authentic voice of the people of Pakistan . . . by virtue of the verdict that you gave in the national elections . . . *I would not like to see Martial Law remain one day longer than necessary . . . We have to rebuild democratic institutions* . . . we have to rebuild a situation in which the common man, the poor man in the street, can tell me to go to hell.[22] (Emphasis supplied.)

However, his 'own man' Zia could not brook his autocratic functioning and interference with the integrity and new-found Islamic identity of the army and overthrew him unceremoniously in another military coup. Subsequently, the Lahore High Court by an in-camera trial convicted Bhutto of conspiracy to commit murder, and he was ultimately hanged in Rawalpindi on 4 April 1979.[23]

The army was back in power, exterminating all remnants of civilian rule.

17

Zia's Reign

'In March 1976, my father [Zulfikar Ali Bhutto] elevated General Mohammad Zia-ul-Haq to Army Chief of staff, jumping over several more senior officers. This would prove to be a tragic mistake.'

—Benazir Bhutto, *Pakistan: The Gathering Storm*

The era of civilian rule under Zulfikar Bhutto proved more dictatorial than that of the generals before him. Apart from the fact that an appetite for democracy had not developed in Pakistan as a result of weak structures and traditions, Bhutto himself was a highly ambitious and egoistic leader (bred on the principles of Napoleon) and suppressed democracy, resisted accountability and politicized the bureaucracy. He also offended the military by creating his 'personal' paramilitary outfit—the FSF. His iron hand crushing of the protests against the 1977 election results not only made him a detested leader, but fatally, also compelled him to rely upon the army to bring about law and order.[1] Equally, he had no rapport with the army.

This was the Achilles heel of all civilian leaders in the history of Pakistan—the need to rely on the army to sustain their legitimacy and status, as also to call in the army to quell frequent and violent internal disturbances. The crafty General Zia seized the opportunity and overthrew Bhutto, and later had him executed. Had Bhutto kept the army on his side, civilian rule might have continued in Pakistan for a while longer, though not *democratic* civilian rule.

Bhutto was arrested by the army on 5 July 1977, and put to death allegedly for violating Article 6 of the 1973 Constitution of Pakistan, which dealt with the offence of 'High Treason'.[2] General Zia-ul-Haq, an Islamist at heart, replaced Bhutto, and thus began another era of military rule in Pakistan.

Soon after his investiture, General Zia made the (now customary) hollow promise of elections, this time, in a short span of ninety days. He was to soon thereafter brazenly contradict himself, when he said:

> It is not in the Quran nor has it been revealed to me that elections will be held on October 18 and nothing will happen thereafter . . . In my opinion the presidential system, which is closer to Islam, is more suitable for Pakistan. I will put it up to the National Assembly on October 28 and leave the decision to the next government . . . My Government is an interim government . . . *This country can be kept together by the armed forces and not by politicians.*[3] (Emphasis supplied.)

This statement betrayed the religious and palpably political role that the army played in Pakistan. The rhetoric shielded the shrewd knowledge of Zia that the elections held soon after Bhutto's execution would give the PPP a strong chance of victory based on a sympathy wave. Indeed, throughout Zia's reign, he suffered the paranoia of Bhutto's killing and tactfully avoided any semblance of democratic governance.

While Zia respected the secular theories of governance, he was convinced that a deeply religious soldier (or any other professional) would be a better fighter.[4] Significantly, he represented a 'postcolonial', non-military background of a modestly wealthy set of military officers who had moved from the theories of professional soldiering to more activist perceptions of governance, ideology and purging of the political system. Naturally, he restored the pre-eminent position of the army to politics in Pakistan and went on record to declare that '[the] preservation of that Ideology [Pakistan's ideology] and the Islamic character of the country was . . . as important as the security of the country's geographical boundaries'.[5] This directly contravened Jinnah's purported secular vision of Pakistan. Significantly, this started the process of the Islamization of an army, which hitherto was largely areligious in character as an institution.

Zia even directed his army commanders to appoint *Nazim-us-Salat* (prayer leaders) in their areas, to ensure that the people duly performed their ritual prayers. Army officers were encouraged to partake in these prayers and even their confidential reports contained an assessment of their 'moral and religious behaviour'.[6] Zia 'upgraded' the position of maulvis attached to army units—whom Omar Noman described as 'hitherto, comic figures'[7]—so much so that they accompanied the troops led by 'religiously-inclined generals'.[8] The motto of the army was changed from Jinnah's 'Unity, Faith, and Discipline' to the revealing '*Iman, Taqwa, Jihad fi sabeelillah*', meaning 'Faith, Obedience to God, and Struggle in the path of Allah'.[9]

The army was therefore now the protector of ideological standards for the nation as well. An army that owed its allegiance to a notionally secular constitution was not hesitant to venture into Islamization not only for itself, but for the country as well, through the implementation of *Nizam-i-Mustafa* or the Rule of the Prophet.[10] It was hence natural that Zia started this process with 'his own constituency'—the army, before moving on to the larger frame of the country. On display were the interpretation, usurpation and transformation of the very constitution by the army in Pakistan, which obviously had serious ramifications on the growth of democratic institutions and constitutionalism. Benazir Bhutto had lamented that Islam is 'not to be allowed to become a plaything for dictators'.[11] The situation was precisely that.

This communalization of the army created the triumvirate that the modern State of Pakistan is unable to ignore—with the army, the ISI and the Taliban largely in sync and the civilian leadership increasingly marginalized. While the corps did not necessarily accept this Islamization of the army, the attempted coup in September 1995 led by Major General Zahir ul Islam Abbasi, a stated Islamist officer, belied this theory.[12] These later acts were the fruits of General Zia's potent mix of religion and the military.

Cohen quotes Hasan-Askari Rizvi as saying that the middle- and junior-level officers in the Pakistan Army were the 'product(s) of an era' when a 'public display of Islamic orthodoxy and conservatism was an asset and even a method of career enhancement'.[13]

Zia's closest advisers were former generals, as well as civilians who had advised Ayub and Yahya in the past. Particular emphasis was laid on legal advice for the implementation of martial law with an Islamic flavour under the constitutional framework, which itself underwent dramatic changes under his leadership. A.K. Brohi and S.S. Pirzada were two such lawyers that advised the general.[14]

Zia's leaning towards an Islamic regime was reinforced by his alliance with some Islamic parties such as the Jama'at-i-Islami, purportedly in order to neutralize the impact of the PPP. However, this alliance spent itself once Zia strengthened his position. All along, the remnants of democracy, such as a party system and political rallies, were methodically suppressed.[15] The nuclear arsenal was also back with the army, as was internal security with the disbanding of Bhutto's paramilitary FSF.

The dominant Punjabi class enjoyed its place in the sun in Zia's regime, in matters of politics and economy. The United States supported Zia in order to confront the Soviet Union in Afghanistan through the Afghan Mujahideen. In February 1985, non-party elections were carried out and martial law was relaxed later that year in December after receiving a 98-per cent approval vote in a national referendum that was 'undoubtedly rigged'.[16]

The sham democracy was apparent from the fact that Zia prohibited political parties from contesting the elections, allowing only independents, and dismissed Prime Minister Mohammad Khan Junejo in May 1988 as a reaction to the latter's independent stand on matters of foreign policy. As Cohen says, 'The result was a narrow political elite that drew heavily from the ranks of retired officers, shorn of idealism, suspicious of democracy, and convinced that it was the 'saviour' generation, rescuing Pakistan from grave domestic and foreign threats.'[17]

The Zia–Junejo combine was the proverbial square peg in a round hole. They clashed on matters of policy and on the appointment of bureaucrats and army officers. Moreover, they differed in perception on the dosage of religion in institutions of governance, with General Zia, obviously being in favour of a large role for religion in matters of the State.[18]

Ultimately, Zia removed Junejo. This was a direct outcome of the constitutional amendment in 1985, whereby the President reserved the right to unilaterally remove the prime minister. The constitutional development in India, by such time, as a result of the judgment of a thirteen-judge bench in *Kesavananda*[19] ensured that no amendment to the constitution could alter its basic structure—a judicial precedent and attitude that was sorely missing in Pakistan at the time.

By this time, the army had penetrated deep into civilian governance, with military officers holding senior positions in the bureaucracy and the economy, and retired generals being appointed to ambassadorial and gubernatorial positions of eminence. The intelligence apparatus in Pakistan consisted of the Intelligence Bureau which was responsible for local intelligence, the Directorate of Intelligence for military intelligence and the military-heavy Inter-Services Intelligence Directorate (better known as the ISI). The ISI was founded in 1948, headed by a lieutenant general who reported directly to the prime minister, and was focused mostly on foreign intelligence. It grew in strength during the Soviet occupation of Afghanistan after being focused earlier on India and East Pakistan, leading up to the creation of Bangladesh.[20] Ironically, despite an ISI that was comprised mostly of military officers, Zia faced two coups from within the army to oust him from power—one headed by Tajammal Hussain Malik in 1980 and the Attock Conspiracy case-II in 1984.[21] Both were unsuccessful.

The ISI was, by now, a dominant player in the politics of Pakistan, and had differences of opinion with the CIA on the nature and timing of operations in Afghanistan, where the Soviets had a stranglehold. It was against this backdrop of simmering instability that General Zia was vulnerable to opponents—locally and internationally.[22]

On 17 August 1988, General Zia boarded a C-130 Hercules cargo plane with a few loyalist army officers from the Tamewali firing range close to Multan. It took off only to abruptly come crashing to the ground, killing Zia and all his co-passengers. Conspiracy theories (the hallmark of most deaths of leaders in Pakistan) did the rounds, and Zia's death still remains a mystery.[23]

Zia's influence was unmistakable in three prime areas. Firstly, the emphasis on Islam. Secondly, his emphasis on low-intensity conflict (with India). And finally his emphasis on the nuclear programme.[24] While the last was a direct outcome of the humiliation of 1971, both in terms of the loss of East Pakistan and a loss to the Indian Army, the short-sightedness of this programme resulted in a change in the balance of power in South Asia with a race to amass nuclear weapons. This led to 'open' nuclear testing—Pokhran-II in 1998 during Prime Minister Vajpayee's time being a case in point—and more diabolically, the serious threat of Pakistan's nuclear assets falling into the hands of non-state players such as the Taliban.

Inexplicably, Zia and his military coterie believed they were being progressive when they sought to enforce brutal Islamic laws such as public whipping and chopping of limbs, on account of Pakistan not yet being a fully developed or modern society.[25] No emphasis was laid instead on the development of democracy and economic growth which were more civilized methods of development than archaic legislation. On General Zia's death, the army decided against imposing martial law and called upon former bureaucrat Ghulam Ishaq Khan, the chairman of the Senate, to assume the role of President of Pakistan. Ishaq Khan correspondingly appointed General Mirza Aslam Beg the chief of the army. However, the first cabinet meeting was attended absurdly by all the three service chiefs of the army, navy and air force and the stranglehold of the military was unmistakable. Significantly, the cabinet, including General Beg, resolved inter alia to 'sustain democracy until 16 November 1988 when the elections were slated' to be followed by the installation of a new government thereafter.[26]

Benazir Bhutto also comments on the resulting situation in that Zia failed to hold promised elections for almost eight years after 1977 and, by his conduct, 'set the cause of democracy in Pakistan back by a generation', by his 'political-Islamization' and the brutal suppression of pro-democracy sections of civil society.[27] Though she could be prejudiced due to Zia's execution of her father, the comment is still accurate. The balance of power in Pakistan by this time was well and truly vested in the army, and even civilian governments seemed to draw their source and legitimacy from it.

18

'Decade of Democracy'

'The President, the Army Chief, and the Prime Minister would become the troika *that would run Pakistan's fissiparous politics for the next eleven years, till the cycle repeated itself with another coup d'etat in 1999.'*

—Shuja Nawaz, *Crossed Swords: Pakistan, Its Army, and the Wars Within*

Polish–British sociologist Stanislav Andreski, in his epochal work *Military Organization and Society,* distinguishes four types of 'militarism'—(a) idolization of the military, (b) rule by the military, (c) peacetime militarization of society, even under civilian rule, and (d) the gearing up of society for war.[1] The previous regimes in Pakistan showed traits of the first two forms of militarism. However, the next decade would display a pronounced absence of the military in direct power, though it never lost its place at the political high table.

General Zia's regime ended with the suspicious plane crash in August 1988, resulting in what is known informally as the 'decade of democracy'. True to his word, General Beg ensured that elections were duly held in November 1988—the beginning of an era, which saw the emergence of Benazir Bhutto and Nawaz Sharif as the torchbearers of civilian leadership.

Reflecting on this period, Cohen comments:

> There were elections in 1988, 1990, 1993, 1997 and 2002, but the actual turnout in each succeeding election declined from 50 percent in 1988 to a government-declared 35 per cent (but probably closer to 26 percent) in 1997, and 25–30 per cent in 2002. Reflecting the elite nature of Pakistan's politics, turnout has generally been low—except when there have been provincial grievances, or during the Bhutto years. Many elections have been rigged—often with the connivance of Pakistan's ineffective Election Commission.[2]

The brand of democracy that was to be found in Pakistan post-Zia was but a diluted version of the ideal, with higher involvement of political parties and leaders, and a lesser emphasis on the military and religion. However, the army could never be kept out of matters of foreign policy and defence. Significantly, both the national leaders realized that the stand on Kashmir and the parameters of relations with India, followed by the army, were set in stone.[3]

Benazir Bhutto was the Oxford-educated daughter of Zulfikar Ali Bhutto and his successor in the PPP, while Nawaz Sharif was a wealthy Punjabi who controlled the Muslim League. Benazir Bhutto was prime minister from December 1988 to August 1990 and again from October 1993 to November 1996, while Nawaz Sharif was prime minister during the interregnum from November 1990 to July 1993 and later from February 1997 to October 1999.

Though elections were held in November 1988, by this time Pakistan had seen over a decade of military rule and the power centre was still the army, with the bureaucracy in tow. As such, adjusting to a democratic regime that required bequeathing power to the people and the people's representatives was virtually impossible for the army, whose manoeuvrings ensured that neither Benazir nor Sharif served full terms. Shuja Nawaz describes the scenario as a 'troika' and says that the consequence of what he calls this 'delicate balancing act' was a scenario in which presidents, prime ministers and even army chiefs came and went. In such a scenario, the ordinary people of Pakistan had to, as Nawaz says, 're-learn democracy over and over again', though they never lost hope.[4]

The elections of 1988 were peaceful and fair, as compared to earlier elections, with Benazir Bhutto's PPP winning ninety-three out of 207 seats (38.5 per cent) and Nawaz Sharif's Muslim League (which contested under an umbrella organization—Islami Jamhoori Ittehad [IJI] winning fifty-five seats (30.16 per cent). Bizarrely, the IJI was strung together by Major General Hamid Gul, who headed the ISI, who had been told by the ISI of PPP's likely success and who felt the need to strengthen the Opposition![5] The IJI received 'logistic support' from General Beg in the form of ISI funds of $58,000 to Nawaz Sharif's account, $83,000 to IJI's and remittances to other IJI leaders.[6]

Not one to let democratic will flow freely, General Gul waited ten full days before 'permitting' Benazir to form the popular government, and simultaneously obtained a tacit agreement from her that there would be no change in policies relating to Afghanistan, nuclear matters, defence and civil administration.[7] India would have been understood to be part of 'defence'. A crippled democratic government hence assumed power after the elections, with the President, the army chief and the prime minister all grappling for political space.

General Beg initially kept aloof, permitting the government to function without hindrance and playing the role of a mediator of sorts between the two major parties. However, as the army chief, he dispensed with Zia's religious 'audit' of his officers, and introduced a military exercise called *Zarb-e-Momin* (Attack of the True Believer) which involved massive war games in the desert in Sind aimed at displaying the might of the Pakistan Army and potentially taking on its arch-rival—India.[8]

The dominance of the army was to resurface in the control for the nuclear assets of the nation. Hitherto, the President had enjoyed final control over the nuclear programme. However, Bhutto, perhaps unwittingly, got the army chief involved in the launch of her nuclear programme and the army was thereby to play a critical role in the control of the nuclear policy and nuclear weapon pile.[9] The troika that Shuja Nawaz speaks of was well and truly in motion.

Benazir Bhutto indicts the ISI for 'having failed to stop the PPP winning a parliamentary majority. [And] now began plotting to dismember the PPP.'[10] Differences emerged—or were created—between Bhutto and the ISI (headed by Major General Hamid Gul) in the matter of operations in Afghanistan. Besides, through a videotaped sting operation on Brigadier Imtiaz Ahmed, Bhutto learnt of manoeuvring to get her party members to defect, reportedly as 'the army did not want her'.[11] Faced with the threat of overthrow or assassination from the ISI, Benazir proceeded to remove General Gul as the chief of the ISI.[12]

The conflict between President Ishaq, Prime Minister Bhutto and General Beg was accentuated by Benazir Bhutto's inquisition of the role of the ISI and, significantly, the appointment of Lieutenant General Ahmed Kamal as the chairman of the Joint Chiefs of Staff Committee (JCSC) in place of Admiral Sirohey. President Ishaq, in exercise of powers under the 8th Amendment to the Constitution, reversed the decision and battlelines were drawn. Bhutto however suffered the same weakness as other civilian leaders in depending on the army to enforce law and order (in Sind, in her case) and indirectly suppress political opponents. All this while, Bhutto naively believed that with the support of the US, she would remain entrenched in power, and even took on the army in the matter of promotions, which she made contrary to the advice of the army chief. These steps led to the inevitable outcome.

On 21 July 1990, General Beg, in consultation with his corps commanders, conveyed the army's dissatisfaction with the PPP. President Ishaq conveniently took cognizance, and exercising his powers under the aforementioned 8th Amendment, dismissed the Bhutto government in August that year.[13]

Strangely, democracy in Pakistan permitted the dismissal of a popular government at the whims of the President, rather than by the decision of the electorate at the next elections (or by recognized exception such as 'no-confidence motions' or 'right of recall').[14]

The dismissal of Bhutto's government was followed by elections in November 1990, which Nawaz Sharif's IJI won convincingly with 105 out of 216 seats. General Beg did his bit to 'help' Nawaz Sharif, by allegedly distributing approximately Rs 14 crore to Benazir Bhutto's opponents through the 'good offices' of the ISI.[15] Sharif himself came from a wealthy, industrial family that lost most of its wealth to the nationalization policies of Zulfikar Ali Bhutto, and did not brook much bureaucratic control of business. He 'liberalized' the economy by a higher degree of participation and was seemingly comfortable with having the President and the army chief share political space with him, as prime minister. However, the typical confrontation arose when it came to the appointment of the next army chief on the superannuation of General Beg in August 1991.

Sharif was in favour of the seniority principle by which the Indian-born and well-regarded Lieutenant General Shamim Alam Khan—one of nine brothers, all of whom went to the forces[16]—ought to have become COAS, ahead of Lieutenant General Asif Nawaz and the popular but radical Lieutenant

General Hamid Gul. However, the President, who made the appointment of the COAS on the recommendation of the prime minister, viewed this as his prerogative and resolved to appoint General Nawaz as the COAS, ahead of the other two generals.[17] Naturally, Nawaz Sharif felt slighted by this one-upmanship.

General Nawaz was himself a professional and competent officer. Soon after assuming office as COAS, he delivered a clear message to his troops that as the democratic process has now taken hold, he would like it to be clearly understood that 'the Army must have nothing to do with politics' and ought to let the elected representatives do their job and at all costs '*must avoid involvement in politics and devote ourselves to our profession*'.[18] (Emphasis supplied.)

Cloughley points out that there was 'a sigh of relief from the bureaucracy' and politicians alike when General Gul handed over the reins to General Asif Nawaz who was 'straightforward' and interested in 'foreign policy and relations', though with no intention of 'making' the said policies or 'interfering' in the said relations.[19]

General Nawaz inherited not only an army but also a virtual economy, in the form of the various businesses and enterprises that the army controlled in Pakistan.[20] He was in charge when Kabul was liberated from the Soviets and was equally interested in extending the operations of his army to peacekeeping missions of the United Nations in places like Somalia, and not fixated with India.

But for all the sagacity of the army chief, the other two players in the piece—the prime minister and President were having a showdown over the powers of the latter under the notorious 8th Amendment to the constitution. The prime minister believed that his advice to the President thereunder was binding upon the President,[21] while the President liked to believe that his powers under the 8th Amendment were unbridled. A strange hybrid of presidential and parliamentary systems was at play.

Equally, the prime minister and the new army chief differed in their approaches to matters of administration, with the former unabashed in using family and tribal connections in matters of appointment and promotions, while the latter being merit-driven. The general would get a rude shock when Prime Minister Nawaz Sharif appointed the overtly Islamic Lieutenant General Javed Nasir as the ISI chief.[22]

All the same, Nawaz Sharif deployed the army in Sind to oppress political rivals, though the army was reluctant to undertake this exercise and made a case for its release. The (Punjabi) political powers viewed this as the army's collusion with their bitter Sindhi rivals and, once more, there was an impasse. General Nawaz came under increasing pressure to impose martial law and overthrow the belligerent government—a temptation he was the first army chief to resist. Even in matters of military aid to civil power, General Nawaz did not believe in 'half measures' and insisted that such measures be 'introduced by Parliament'.[23] Soon after, in January 1993, General Nawaz died of a heart attack while on his treadmill, amid cries of an arsenic poisoning conspiracy.[24]

This was perhaps one of the few times in the history of Pakistan that an army chief functioned as a dispassionate and apolitical soldier, as his tribute in the British newspaper the *Independent* stated,

> The last of the Sandhurst-trained generation of Pakistani officers, Nawaz was known as a 'soldier's soldier' who had no political ambitions. His aim was *to keep the army out of politics* and restore the military's credibility both at home and abroad after long bouts of martial law . . . As a

> strong believer in liberal values, he was trying to improve the military's relations with India and take Pakistan out of the dead-end legacy of Islamic fundamentalist rhetoric led by his predecessors, General Ziaul Haq and General Aslam Beg . . . Unlike so many of his predecessors, Nawaz was incorruptible.[25] (Emphasis supplied.)

The customary acrimony relating to the appointment of the next army chief followed between the prime minister and the President, before they agreed on the name of Lieutenant General Abdul Waheed Kakar, superseding many other senior officers and causing considerable heartburn among the top brass. Meanwhile, Nawaz Sharif was aligning with rival PPP in order to try and muster support to repeal the notorious 8th Amendment and thereby curb the powers of President Ishaq.[26] President Ishaq responded in volatile fashion, dismissing Sharif's government and announcing another round of elections, with Balkh Sher Mazari being appointed caretaker prime minister. Again, democracy was uprooted using the infamous 8th Amendment. However, this time, the Supreme Court rose to the occasion, declaring the dismissal illegal and Sharif remained in power.[27] However, unlike the position in India where the Supreme Court is the ultimate arbiter of rights, in Pakistan, even the verdict of the Supreme Court appeared to be subject to the discretion of the army. And the army was unimpressed with the political see-sawing.

Rather than permit Sharif to continue as prime minister—in a situation that has been described as 'laughable'—Army Chief General Waheed stepped in and 'by a combination of tact, forcefulness, honour and tenacity' convinced *both* President Ishaq and Prime Minister Nawaz Sharif to resign in July 1993 and announced elections later that year.[28] Clearly, the popular will or the judgments of the Supreme Court of Pakistan were subordinate to the will of the army. This was Pakistan's brand of democracy in the much touted 'decade of democracy'.

The army backed an ex-World Bank official Moeen Qureshi as caretaker prime minister, and the elections of October 1993 resulted in the return of Benazir Bhutto's PPP, with a narrow victory over its rivals. By such time, the army had become increasingly Islamized and Benazir faced an unsuccessful coup (that was swiftly stifled by military intelligence) from a radical faction of the army, headed by Major General Zaheer-ul-Islam Abbasi, who intended to overthrow both the civilian government as well as the military leadership, and declare Pakistan an 'orthodox Islamic state'.[29]

General Waheed's retirement in 1996 and his admirable refusal to accept an extension led to the usual hobnobbing for the post of the next army chief. Ultimately, General Jehangir Karamat was appointed, more at the instance of the President (Leghari) and the previous chief, and not entirely with Benazir Bhutto's approval.[30] President Leghari went a step further. Having received repeated reports of gross corruption on the part of Bhutto's government—particularly her husband and investment minister Asif Ali Zardari—and taking serious note of these omissions and 'commissions', dismissed the Bhutto government in November 1996.[31]

For the fourth time in eight years, a new government was sworn in. The pendulum swung back towards Nawaz Sharif who found himself in the seat of the prime minister. This time, *with* the tacit approval of the army and the President, he deleted the 8th Amendment from the Constitution of Pakistan.[32] This effectively swung the balance of power largely in favour of the prime minister, which, in principle, was preferable for a sound democracy. Qureshi had sagaciously observed that this was 'the last chance' for parliamentary governance 'of the kind (available) in Pakistan' which, if unsuccessful, would compel the people of Pakistan to 'consider a presidential form of government'.[33]

But, as was the wont with civilian leaders in Pakistan, the spirit of democracy and constitutionalism was absent. Sharif took on the judiciary, provoking revolts among the sitting judges of the Supreme Court against Chief Justice Sajid Ali Shah, whom Sharif saw as being adverse to his interests. Sharif sought to appoint a chief justice of his choice and even had party workers storm the court of law when contempt proceedings were initiated against him.[34] He further sought to impose Islamic law in Pakistan and take all government actions beyond the pale of judicial review vide the proposed 15th Amendment, which however was defeated on the floor of the Senate.

Prime Minister Nawaz Sharif's adventurism did not go down well with General Karamat, who publicly criticized Sharif. Sharif, in turn, took serious objection to the army chief's comments and using his political clout—which now surpassed that of the President—prevailed upon General Karamat to resign two months prior to the date of his superannuation. In his place, Sharif appointed an officer over other senior generals, on the belief that he would be more supportive to him and his policies.

That officer was General Pervez Musharraf.

In this period of so-called democracy, the two prominent leaders—Benazir Bhutto and Nawaz Sharif—participated in political musical chairs. Periodically, both were dismissed by the President with the connivance of the army, and the election process was often manipulated at the army's behest by the internal wing of the ISI.[35] Nawaz Sharif showed signs of insecurity by interfering with the operations of Pakistan's judiciary and indulging in other abuses of power. At most times, the governments were permitted to continue in office at the sole discretion of the army chief and/or the President of Pakistan, and the time when democracy prospered was ironically when

General Nawaz lived up to the professional standards of an apolitical soldier who did not obstruct its free flow.

Bhutto and Sharif themselves often proved undemocratic and autocratic. Under their governments, sectarian violence increased in the key Punjabi and Sindhi strongholds of Lahore and Karachi, and corruption was rampant. Perhaps it is these factors that convinced the populace to accept a return to military rule where though democracy was a casualty, stability and discipline were on hand. While this phase appeared to enjoy a semblance of two-party democracy, the army was always lurking in the wings and remained the centre of power in realpolitik. Inevitably, the army returned to power when, in October 1999, General Pervez Musharraf dismissed Nawaz Sharif's government and assumed power as 'chief executive'.

19

Musharraf's Coup

'*[W]henever the army gets involved in martial law, it gets distracted from its vital military duties. [Also] when we superimpose . . . the military over the civilian government, the latter ceases functioning.*'

—Pervez Musharraf, *In the Line of Fire: A Memoir*

In the typical ironies that abound Pakistani politics, one of the earliest commands given by General Pervez Musharraf to his corps commanders on becoming army chief was that all officers were to 'stay away from politics and politicians' and only the COAS would interact with the government to present the army's viewpoint though the Chief would 'indeed discuss all matters with his subordinate commanders to form opinion on national issues'.[1]

The doublespeak would prove to be unmistakable.

Soon after taking over as COAS, Musharraf explored the option of deploying the Pakistani forces in Kargil, India. This was seen as an act to avenge the loss of critical positions on the Siachen glacier to the Indian Army as part of its Operation Meghdoot in 1984, an operation in which Musharraf as a junior officer was at the receiving end.[2]

While the initial forays by the Pakistani forces, assisted by the Afghan Mujahideen, proved debilitating to the operations and morale of the Indian troops, the end result showed Pakistan in poor light.[3] Musharraf however made bold to state that the Kargil conflict, though a 'tactical maneuver of limited dimensions', had strategic effects and was the sole reason for any 'movement . . . in the direction of finding a solution to Kashmir'.[4]

The strong Indian response and the glare of the international community brought to the fore the serious differences between Prime Minister Nawaz Sharif and his army chief. Till date, it remains unclear as to whether Sharif was fully in the know of the Kargil plan, with him and Musharraf diametrically differing on the subject in their public responses. Shuja Nawaz brands this the 'Rashomon effect'[5]—where each key member of an incident has a divergent perspective of the facts. Musharraf on his part is categorical that,

> The army briefed the Prime Minister [Nawaz Sharif] in Skardu on January 29, 1999; and in Kel on February 5, 1999. During these briefings our defensive maneuver was explained as a response to all that was happening on the Indian side. Subsequently, the Prime Minister was also briefed on March 12 at the Directorate General Inter Services International, which included a detailed survey of the situation inside Occupied Jammu and Kashmir and also the LOC. As the operation developed, he [the Prime Minister] was briefed in detail by the director general of military operations on May 17. Later briefings were also arranged on June 2 and June 22.[6]

On the contrary, Sharif states that he was 'hoodwinked' by the army, who told him that the operations were being carried out by the Mujahideen.[7]

It is undisputed that Nawaz Sharif was opportunistic enough to permit the operations (by whatever manner or mode they were informed to him) to continue till such time Pakistan had the upper hand. Upon realizing that the plans had seriously backfired, he desperately rushed to Washington on an unsolicited visit to seek the immediate interference of President Clinton to prevail upon India to stay its hand. Bennett Jones points to the fact that there clearly was 'no thoroughgoing debate' on the implications of Kargil and the possibility of a major Indian counterattack, which was 'a remarkably casual way for a nuclear power to run a war'.[8]

The Kargil imbroglio ended in an 'unofficial'[9] ceasefire. The relationship with his prime minister is summed up by General Musharraf as having shifted from being 'perfectly good in the beginning, with some minor disagreements' over matters of appointments and removals of senior officers, to having 'soured only with the Kargil episode and Nawaz Sharif's sudden capitulation before President Bill Clinton in Washington on July 4, 1999.'[10]

Musharraf also suspected Sharif of plotting to remove him and promote him to the largely decorative position of Chief of the Joint Chiefs of Staff (CJCS). Mary Anne Weaver remarks:

> The ensuing battle of wills (sic) between the Chief of the Army Staff and his prime minister grew bitter and intense. The die had been cast for Musharraf's dismissal and for an Army coup. The only remaining question was, which would come first.[11]

When Musharraf was on a flight back from Colombo to Karachi on 12 October 1999, the aircraft was denied permission to land anywhere in Pakistan and directed to turn to any other destination, excluding Dubai. Sharif had, meanwhile, unilaterally appointed Lieutenant General Ziauddin as COAS though, to his chagrin, the senior army commanders supported Musharraf and, in a swift reaction, nullified all of Sharif's manoeuvres and enabled Musharraf to land in Karachi with just seven minutes' fuel remaining in his aircraft. Musharraf accused Sharif of attempted murder, summarily overthrew and exiled him to Saudi Arabia with forfeiture of his assets. Sharif was spared criminal trial for treason, while Musharraf assumed power as chief executive in what he describes as the army's 'countercoup'.[12] Former US ambassador Robert Oakley pithily stated, 'When one deals with the army recklessly in Pakistan, one usually pays the price.'[13]

In the fallout of this encounter, democracy was again the casualty. Soon after his takeover, Musharraf would proclaim that the Constitution was 'but a part of the nation therefore I chose to save the nation' and the Constitution was only temporarily held in abeyance. '*This is not martial law, only another path towards democracy,*' he would assert, adding the hackneyed caveat that 'the armed forces have no intention to stay in charge any longer than is absolutely necessary to pave the way for true democracy to flourish in Pakistan.[14] (Emphasis supplied.)

Incredibly, the army remained in power for approximately a decade, being itself the sole arbiter of the concepts of 'nation' and 'national good', overriding the Constitution.[15]

Musharraf is candid enough to admit:

> It is not unusual in Pakistan for the general public and the intelligentsia to approach the Army Chief and ask him to save the nation. In all crises, everyone sees Pakistan's army as the country's saviour. Whenever governments have malfunctioned [as has frequently occurred], whenever there has been a tussle between the President and the Prime Minister [especially during the 1990s], all roads led to the

> general headquarters of the army. The Army Chief was regularly expected to put pressure on the Prime Minister to perform—to avoid corruption, nepotism, and sometimes, downright criminality. The Army Chief was also dragged in to mediate all disputes between the President and the Prime Minister.[16]

There was a new-found volatility in Pakistan in 2001. The events of 11 September 2001 and the attack on the World Trade Center, New York, affected Pakistan 'more than any other Muslim state except Afghanistan', leading to 'major concessions' such as the abandonment of the Taliban, provision of extensive military and intelligence support to the United States and allowing its territory to be used by the American forces fighting in Afghanistan.[17]

Though Musharraf claimed to pave the way for democracy, Pakistan's intelligence services ensured that in the October 2002 election, both the PML and the PPP were unable to assert themselves. A coalition of Islamic parties—the Muttahida Majlis-i-amal (MMA)—assumed power in the volatile NWFP and also shared power in Balochistan.

The election resulted in a hung parliament amidst cries from the PML and PPP of 'the government machinery conducting massive pre-election rigging' as well as of 'doctoring results' of the election itself.[18] Musharraf, as President, appointed Baluch Mir Zafarullah Khan Jamali as prime minister, only to replace him after forcing his resignation after eighteen months.[19] Musharraf also 'provided' for a victory to the Islamist coalition—the MMA—in Balochistan and the NWFP. According to Benazir Bhutto, this was done to 'exaggerate the so-called strength of the Islamist threat to Pakistan and to paint his [Musharraf's] authoritarian regime as a bulwark against it'.[20] An unelected army was again calling the shots politically.

Musharaf inducted 'more and more army officers into the civil services' and 'spent more time playing the politician on the basis of the military's latent coercive power rather than a broad base of political support'.[21] This phase also saw the introduction of orthodox Islamic ideology, including that of the Tablighi Jamaat, in the echelons of the army and 'the formation of Pir Bhai networks of spiritual bands that included civilians and military men and threatened the discipline and rank order of the military . . . (with) senior officers opening the door for a junior officer who outranked them in the Pir Bhai network.'[22] This was a far cry from the signature traditions of a British Army from which the Pakistan Army drew its DNA.

Milam does defend Musharraf to an extent in commenting that 'those who justified military government on the basis that it could turn back the rising tide of Islamism found . . . that things were not so simple' and 'if Musharraf did not live up to their expectations it is because, in part, of the deep roots Islamists (had) established in Pakistani society, the legacy primarily of the previous military regime, as well as the sad state of general education in Pakistan, the legacy of all previous regimes.' He clarifies that 'each time the Musharraf government ventured to push Islamists back by modifying some of their favourite levers of social control, it found that Islamists have the means to push back equally forcefully', noting that several times, President Musharraf did indeed come into conflict with Islamists, but 'usually backed down'. Citing, for instance, the proposed changes in the blasphemy law in 2000—at a point in time when Musharraf was in 'direct charge of the country with no parliamentary body to answer to', but nonetheless, 'resistance from the Islamists was still too much for him and the army leadership.'[23]

The role of non-State actors in the functioning of parliamentary democracy in Pakistan was more and more apparent by now. The army had contributed to the hollowing out of civilian institutions and was now itself being arm-wrestled by other groups that did not enjoy constitutional status.

Enigmatically, Musharraf, a Mohajir, was able to become COAS as also President of Pakistan, without demur from the dominant Punjabi community. This can be put down to the fact that Musharraf was propped up by a Punjabi prime minister—Nawaz Sharif, who thought a Mohajir would be more 'amenable to his orders'.[24] Instead, Musharraf ended up not only overthrowing Sharif but even creating a political party—the PML (Q) which was shored up by the Punjabi elite!

In the face of claims of democracy, after his initial three-year tenure, the referendum in 2002 enabled Musharraf to remain in power for a further five years. After a farcical national referendum held in April 2002, Musharraf declared himself President on 20 June that year. The resolution for the referendum, put before the people of Pakistan, was almost rhetorical and read:

> For the survival of the local government system, *establishment of democracy,* continuity of reforms, end of sectarianism and extremism, and to fulfill the vision of Quaid-e-Azam, would you like to elect General Pervez Musharraf as President of Pakistan for five years?[25] (Emphasis supplied.)

A general was able to convene and participate in a pan-Pakistan referendum but otherwise be pusillanimous in the matter of holding regular, free and fair elections. This was the sinister effect of the army on democracy in Pakistan. The prime ministerial authority was subordinated to that of the President in 2002 by an extra-constitutional Legal Framework Order (LFO). In 2004, substantial parts of the LFO were incorporated into the constitution by a majority vote of Pakistan's electoral college, comprising members of the national and provincial assemblies.[26]

Cohen tersely opines that Musharraf's version of military rule was 'far more tolerant than that of Zia, but as with previous military regimes, the army appears unable to govern Pakistan itself but will not allow anyone else the opportunity to do so either.'[27]

20

'An Army's Nation'

'The road ahead is no highway to democracy.'
—Murtaza Razvi, *Musharraf: The Years in Power*

Soon after Musharraf's coup of 1999, 'many of the contradictions in Pakistan's political, economic, and social structure' were 'painfully evident'.[1] Pakistan's nuclear programme, its increasing domestic violence and its support for Islamic radicalism in Afghanistan (and at home) worried the international community at large. The human rights track record was also abject. The 2002–03 Annual Human Rights Report of the US State Department named Pakistan as one of twelve states where human trafficking is rampant and religious freedom is absent, while the Pakistan Human Rights Report of 2001 listed mass violence against women and children, including rape, honour killings and illegal death sentences.[2] Equally disturbing was the abuse of hundreds of Indian POWs in Pakistan, stated to be 'abandoned' by the Indian government.[3] Other negative episodes involved attacks on foreigners, such as the gory videotaped beheading of the American journalist Daniel Pearl.[4]

Benazir Bhutto caustically comments, 'Though Musharraf quickly installed first Zafarullah Jamali and then Shaukat Aziz as Prime Minister in 2002, there was no doubt in Islamabad, Washington or London, [as to] who ruled Pakistan.'[5]

Because of its renewed relationship with India, the United States pressed Pakistan to end its support to cross-border terrorists moving across the Line of Control (LoC) into Kashmir. The United States (earlier under President Clinton and later, George Bush) was already 'worried because of the rise in India–Pakistan tensions after the (Musharraf) coup'.[6] This led to the Indo–Pak summit in January 2004 during the South Asian Association for Regional Cooperation (SAARC) meeting in Islamabad, and after the May 2004 national elections in India, the two countries resumed talks on nuclear issues and Kashmir that remained inconclusive.

On the resulting situation, Musharraf plainly stated:

> [That] the spirit of democracy is entirely forgotten. What we in Pakistan have consciously constructed instead is rule by a small elite—never democratic, often autocratic, usually plutocratic and lately kleptocratic—all working with a tribal–feudal mindset . . . *with democratic camouflage* . . . People generally do not vote . . . across their tribe, caste, or clan boundaries. Elections therefore involve shifting coalitions . . . rather than appeals to independent voters . . . It creates the *illusion of democracy* because we do have elections; but we forget that elections are but a tool of democracy, not an end in themselves.[7] (Emphasis supplied.)

These were astute observations, except they entirely discounted the sinister effect the army had in causing the status quo. Musharraf's sentiments are to be contrasted with those of the Pakistani academia at the time. Professor Pervez Hoodbhoy observes that to stay put in power, Musharraf and his generals 'will protect the source of their power—the army' and 'accommodate those they must—the Americans', while they 'pander to the mullahs' and 'crush those who threaten their power and privilege.' His epithet is scathing, 'No price is high for them (the generals). They are the reason why Pakistan fails.'[8]

Post the 2002 elections, while 'scores of Shias were murdered in the suicide attacks by the jihadis on Shia mosques' and civil society looked on,[9] Musharraf evolved his doctrine of 'Enlightened Moderation' whereby a progressive interpretation of Islam was sought to be promoted in Pakistan. However, this did not go down well with the Islamic-coalition—the MMA, which was in power in the NWFP and keen on applying Islamic Sharia Law. The MMA fell out with Musharraf, ostensibly for his failure to 'doff his military uniform'.[10] Musharraf's reason for refusal to shed his military hat was that the MMA, along with Nawaz Sharif's supporters, was attempting to 'destabilize the country and the democratic system' that Musharraf claimed he 'had put in place'![11]

Musharraf's regime smacked of doublespeak in the matter of tackling jihadi terror or, for that matter, the Islamization of the state. Richard Weekes, circa 1964, viewed religion as the magnet that bound 'diverse Pakistanis together, when logic seemed to demand their disintegration'.[12] Wilson John has, in his work *The General and Jihad*, extrapolated how the jihadi groups had, over the years, become a 'strategic tool', a necessary evil and a redoubtable rival to the army, in what has comically been described as 'An Army's Nation'.[13]

Zahid Hussain records that Musharraf's unwillingness to cede power and 'the lack of democratic progress were the main reasons why no headway was made in countering Islamic extremism.' In his assessment, the fact that the Musharraf government 'had failed to build an independent state and political institutions, or establish free and fair elections', created a 'conducive environment for extremism to flourish.' Any positive steps Musharraf took to introduce a 'modicum of democracy were countered by measures to increase his or the military's power.'[14]

In the vicious circle that is Pakistan, the assumption of power to enforce democracy, the inability to yield power, the absence of institutions, the suppression of democracy and the resultant extremism were in full display by this stage in its political history. Immersed in this ad-hocism, Musharraf made an unprecedented and 'critical error' in going after judges and lawyers in Pakistan and removing Supreme Court Chief Justice Iftikhar Muhammad Chaudhry for probing the 'scandal of missing persons' and then placing him under house arrest.[15]

Later, unable to tackle the strong agitation and opposition from the lawyers in Pakistan to his taking on the judiciary, Musharraf imposed Emergency Rule in November 2007, suspending the Constitution and thereby 'establishing the action as martial law'.[16] The imposition of Emergency was quashed by the Supreme Court, in the wake of Musharraf demanding that the judges take 'fresh oath of office under the new emergency rule'.[17] This was a refreshing judicial intervention upon the arbitrariness of the army.

Imran Khan refers to this moment in graphic detail:

> The lawyers' movement was a significant development for Pakistan, offering hope of a plank of civil society activism that did not represent any particular religious or political group. The way in which the surge in independent media had sharpened political consciousness in Pakistan was consistently underestimated by Musharraf, and later by Sharif and Benazir . . . One of my party's main demands when I had founded it in 1996 was for an independent judicial system, and for years ours was a cry in the wilderness. Finally it was

> an idea whose time had come . . . (Chief Justice) Chaudhry set off on a tour of courts and lawyers' associations around the country, drawing huge crowds of people who tossed rose petals at his cavalcade and called out anti-Musharraf slogans . . . It was then that I realized something quite incredible was taking place in Pakistan. There was a general awakening of the public for the first time since I had entered politics. As the sun came up a man shouted from the distance, 'Imran Sahib, a new dawn is rising!' I'll never forget that. Pakistan had changed.[18]

General Musharraf then shed his army uniform in favour of General Pervez Kayani (an ex-ISI chief and a loyalist) purportedly to hold only one office of a 'bona fide' civilian leader. Simultaneously, Musharraf announced the conduct of elections in February 2008 in what have been described as 'the second of the fairest elections ever held in Pakistan'.[19] The elections witnessed the rout of pro-Musharraf parties and right-wing parties, and the success of a popular coalition of Benazir Bhutto's PPP and Nawaz Sharif's PML(N), with Yousaf Raza Gilani as prime minister. His popularity having waned tremendously and his impeachment (and possibly, assassination) looking inevitable, Musharraf resigned from the office of President (making way for President Zardari) and relocated (in exile) to Saudi Arabia.

Musharraf's address to the nation on the eve of these developments on 12 July 2007 did not have a *single* mention of 'democracy' or 'elections'.[20] On the contrary, Nawaz Sharif and Benazir Bhutto's 'Charter of Democracy' dated 13 May 2007 (ironically, signed while both were still out of Pakistan; in London), while expectedly condemning 'military involvement' as the cause of the breakdown of democratic institutions, contained the following clause as a part of the 'Code of Conduct' under the Charter: 'We shall not join a military regime or any military sponsored government. *No party shall solicit the support of [the] military to come into power or to dislodge a democratic government.*'[21] (Emphasis supplied.)

This clause was a faux pas, a confession of one of the most direct causes for the breakdown of democracy in Pakistan. Benazir Bhutto returned to Pakistan in October 2007 after a lengthy exile, in the midst of hectic lobbying and politicking between her and Musharraf and other players in the frame. The quid pro quo was Benazir supporting Musharraf's continuance as President after the 2008 elections, in return for immunity from prosecution to her and her husband, Zardari.[22] Benazir returned to crowds in Karachi unable to 'stop the tears', with a sense of awe and belief that this was going to be 'the beginning of a long journey for Pakistan back to democracy'.[23] Not much later, on the evening of 27 December 2007, while she was leaving a rally in Rawalpindi 'happy (and) thrilled', she was shot dead with bullets to the neck and head.[24] Her position was vindicated posthumously with the ouster of Musharraf and the return of a democratically elected government in the 2008 elections.

For all the rhetoric, the last few months of Musharraf's regime witnessed the high-handed suspension of the chief justice, the forcible deportation of Nawaz Sharif to Saudi Arabia (only to let him return later), the imposition of Emergency for a month in November 2007 and ultimately the assassination of Benazir Bhutto (allegedly by the Al-Qaeda, but under the nose of the army at Rawalpindi, which was the army GHQ). Benazir's death has been attributed by some to the acts of the anti-Shia fundamentalist extremist group, Lashkar-e-Jhangavi, for her being 'anti-Islamist'.[25] Others have speculated that 'the US was somehow involved' since the Americans had 'always distrusted the Bhuttos'.[26] None of the theories were corroborated. The Taliban, on its part, 'claimed' the murder.[27]

Musharraf would face the ignominy not only of having the Supreme Court declare his proclamation of Emergency in 2007 illegal, but also of facing charges for treason and 'personal aggrandizement and a consequential vendetta' for unilaterally seeking to amend the constitution—which gave a momentary 'glimpse of civilian triumph'.[28] Musharraf would evade the proceedings by fleeing to London (after time spent in Saudi Arabia), where he remained in exile.

Each of these incidents represented a complete breakdown of stable civilian governance and a rank subversion of democracy in Pakistan. Razvi concluded at the time:

> With each military coup and derailment of democracy in Pakistan, the country has been pushed back decades in terms of political sustainability and economic stability . . . Unless politicians like Zardari and Sharif show the will to learn from their mistakes, and respect the public mandate given to their respective parties to rule in accordance with the law, while at the same time empower parliament to carry out the much-needed and overdue reforms in the basic law, *an Ayub, Zia or a Musharraf will keep waiting in the wings to pounce on them.*[29] (Emphasis supplied.)

2008 and After: The Flux

'Nothing in Pakistan happens the same way twice. On no institution can you entirely rely.'

—Wasim Akram, *Sultan: A Memoir*

Upon Musharraf's exit, general elections were held in Pakistan in February 2008 and the PPP and PML-N returned to power in a coalition. The PPP was now under the leadership of the late Benazir Bhutto's son Bilawal, while PML-N saw the revival of fortunes of the ever-present Nawaz Sharif. Yousaf Raza Gilani was the negotiated name for prime minister. The PML-N however exited the coalition within a week, and the PPP was now in alliance with other smaller parties. The army sat back in its cyclical style, to enable one term of democracy at least. The elections of 2013 saw the entry of Imran Khan's Pakistan Tehreek-e-Insaf (PTI) into the political fray. This time, the PPP and PML-N were able to cobble together a pre-electoral alliance, though Parliament was hung. Independents who supported PML-N helped Nawaz Sharif return as PM and enjoy a term in power, though riddled with allegations of corruption.[1] Sufi cleric Tahir-ul-Qadri led a countrywide march in 2013 to protest against corruption, reminiscent of the Anna Hazare movement in India a little earlier. Imran Khan supported this call against the corruption of power and made this the sheet anchor of his campaign over the next five years. Surprisingly, the army was able to afford the civilian government another shot. Nawaz Sharif had managed the delicate decision of appointing the new COAS upon General Kayani's premature retirement. General Raheel Sharif was the dark horse who replaced him and kept things quiet till his retirement in 2016, when General Qamar Javed Bajwa took over. He was regarded as being 'pro-democracy', which perhaps prompted his appointment. Ironically, politicians would accuse him of influencing the outcome of the next elections to come, with Nawaz Sharif going so far as to accuse him of rigging and forcing Sharif's ouster in 2018.[2]

Pakistan's election of 2018 saw a popular Imran Khan lead the PTI to victory. Though analysts considered him to be a 'nominee' of the army and often disparagingly referred to his new government as a 'hybrid' (civilian–military),[3] Khan was independently popular with the common folk owing to his lack of dynasty and, of course, his cricketing fame. In his initial period, he was close to the military establishment and, particularly so, to the COAS General Bajwa.[4] His regime let the army call the shots on areas that were traditionally regarded as being their 'portfolio'—defence and foreign affairs. But with the passage of time, his ambition and clout increased and he was able to hit against the spin. Khan replaced the director general of the ISI—always a sensitive move, and also began to assert himself on the economic front. While Pakistan saw some of its hardest economic times under him—with unparalleled inflation and foreign debt—the Covid pandemic was always a fallback. Intriguingly, Khan was opposed to imposing lockdowns in the country but was publicly overruled by the army spokesman! This was signature Pakistani democracy at play. Khan was able to see an economic rebound, which increased his popularity with the common citizens and smaller traders, while his austerity drive earned him enemies from within.[5]

The extension of the term of office for General Bajwa in November 2019 turned out to be a crucial (if not comical) episode with the PM first granting him an extension, only to be advised that it was the President's prerogative. The resolution was accordingly recalled to enable the President to grant the extension, which was done bereft of the recommendation of the council. After a third round of paperwork, the extension found itself challenged in the Supreme Court which, by an unprecedented order, stayed its implementation. Such assertion by the court, especially in a matter involving the very top brass of the army, was delicate and could well have triggered a reaction from the military. In an equally unexpected development, the army did nothing and awaited the orders of the Supreme Court, which ruled that there existed no legal provision to grant such an extension. But it stopped short of quashing the extension and permitted the government to bring in appropriate legislation to deal with the situation.[6] The law came to be suitably amended in January 2020 and the COAS remained in office. The sensitivity of the matter was such that the law minister resigned his office to appear for General Bajwa as counsel!

A change in defence minister in early 2022 led to a bold pushback by the government in response to the army's budgetary demands. While the demand was for a whopping 12 per cent increase, the government was able to plead insufficiency of funds and keep it at 3 per cent. Again, this was the sort of thing that could fire up the army enough to cause political disruption. But for a variety of reasons, it stayed passive. These reasons could include the increasing popularity of Imran Khan as a mass leader, a greater sense of the spirit of democracy among the younger Pakistanis, the increasing institutional assertion of the Supreme Court and a proactive (global) media that would not sympathize with a military coup. The absence of international examples of military rule at the time could well also be a factor.[7]

Khan's popularity came to the fore after a no-confidence motion was passed and he was ousted from Parliament in April 2022. A truly non-partisan, emotional uprising among ordinary citizens rose in his support, with hundreds thronging the courts when he sought bail and thousands lining the streets during his rallies. Khan has become a sort of sui generis leader, sans the dynastic, sectarian and corrupt trappings of his predecessors. Though his colleagues in the government have faced allegations of corruption, the perception remains that Khan himself was always above board. His affinity to orthodox Islam over 'otherworldly' Sufis is driven by his adoration for Alama Iqbal and endears him to the everyday Pakistani.

As things stand in March 2024 Nawaz Sharif's brother Shehbaz Sharif is back as the prime minister and the army is letting democracy work itself out. The army under General Asim Munir appeared to back the return of the Nawaz Sharif camp in the game of thrones that is Pakistan.[8] This phase of a 'non-coup' is the longest in the country's history and it would perhaps take a significant shift in the army's mentality for it to abruptly re-enter the polity. It seems content for the moment to enjoy its back-seat power, financial assets and a new-found legitimacy in Pakistan's new-found democracy.

* * *

The noteworthy development in India since 2008 was the creation of the institution of Chief of Defence Staff (CDS). The long-standing demand for a CDS came to fruition in 2020 with General Bipin Rawat, former COAS, assuming charge. The stated objective for the CDS is to bring about 'jointness in operations, logistics, transport, training, support services, communications, repairs and maintenance of the three Services'.[9] Sushant Singh argues interestingly that the creation of the CDS as a 'Super-General-Super-Bureaucrat' (a phrase coined by former defence secretary G. Mohan Kumar), eliminates the 'layer of civilian bureaucracy between the politician and the military' and shifts the control of the military directly to the political class.[10] This, he observes, resembles the political control over the Indian Police Service and significantly reverses the 'critical coup-proofing and balancing measures initiated by the government in the first decade of India's independence.'[11]

While the implicit idea behind the CDS was to have an enhanced and unified level of contact with the civilian bureaucracy, it came to be felt that General Rawat paid less attention to the other services, especially the air force.[12] He oversaw the initial plans for the proposed merger of seventeen theatre commands into five Integrated Theatre Commands (ITCs) to operationally combine the three services, in which formula he perceived the IAF rather disparagingly as a 'support arm' of the army's combat units.[13] This was tone-deaf to the (stand-alone) Balakot strikes by the air force in response to the Pulwama attack of 2019—strikes that the government had taken pride in.[14] Significantly, the Ministry of Defence has stonewalled the move to have such ITCs in place, in no small measure due to the change in the pecking order between the new commanders of the ITC and their corresponding IAS colleagues. The arm-wrestle between the civil–military apparatus was magnified via a Twitter ('X') exchange when former CNS Admiral Arun Prakash criticized the fact that a financial adviser to the defence ministry affixed the naval flag on their car, only to have the spokesperson of the ministry respond by questioning the use of jawans for personal chores by senior military officers.[15] (The spokesperson was sent on leave soon after, to diffuse the potential storm that was beginning to rage between veterans on both sides.)

Some of General Rawat's statements in (and on) Kashmir sounded more political than one would expect from an officer—he was open in endorsing the 'lynching' of terrorists in the act of self-defence.[16] His comments on China being an ally of Islamist sections (read: Pakistan) made the foreign ministry uneasy.[17]

He was unfortunately killed in a helicopter crash in the Nilgiris in December 2021, after which the government needed to amend the rules for the appointment of a CDS. After a rather long wait of nine months, the new CDS was appointed in September 2022. The officer so appointed—Lieutenant General Anil Chauhan, who was brought out of retirement—also belonged to the 11 Gorkhas as did his predecessor. That it was another infantry officer, when the pool of selection transcended not only the regiments but the tri-service, is an indicator of the political heft of the infantry in India.

In this context, it is to be said that General Rawat was appointed COAS by superseding two officers, lieutenant generals Praveen Bakshi and P.M. Hariz—both well-respected officers, of whom Hariz was Muslim. For the record, India has never had a Muslim COAS, though it has seen a Muslim chief of air staff in Air Chief Marshal Idris Latif. The supersession was called out by the Opposition, but drew no reaction from within the Service or from the two officers themselves. Tongues wagged about the regimental (infantry versus armoured corps), territorial and religious biases that permeate the politics of appointment of army chiefs. But as has been the practice, the officers take it on the chin and move along, dissipating any politicization of the matter.

In mid-2020, Indian forces faced off against their Chinese counterparts at Galwan, in a pitched encounter that saw the loss of twenty-five or more lives on either side. Not since 1962 (or possibly 1967) had the two sides clashed in such a manner. While the official position remains that India did not cede any territory, the scale of the infiltration and the intensity of the exchange points to a renewed threat from a domineering China.[18] A la 1962, one wonders about the ability of the government to recognize the threat over the attention paid to Pakistan, and whether senior army commanders would be able to advise the government plainly on the lopsided territorial, military and cyber-offensive risks from China. This assumes importance in the light of an increasing politicization/communalization of the army, about which retired officers have themselves spoken out in public fora.[19] A dominant executive has also interfered in the seniority of officers while making appointments. Apart from the instance of General Rawat's promotion as COAS, the government named Vice Admiral Karambir Singh as CNS, passing over Vice Admiral Bimal Verma (who then moved the Armed Forces Tribunal to no avail). The government also introduced an unprecedented direct recruitment scheme for enlisting entry-level candidates for 'Agnipath', a four-year tenure in the army. Opinions are divided on its need and efficacy, and especially on its effects on the professionalism and morale of the candidates and the regiments alike.[20] The religious objectivity with which the Agniveers (as the recruits are known) perform will determine the success of the scheme and, more importantly, the status of the army in changing times of civil–military relations in India.

A soft spot in the equation before the military and the bureaucracy has always been the matter of pay scales. The recommendations of the Sixth Pay Commission undermined the uniformed services like never before, and led to retired soldiers returning their gallantry medals to the President of India in a visceral protest against their inequitable treatment. Some of the veterans were manhandled during their protest in New Delhi, reflecting a new low in the treatment of retired soldiers. The 7th Pay Commission offered some course correction alongside the One Rank One Pension ('OROP') scheme, though the anomalous position remains not only inter se the officers and their civilian counterparts. After the 7th Pay Commission was implemented, officers of general rank stood to earn lesser than their *junior officers* in the army (brigadiers), owing to a variable called Military Service Pay. This was corrected by the government only after a High Court direction.[21] Even with respect to pensions, a group of ex-servicemen was constrained to move the Supreme Court challenging the disparity in having 1 January 2016 as the cut-off for implementing revised pensions, only to be asked to move the ditto. Unsurprisingly, the veterans (and serving officers) feel hard done by with the lukewarm treatment meted out to them by the executive. There are demands that the military needs its own pay commission, owing to its peculiar needs and circumstances. Such a move on the part of the government would bolster the morale of the forces, who often find themselves unfairly clubbed with civilian government servants and often sans parity.

For now, the Ministry of Defence has directed defence establishments to set up 'selfie points' to showcase the policies of the government (that go beyond matters of national security) and draw the armed forces into practically aligning with the politics of the day. This is accompanied by a 'recommendation' from the army HQ that soldiers on leave undertake outreach within their local communities on subjects of their choice. Written between the lines is the directive to carry positive messages of governance at the Centre. Major General S.G. Vombatkere (Retired) refers to Rule 20 of the Army Rules, 1954[22] (framed under the Army Act, 1950) to point to the embargo on associating with political purposes or causes, and finds that these schemes are an instance of directly politicizing the armed forces by having them propagate the policies of the government of the day.[23] Veterans and commentators have roundly criticized these endeavours as reducing the armed forces to being 'social warriors'—a term coined by Lieutenant General H.S. Panag (Retired)—or 'BJP cadres', and worse still, tempting senior officers to identify with the prevailing political ideology to further their careers.[24] The serving armed forces, however, appear to see these directives as part and parcel of their customary obedience.[25]

The balance of power between the military and the civilian establishment in India and Pakistan is poles apart. The effects of these relationalities are commensurately felt on their respective democracies—for better or for worse.

If this chapter begins with a quote from a fast bowler, it is fitting to have one at this end too. Imran Khan says:

> [O]nly a credible government can save and strengthen the Pakistan army by making sure that it remains within its constitutional role. The example for Pakistan is that of Turkey, where the Army—which kept destabilizing democratic governments—had a constitutional role to uphold its secular ideology. It took a credible leader of the stature of Erdogan whose dynamic leadership and great moral authority has put the army in its rightful place and taken Turkey towards a genuine democracy.

The layers within these lines are tantalizing.

Bangladesh: The Experiment

'(T)he military had been forced to take over because it was the only organized national institution which could be relied on to defend the national interest, and that it would rule until new elections could be held.'

—General Ershad, quoted in William B. Milam, *Bangladesh and Pakistan: Flirting with Failure in South Asia*

Pakistani journalist Anthony Mascarenhas, in his stirring, no-holds-barred work *The Rape of Bangla Desh,* observes that the idea of having a 'separation of East Bengal' was regarded as 'suicidal for any politician living in West Pakistan', as this was more sacrosanct to the polity of the time than even Kashmir, and would 'automatically stir up a similar demand from three of the four provinces in West Pakistan' leading to not two, but 'five Pakistans'.[1] As things panned out, Bangladesh was liberated nevertheless, in no small measure, owing to India's military intervention. Chandrashekhar Dasgupta observes that with 'the minor exception of the 1965 clashes in the Rann of Kutch, the 1971 conflict was the only Indo–Pakistan war in which India's primary objective was not focused on Kashmir. The strategic aim of the war was to speed up the liberation of Bangladesh, not to resolve the Kashmir question.'[2] That liberation was swiftly obtained in December 1971.

On 10 January 1972, Mujibur Rahman returned to newly formed Bangladesh from prison in Pakistan—via London and New Delhi (to call on Indira Gandhi)—and led an Awami League government in the spirit of parliamentary democracy. He relinquished the office of President in favour of becoming prime minister. By early April 1972, all the permanent members of the UN Security Council, except China, had recognized the People's Republic of Bangladesh. A new constitution was adopted in November 1972, with 'Mujibism'—nationalism, socialism, secularism and democracy—at its heart. However, the radical opposition (mostly comprising militant student unions) aspired for a revolutionary paradigm shift away from the agrarian–business groups that were representative of Pakistani power structures, and sought a more authentic, democratic model that represented the aspirations of the working classes. Mujib sought to pursue populist policies of land reform and nationalization in the teeth of resistance from various quarters. Ayesha Jalal reflects on the initial Bangladesh experiment by observing that what made the 'Bangladeshi experiment with populism' different from the Indian and Pakistani instances was Mujib's reliance 'on the Awami League's political networks than on the non-elected institutions of the state'. As she puts it, 'Effective steps were taken to build the ruling party's organizational machinery down to the district level and elective control over the administrative arms of the state was sought to be established. Yet Mujib failed since the Awami League reflected the broader ideological divisions in Bangladeshi society which more than outweighed the merits of its organisation.'[3]

The divisions were more than ideological, and manifested themselves as a socio-political gridlock, and as internal differences within the Awami League itself. Interestingly, the (re)organization of the military establishment also faced an identity crisis—would it continue in the colonial format as available loosely in neighbouring India and Pakistan or would it integrate the Mukti Bahini, who were the 'freedom fighters' who had fought for Bangladeshi liberation and now merited their place in the sun? The armed forces themselves were 'hostile to Bengali aspirations' because of their demands for provincial autonomy, normalization of relations with India and a non-aligned foreign policy', all of which were opposed to the 'institutional interests of the military'.[4]

Finding himself tentative on this significant matter of the integration of the Mukti Bahini and unsure of how the army would respond, Mujib 'followed Bhutto's example by setting up his own paramilitary force, the Rakkhi Bahini, (whose) membership . . . was based entirely on demonstrated loyalty to Mujib and the Awami League'.[5] They would come to be regarded as an affront to the standing army.[6] And, as was the case in Pakistan, the Rakkhi Bahini, or the National Security Force, became Mujib's personal unit to extract loyalty from the electorate and to keep the (small) Opposition in check.[7] This despite winning the 1973 elections with over 90 per cent of the seats!

Soon enough, authoritarian precedents from Pakistan were being replicated in Bangladesh with Mujib assuming a dictatorial position, in the face of allegations of poll rigging and suppression of press freedoms. In December 1974, he declared Emergency invoking national security powers under Article 2 of the constitution, which he used 'to abridge civil rights and drastically curtail the judiciary's authority and scope to check and review executive actions'.[8] He also sought to make Bangladesh a one-party state with the formation of the Bangladesh Peasants and Workers Awami League/ Bangladesh Krishak Sramik Awami League (BAKSAL) and pushing the country into further economic debt and political chaos,[9] reminiscent of the last days of Mao in China.

Mujib, it seems, betrayed a strong bias towards those with 'sound liberation credentials' and this also influenced army appointments with fatal consequences.[10] Officers taken off duty by the Pakistan Army and interned in West Pakistan found to their horror that on their return, they had to report to their juniors who had been promoted because of their role in the liberation. There was mutual suspicion, in the face of the cult that Mujib encouraged around himself; some of the older officers 'found it harder to reconcile their professionalism with the new ideological demands'.[11]

Milam analyses Mujib's distrust of the 'repatriates'—those who had served the Pakistan Army pre-1971, and his preference for the pure 'freedom fighters', i.e., those who had never served the West over those who 'escaped' the West to join the freedom fighters in the East.[12] He finds this nuanced preference of one category of 'freedom fighters' over the other in Mujib's decision to ignore General Ziaur Rehman as COAS despite his credentials as a fine soldier and a 'national hero', and in denying soldiers like him promotions and plum postings.[13] A similar bias was on display with the civil service, with a rank preference for those novices who opted for the services in East Pakistan being preferred over the old guard. Unsurprisingly, Mujib alienated the military who now saw his regime as deleterious to the future of Bangladesh and, in keeping with the familiar playbook in (West) Pakistan, eliminated him.[14]

In August 1975, Mujib, his wife, three sons, two daughters-in-law, and a host of other relatives, personal staff and a brigadier general of the Bangladesh Army were assassinated in a military coup orchestrated by serving and retired officers, swiftly ending Bangladesh's first bite at the democratic cherry. On the coup, B.Z. Khasru comments:

> Although the entire military did not directly take part in the August coup, the top brass in general tacitly accepted, with only a few exceptions. There was hardly any active resistance or revolt against the coup. When General Shafiullah learned about the coup early in the morning, he ordered Dhaka brigade commander Colonel Shafayat Jamil to counter it, 'but the brigade commander was undone as the loyalty of his brigade was with the Sena Parishad'. When the army

chief asked Brigadier Khaled Mosharraf, he simply replied, 'There was nothing that possibly could be done to reverse the process.'[15]

Salil Tripathi studied this episode in his book, *The Colonel Who Would Not Repent*, and records:

> The men who killed most of Mujib's family were junior officers in the Bangladesh army. Several of them had personal scores to settle with Mujib—some had been sidelined and others had been dismissed from positions in the army. The disaffected officers and the troops loyal to them personified the grievances many army professionals felt over the slights the army faced at the hands of Mujib's supporters, in particular, the wayward fighters of the Rakkhi Bahini. Later, they also claimed they were concerned about growing corruption, and as Farooq would tell me a decade after the assassination, *they were concerned about Mujib aggrandising all power to himself and effectively destroying parliamentary democracy.*[16] (Emphasis supplied.)

The Bangladesh Army also had the 'past legacy for its political role, first inherited from Britishers and then from Pakistan. It had the experience under the military regimes of Ayub and Yahya, such a politicized army [which] fought for the liberation of the country, harboured some ambitions of having some representation in the political affairs of the country after liberation.'[17]

As was often the case in Pakistan, the new incumbent would often be the bête noire of the vanquished. After Mujib's assassination, martial law was imposed and Khondakar Mushtaq Ahmed served as President. A 'pro-Awami League counter-coup . . . led by Brigadier Khaled Musharraf' was 'squashed',[18] while the former Awami League leadership, including Prime Minister

Tajuddin Ahmad, were murdered in prison. Other attempted coups by the 'Revolutionary Army' and the radical factions of the army were ineffective, including one by the air force chief. Charulata Singh quotes scholar Lawrence Lifschultz as describing these as 'soldiers uprising(s) that had not been seen in the subcontinent since 1857, when the colonial army of Indians rebelled against the British. Thus the ideological orientation of military officers in Bangladesh army has been responsible for various military Juntas.'[19]

Colonel Abu Taher led the Biplobi Gana Bahani (Revolutionary People's Army) with the intent of having a class-free army and society. His 'twelve demands' looked at a radical overhaul of the military as being a blueprint for larger societal change.[20] These demands included the confiscation of the properties of corrupt public servants, ending discrimination between the officers and sepoys, and making recruitments more equitable and less lopsided towards those belonging to the privileged sections. Intriguingly, Ziaur Rahman—who was now the de facto centre of power—agreed to these demands, knowing fully well their sensitivity and imminent resistance from within the forces. He not only reneged on the commitment but, in November 1975, had Taher charged for treason with several other military and political leaders. Colonel Taher was tried in camera and sentenced to death. This episode demonstrated the class loyalties that pervaded Bangladesh's power structures—that a fellow army officer could be put to death by the general showed class trumped institution by a long shot.

Ziaur Rahman would ultimately call on the professional corps of the army to orchestrate a coup, that saw former Chief Justice Abu Sadat Muhammed Sayem become President and CMLA, and Rahman himself his deputy.

Though Ziaur Rahman's policies closely resembled his Pakistani namesake Zia ul Huq's in their 'Jacobin crushing of political parties and civilian politicians, and their suppression of dissent and protest',[21] he also had the onerous task of dealing with recalcitrant factions in the army, who had grown accustomed to indiscipline and political adventurism. To his credit, he established local self-governments at the village level and sought to introduce a modicum of democratic tradition and development of judicial independence that was hitherto absent in the young country. He rescinded Mujib's one-party system, retaining the powers vested in the President. Growing in stature and power, he held a referendum in May 1977 on the basis of a self-serving nineteen-point policy programme and claiming 99.5 per cent support. This was followed by a presidential election in June 1978, where he emerged successful, defeating another officer, General Abdul Shani Osmany of the Awami League. After the elections which now saw a general as an elected leader of a democracy, President-General Ziaur Rahman moved an amendment to the constitution to insulate all martial law actions from the scope of judicial review. To quote Milam:

> Such amendments are common in martial law regimes to indemnify military rulers from retrospective legal action by subsequent civilian governments, primarily for their (usually unconstitutional, and possibly treasonous) seizure of the government. In this respect, Ziaur Rahman, Muhammed Ershad, Zia ul Huq, and Pervez Musharraf have acted exactly alike.[22]

Ziaur Rahman further consolidated his power, undertook economic reforms and oversaw the creation of the Bangladesh Nationalist Party (BNP)—as an alternative to the Awami League and essentially anti-India in doctrine and nationalist at heart. Despite Pakistan having 'promulgated genocide in Bangladesh', General Zia shared an anti-India phobia with Pakistan. The very formation of the BNP, comprising an admixture of 'religious zealots (and) pro-Chinese Maoists', was with the common 'defining impulse (of) a 'loathing of the Awami League and that party's chief patron, India'.[23] The history of Pakistan till such time itself had shown 'that religion makes poor binding without resin of a common hatred',[24] which India and Partition provided in ample measure. Zia would replace 'secularism' in the constitution with 'absolute trust and faith in Almighty Allah' and institutionally encourage madrasa education and a national religious identity.

His popularity grew as did his hold over the military, which welcomed a more Islamic identity in nouveau politics. The creation of the BNP was also to 'establish legitimacy for his government', though he remained 'a military man intent on using military methods to control the destiny of a nation'[25]. His second in command, interestingly, was a civilian—former justice Abdus Sattar.

Notwithstanding his ability to manoeuvre the political systems and processes to his advantage, Rahman, like any leader in Bangladesh or Pakistan, was always vulnerable vis-à-vis the army. The sharp divide between the 'repatriates' and the 'freedom fighters' was to cost him dearly, despite his nationalistic endeavours. After facing nineteen 'abortive coups' between 1977 and 1981—including the bloody Dhaka mutiny of 1977 which had the rebels killing serving air force officers, only to be suppressed by the army—Ziaur Rahman was assassinated in Chittagong on 30 May 1981 by a freedom fighter (Lieutenant Colonel Motiur Rahman) from the very same army.[26] Once again, the army had the last word in these fledgling democracies. One of the three senior army officers—Major General Muhammed Manzur, who was earlier passed over for appointment as COAS—was the mastermind behind the assassination of the President. He and his cohort would be either killed by the loyalist army or hanged after trial.[27]

On the aftermath of the Dhaka mutiny, Milam says that 'If the dangers of a politicized military had not previously been fully visible to Zia, they certainly were after the (Dhaka) mutiny' and he now 'strengthened his determination to isolate the military from politics and after a few months of minimal political activity to quiet fears and stabilize the country (and the military) proceeded quickly with his strategy to 'civilianize' the government more fully'. To this end, he dropped his description as 'General', opting for 'President,' and '(a)ll the other officers in the cabinet were required either to resign from the military or from the cabinet.' The thirteen civilian politicians that were appointed to the cabinet 'were mainly associated with his (Zia's) new political party or with its allies from parties that made up the national front, called JAGODAL, which would support Zia's candidacy for President.[28]

The return to a presidential form of government was an antithesis to any pretence of broad-based, party-driven democracy. Military rule lasted until February 1979 though, by all accounts, Ziaur Rahman brought in political stability and social reform, and was 'steadily more disinclined to perpetuate the army in power and was to lead Bangladesh back to a democratic political structure in which civilian politicians would dominate'.[29] Paradoxically, this disenchanted the radical factions of the army that would take his life for 'betraying the army and threatening the nationalist cause by his civilianization of the government'.[30] The military would now discover the absence of its connection to national policy and feel politically isolated.

Sattar, who was now acting president, called for fresh elections and maintained political status quo. But he was no general and did not enjoy the rapport or confidence of the army. Major General Ershad—a repatriate from Pakistan—had earlier replaced Ziaur Rahman as COAS and was waiting in the wings. The elections of November 1981 saw Sattar defeat lawyer Kamal Hossain of the BNP in an overwhelming victory. The electoral victory lulled Sattar into believing that the army could be kept out of the political apparatus and all senior posts in the government filled with civilian leaders. General Ershad called for an 'institutionalized role for the military in policy making',[31] only to be initially rebuffed. Once the army upped the ante, Sattar established the National Security Council (NSC) comprising a troika of the President, vice president and the prime minister on the one side and the three service chiefs on the other. As the army was still not satisfied, Sattar would remove senior ministers as a token of appeasement. But in an affront to the military, he would also repatriate military officers serving within the lower echelons of government to their official posts.

The pendulum of political power would once again shift towards the military, with a direct coup removing Sattar and his cabinet, declaring martial law and having General Ershad assume power as CMLA. Ershad would go on to become the President in 1984, echoing what several generals had earlier said, in their weak defence, on the assumption of political power that 'the military had been forced to take over because it was the only organized national institution which could be relied on to defend the national interest, and that it would rule until new elections could be held'.[32] With the constitution suspended, democracy in Bangladesh was again on the mat. This military phase would last in varying degrees for close to a decade.[33]

Ershad would wrest control over the tiers of administration gradually and privatize several large government jute, textile and other industrial mills. He would call for local body elections and 'use the newly elected councillors to secure the government's victory for the parliamentary elections',[34] where his party, the Janadal, would come to power. Mujib's daughter, Hasina Wajid, and (ironically) Ziaur Rahman's widow, Khaleda Zia, would be the main opposition to the JAGODAL and demand the restoration of a rights based, civilian democracy. However, the military was now entrenched in the political system and controlled the bureaucracy substantially. The factionalism within the Opposition enabled Ershad to have greater political domination. He appointed several serving and retired army officers to various civilian and administrative posts, sidelining the civil services who rightfully belonged there. The trust deficit was mutual, but Ershad maintained a moral superiority to justify his decisions. The army also betrayed a strong ideological and religious leaning, with Islam being the guiding force for political identity and reform. As Charulata Singh observes, 'Military governments need ideology to legitimize their rule and ensure their stability'[35] and religious fundamentalism often became the metric to judge the functioning of the civilian governments. Invariably, the latter were found short of the army's expectations.

Bangladesh's economic condition remained precarious and there was little a general in power could do to redeem that. Though he plodded along in power till 1990, the student-driven protests headed by the All-Party Students' Union, galvanized the political parties to come together in rejuvenated opposition to Ershad. It was during this time that the Berlin Wall had fallen and people's resistance was seen as a magic pill that worked. The military high command saw the writing on the wall and spurned any calls to rescue Ershad from this fait accompli. Ershad had no choice but to resign. The Chief Justice of the Supreme Court, Shahabudin Ahmed, replaced him as the Acting President.

Commenting on the Rahman–Ershad era in Bangladesh, Ayesha Jalal notes that: '(T)he shift towards a military–bureaucratic state under (them) suggests that its external aid dependent political economy has done more to promote the interests of senior defence and civil officials than the development requirements of its teeming millions.' She adds, 'Much in the same vein as Pakistan, enterprising military and civil officials could use their privileged positions within the state structure to acquire permits, licenses and aid-related government contracts, thus expediting their entry into the upper echelons of the economy.'[36]

Both leaders fell short of strengthening democratic institutions and condoned corruption. Rahman was prone to favouring political Islam over constitutionalism, and Bengali nationalism gave way to Bangladeshi nationalism—the latter discounting the Hindu Bengali population entirely. He was cognizant of the 'unleashing of anarchic political and military power . . . (and the) perilous danger which the politicization of the military'[37] posed to him and to the country.

As noted earlier, although Rahman took on the army by removing the extreme revolutionary elements from the service that would lead to his elimination, he antagonized the senior cadres of the force by trying to integrate the outliers in the political system, including those who aspired for a hardcore Islamist state. Governing a country that has a predominant military seemed to require kid gloves, which Rahman lacked. He did introduce a multiparty political system, which shows his commitment to the spirit of democracy at one level. But being a general himself, he was always an 'imposter' in the civilian space, and perforce acted authoritarian regardless of his intentions for Bangladesh.

On Islamism, Jalal observes that it has '(A) weaker foothold and a less influential role in Bangladesh . . . In scenarios reminiscent of Pakistan, the Islamist parties in Bangladesh were saved politically by military governments.' She finds that: 'Both Ziaur Rahman and Ershad reached out to Islamic forces to help secure their legitimacy, and thus Islamist parties had regained their former strength by 1991 when the post-Ershad electoral democracy began.' Nonetheless, electorally, she concludes, they have remained parties with small electoral bases, 'able mainly to influence events and policy by joining coalitions with the major parties on specific issues or helping them to form governments after elections.'[38]

Attempts to 'civilianize the military and . . . the alienation between a pro-Pakistan army and pro-India ruling party'[39] exacerbated the role of the army in the political sphere, as did the presence of 'freedom fighters' in its fold who were more politically oriented than a typical professional soldier. This political consciousness drove the army to have a greater role in the polity and indeed in the constitutional framework of the country. This was despite the fractured nature of the army itself, which explains the frequency of the attempted coups and their frequent failures. The factions included the 'rightists, who believed, in Bangladesh ideology; Mujibists, who believed in the principles of nationalism, secularism, socialism and democracy; leftists, who believed in the class-less and socialistic ideology.'[40] Additionally, the liberation army had fought alongside guerrilla groups and was infused with a peculiar blend of soldiering and nationalist revolution. These traits made for a volatile cocktail, especially in the absence of a strong civilian leadership in the early years. Ironically, the systems of democracy to be followed in Bangladesh over the decades after Ziaur Rahman, were originally set in place by him—a general who had assumed power after the ouster of a civilian leader by a military coup.

Ershad, on the other hand, lacked even the basic legitimacy that Rahman might have enjoyed, having ousted a popular elected leader (Sattar). His cliched justification of the army being a national saviour of sorts was straight out of the Pakistan script and did not cut much ice. No elections could be held till 1986 and democracy was paralysed under a military dictatorship.[41] While several reforms that he introduced were either unwelcome or unimpressive, his tinkering with the judiciary saw a strike by lawyers, reminiscent of the Lawyers' Movement in Pakistan in 2009 against General Pervez Musharraf. Lawyers remained a bastion of resistance even during miliary rule. The resistance spread to students and labour groups when he sought to move towards Sharia rule. These protests would turn violent in 1983 when he announced presidential elections, which were then called off with assurances of reverting to a parliamentary system. The absence of Supreme Court rulings on the nature of the Bangladesh constitution being essentially parliamentary or presidential permitted such manoeuvres by a general in power. It was only in May 1986 that parliamentary elections finally took place and a democratic government was in place. Ershad would only end martial law basis the age-old practice of seeking prior indemnification of all (unconstitutional) actions during the military regime—which he was able to wrestle out via an amendment to the constitution. It was only after this immunity that the government could officially function. Though farcical, this seemed the only way for democracy to raise its head in such circumstances.

Ershad would now step down as COAS only to run for President! He won. The army had a president and an 'affiliated' bureaucracy that enabled a quasi-military rule. Parliament was unable to pull its weight—perhaps due to an absence of tradition and the absence of institutional checks. Emboldened, Ershad moved an amendment to the Local Government Act to provide for army officers to participate in district committees, albeit as non-voting members. Sheikh Hasina and Begum Zia and their political supporters were now up in arms over this brazen attempt at integrating the army into mainstream polity. Protests grew in strength and by November 1987, Dhaka was practically in curfew—the episode of civil disobedience coming to be known as the 'Siege of Dhaka'.[42] Ershad declared a state of emergency, in which fundamental rights were suspended, hundreds jailed and, in early December, Parliament dissolved. Democracy remained closeted. A fresh parliamentary election was called in March 1988, which Ershad's Jatiya Party won. The popular vote seemed to suggest that civilian governance was still a non-starter in Bangladesh. By the constitutional amendment of 1989, the President was given two further terms of five years in office—a brazen usurpation of constitutional process and power by a self-serving parliament.[43] At this point, Bangladesh stood ahead of Pakistan in terms of sheer absence of constitutional democratic governance.

President Shahabuddin, who replaced Ershad, steered the transition.[44] Fresh elections were called in 1991 and the BNP won 140 seats and the Awami League eighty-five. Ershad's party was not entirely vanquished, but it was now no longer in power. Khaleda Zia became the new prime minister and 'showed circumspection towards the embedded complexities of governing Bangladesh by selecting a relatively experienced team consisting of former ministers and retired military and civil officials'.[45] The paradox remained as to whether the military was better off *within* civilian governments or without. The experience in both Pakistan and Bangladesh demonstrates that once the military has its foot in the door, there is no driving it back permanently.

The standout feature of this transition was that a judge could spearhead the return to democracy and that non-elected institutional interventions could sometimes lead to positive results. The question before the new government was whether to continue as a parliamentary system or revert to a presidential one. This ought not to be relevant for a mature parliamentary democracy, but phases of military intervention and see-sawing between the two forms kept the pot boiling. (Though it was the civilian leader Mujib who let the country shift to a presidential form in the first place.) The BNP and Awami League agreed to go with a parliamentary system, perhaps more out of political prudence rather than philosophy. The necessary constitutional amendment was carried out and Bangladesh could now claim to be on the road to pure democracy.

It introduced a unique concept of a caretaker government to oversee elections so as to keep all parties out of the zone of influence.[46] Just as Pakistan saw different parties in power in its 'decade of democracy', Bangladesh would fare just the same. Justice Shahabuddin returned to his seat on the Supreme Court and the two parties in power worked together for a while to keep the wheels of governance turning. However, the political chaos that was now inbuilt in Bangladesh did not permit this happy status quo to continue for long. The parties fell out over BNP's policies, more specifically, the rescission of local government schemes that Ershad had introduced and some anti-terror laws that were introduced rather arbitrarily to be used against university protestors. The response was greater protests by the Awami League and the students at the university. With colleges largely remaining closed, bad blood against the BNP had begun to churn in Bangladeshi society.[47] The street protests gave way to a united opposition boycott of Parliament. Ironically, the demand was for a (non-elected) caretaker government to replace the BNP when its purpose was to merely oversee elections, and not govern the country.

Ultimately, in late 1994, the opposition MPs together resigned from Parliament and the political deadlock continued. By-elections were to be called but the Opposition refused to contest the same. The BNP was then left with the curious option of taking 'walkovers' in all these seats, which would be far from respectable. Not willing to lose face, Prime Minister Khaleda Zia called upon the President to dissolve the National Assembly, and general elections were called in early 1996. It was apparent that rather than moving along with citizen friendly policies (at a time when floods had ravaged the country), the polity was caught up in a game of chess. The Opposition refused to participate in these elections, there was no caretaker government in place (when there should have been) and the elections were now a true no-contest. The BNP won practically every seat it stood for and was back in power.

The groundswell was however against the BNP and it seemed to lack the moral authority to govern. It therefore (recursively almost!) called for a fresh general election under a caretaker government, to be held in June 1996. This scenario could have been obviated in the first place but powermongering appeared to come in the way. The elections saw the Awami League pip the BNP to the post, and come into power in an alliance with Ershad's Jatiya Party. It was now BNP's turn to trigger street protests against the new government! This constrained the Awami League from making major policy changes. The lack of democratic traditions and political grace reduced these years of democracy in Bangladesh to mere topdressing. The government's significant breakthrough in bringing about an agreement with the Buddhist tribes of the Chittagong Hill Tracts brought about an end to the long-standing insurgency in those parts. However, the BNP made this a sectarian issue and played the Buddhist versus Bengali card. This led to more street protests. While the 'proper place to question the form of the agreement, of course, would have been in Parliament, the BNP chose to raise the issue primarily in the streets.'[48] Such was the working of civilian democracy in the country.

Street protests often culminated in violence, either inter se the rival groups or by the police forces seeking to suppress them. The two parties found rare common ground as BNP returned to Parliament, ending its boycott. This did not end the public demonstrations that had now come to be part of mainstream Bangladeshi politics. The Awami League survived this turmoil for its term as fresh elections were due in October 2001. The musical chairs this time found BNP with its alliance return to power, as was expected. Significantly, through these years of political upheaval and serious law-and-order breakdown, the army had remained restrained. However, as was wont in the early years of Pakistan, the BNP *itself* invited the army to quell the continuing political violence on the streets.[49] The army was successfully (and brutally) able to restore 'normalcy', but this was typically seen as a failure of the civilian government and gave the army a renewed stature in the polity.

This stature was enhanced when, after the army's retreat, hartals and violence returned to the streets of Bangladesh. The streets wore a greater shade of lawlessness now, with robberies and even murders becoming rampant. Parliament was dysfunctional and the state police apparatus seemed unable to stem the popular unrest. These would be perfect settings for the army to return to power. It however was willing to remain backstage, as the government scraped through till the next election in 2006. All this while, the country seemed marred by a lack of a coherent socio-economic policy, the lack of a strong political leadership and the sheer lack of statesmanship among the leaders of both the BNP and the Awami League. Sheikh Hasina had emerged as a trenchant voice of the latter, challenging most of the important decisions of the government.

On the eve of the elections, the BNP, finding itself immanently out of power, chose to appoint loyalist officers to the Election Commission. There were protests galore in the wake of such gamesmanship. Sensing that the Awami League would have needed the support of Ershad's party, the BNP raked up an old criminal case against him, leading to his disqualification from the election. At this point, the Opposition decided to boycott the elections and predictably agitate on the streets. The violence was severe and neither party would yield ground. In this scenario, the army was inevitably to return to the scene, though on its own this time. The army would hesitate to support the BNP, as it remained 'under warning from the UN that its peacekeeping duties might suffer if it used repression to support such an obviously illegitimate election'.[50] Conscious of its professional duties on an international arena, and equally unable to resist its role in the internal affairs of the country, the army returned to centre stage after a hiatus of sixteen years. At its instance, the President declared Emergency, and appointed a new head of the caretaker government. The army would 'assist' this caretaker government in its functions. It enjoyed legitimacy in contrast with the rather disastrous regimes of both the BNP and the Awami League. General Moeen Ahmed, as the COAS, was vocal on matters of governance and drove the arrest of Khaleda Zia and Sheikh Hasina for corruption.

Though the caretaker government was in control, the army was certainly a tour de force. It had its stamp on the institutional and social change the country would pursue in terms of electoral, judicial and religious reform. Bangladesh's experiment with democracy had well and truly failed. The army had resurfaced as the saviour and had before it now the option (or opportunity) to define how much or how little power it would wield in real terms.

The caretaker government announced that elections would be held in 2008. In the interregnum, with the tacit support of the army, it attempted to carry out some telling decisions (more so for an interim government) by way of taking on corruption, jailing Sheikh Hasina and Khaleda Zia, having a revitalized Election Commission fumigate the voters' list of duplications and flaws, and creating a Truth and Accountability Commission reminiscent of the experiment in South Africa. Ironically, a non-elected caretaker government working with the military was able to demonstrate greater commitment to institutional change and democratic tradition than the elected governments in Bangladesh. It however was unable to 'exile' the two leaders as it desired. The elections, held in December 2008, saw a record voter turnout with the Awami League alliance thumping the BNP and assuming power. The elections are regarded as perhaps the most transparent and violence-free held in the history of Bangladesh until then.

The proximity to Islamist ideology backfired on Bangladesh over the years with India viewing it as a 'safe haven for terrorists and a conduit for arms under the government' of the BNP.[51]

However, the Awami League addressed the issue once it came into power in 2009, bringing to trial several militant groups and individuals who were hitherto almost untouchable.

Citizens could have been forgiven for believing democracy in Bangladesh had now come of age. The paramilitary (this time) had other ideas. The Bangladesh Rifles (BDR) revolted, with fifty-seven officers being killed in the retaliation. These officers were in fact military officers on secondment and the political discontent that the army nurtured manifested itself in the BDR this time. The government made bold to take on the military, dismissing several army officers from service, conducting trials for the mutiny—with the courts meting out the death penalty in over 150 cases, and restructuring the BDR as the Border Guard of Bangladesh.[52] These developments drew international attention from human rights groups and also set the government on a collision course with the military. Moreover, the Supreme Court of Bangladesh, by two judgments in 2010 and 2011, entirely reversed the constitutional immunity granted to the military regimes of 1975–79 as also the Ershad regime. The trial and execution of Colonel Taher in the mid-1970s was branded a 'murder'[53] by the CMLA General Ziaur Rahman, and in many ways the constitutional and political history of Bangladesh was being unscrambled. The court also ordered the revamp of the caretaker government apparatus, which the Awami League took to its logical end by completely doing away with it in law and practice. This was naturally opposed by the BNP as it could well mean a return to partisan government-controlled elections in the future.

In early 2013, public demonstrations by disgruntled youth—known popularly as the Shahbagh Movement because it took place at the Shahbagh square near Dhaka University—began to gain traction. These protests were a reaction to the verdict of the International Crime Tribunal (ICT) constituted to try the human rights violations of 1971. Though the leaders of the Bangladesh Jamaat-e-Islami (BJI) were indicted, the student/ youth groups demanded harsher sentences for the guilty, and even death.[54] Many of the protesters were active bloggers, and one of them was brutally murdered in the name of blasphemy. The country was now polarized along religious lines, with the BJI portraying the protests as being anti-Islam. The BNP, sensing a political foothold, began to ally with the BJI, and soon a new Islamist body—the Hezafat-e-Islam (HI)—came to take centre stage. It made tall demands of the government to practically transform the character of the country to one that was centrally Islamic, and soon peaceful protests by its members assumed violent overtones. In the suppression of these protests, several lives were lost and, as Riaz comments, five sets of 'interrelated but autonomous' events played out in parallel:

> The ICT continued to deliver verdicts; BNP and its allies including the BJI stepped up violent street agitations in support of the demand for the caretaker government; the BJI continued to unleash a reign of terror after each of the verdicts against its leaders were issued; the Shahbagh movement, although beginning to lose its appeal, pressed on for death penalties for all war criminals and proscription of the BJI; and the ruling party and its allies began preparing for an election even if the opposition should boycott it.[55]

The elections were scheduled for January 2014. With the main opposition boycotting it, the Awami League was the beneficiary of the walkover, and General Ershad's party assumed the role of the Opposition. On the anniversary of the election, the BNP called for nationwide demonstrations, which rapidly spiralled into violent strikes and blockades. The backlash from the police resulted in scores of casualties and serious rights violations.[56] This phase coincided with a renewed attack on bloggers, regarded as being blasphemous and anti-Islamist. The government too seemed to condone these brutal attacks and betrayed a tacit support of the increasing fundamentalism in Bangladesh at the time. The promise of democracy seemed only partly fulfilled in this milieu of violence and persecution.

An unusual political calm pervaded for a span of two years or so, while the country bore the brunt of the Rohingya Refugee crisis. For a country with a weak democratic report card, it did exceptionally well in receiving over 70,000 such refugees from neighbouring Myanmar.[57] The army all this while kept hands-off the politics of the day. The 'peace' was broken when the BNP resumed its age-old demand of having a caretaker government for the forthcoming elections in 2018. This seems to be the default option for the Opposition in Bangladesh and drives home the notion that elections held dehors the caretaker apparatus have inevitably been questionable. Meanwhile, Khaleda Zia was imprisoned for five years on charges of corruption, and the expected protests on the street erupted once more.

The political churn saw the emergence of a new party—the Jatiya Oikya Prokriya, who allied with the BNP and sought to enforce the return to a better democracy. In the elections held in December 2018, the Awami League beat anti-incumbency to return to power with a thumping majority with Sheikh Hasina proving her unparalleled popularity. Even the threat of a possible military showdown at the border with the Myanmar army did not unsettle her or the party. The Awami League has remained in power since, bereft of any military interference. One could compare this extended period of civilian governance to Pakistan and be tempted to conclude that democracy has prevailed over the decades. But as is always the case in both countries, the military can never fully be counted out of the equation.

The absence of a military coup in the latter half of Bangladesh's history has also been attributed to the fact that the 'new recruits of Bangladesh armed forces have no experience of the liberation war and they consider politics as a 'dirty game', making them averse to political action'.[58] In the early decades, a greater emphasis on law-and-order management and an inchoate political culture of dialogue and judicial process led to the army consolidating its position. In many ways, the civilian leadership created political vacuums for the army to occupy.

Saral Patra observes that 'weak democratic process(es) in Bangladesh have resulted in increased participation of armed forces in the decision-making process of the state. (While) the war of liberation heightened the political consciousness of people . . . many of the armed bands of the liberation were taken into the Bangladesh army. Such a politicized army could not remain in barracks under the deteriorating socio-economic conditions of the country and (being) constantly influenced by the socio-economic processes that affect the people in general. (W)henever the democratic forces failed, the armed forces came in to play the effective political role.'[59]

In analysing the experience of the army in politics in Pakistan and Bangladesh, Ayesha Jalal observes:

> The (recent) history of Pakistan and Bangladesh demonstrates just how difficult it is to reverse the phenomenon of military authoritarianism. Elections have been held in both countries (of late), but the *ritual of voting cannot be confused with the achievement of substantive democracy*. Political processes in Pakistan and Bangladesh remain hostage to highly inequitable state structures. Continuing imbalances within the state structures and also between them and civil society foreclose the possibility of a

> significant reapportioning of political power and economic resources in the very near future.[60]
>
> So it is the entrenched interests of the non-elected institutions, the military in particular, within the state structure and the opportunities this affords for legal and extra-legal privileges which justifies labelling Pakistan and Bangladesh as the *political economies of defence*. A political economy of defence by its very nature encumbers the state's development activities, especially when economic resources are scarce and the appetites of the non-elected institutions are insatiable. The very dominance of the non-elected institutions in Pakistan and Bangladesh points to a disjunction between state power and class power.[61] (Emphasis supplied.)

Milam compares the two countries that were one in their close resemblance politically, where 'on the surface (they seemed) to take an almost identical path between 1972 and 1990 (and the) one factor common to both was poor leadership and poor judgment by their charismatic but badly flawed leaders, Mujib and Bhutto.' In both, 'These failed democracies were replaced by military governments that slowly, under pressure, assumed a civilian façade, (though) such hybrid arrangements were inherently unsustainable, and were replaced by elected civilian governments.' In those years, he comments 'observers could be forgiven for concluding that one was a pale imitation of the other.'[62]

The formation of Bangladesh had an independent but marked effect on Pakistan, as Anam Zakaria records in *1971: A People's History from Bangladesh, Pakistan and India*:

> The 1971 war had a significant impact on the psyche of India and Pakistan, and subsequent policies in the region. Since Pakistan continues to view the war *as an Indo–Pak war*, it sees itself losing to India and not to Bangladesh. Even when the

> Pakistanis admit to their failure in keeping the country together, more often than not they reinforce that 'had India not interfered, we would have remained one'. This defeat to India impinged on its collective memory for decades to come. Until that point, Pakistan was confident of its military prowess, but the war indicated that its enemy had achieved military superiority. This gave further impetus to the Pakistan army to strengthen itself... The only way to avoid another East Pakistan-like situation was to increase the defence budget. *Military superiority—not democracy, justice, strong civilian institutions and egalitarian polices, which were the key demands of the Bengalis—was going to save Pakistan.*[63] (Emphasis supplied.)

Alongside Kashmir, Bangladesh now became the justification for the military in Pakistan to rake up the India bogey and reinforce public opinion that the army was needed to 'save' Pakistan in the years to come. Ironically, a military defeat built into a narrative that gave the army renewed *locus standi* in non-military matters in the decades that followed.

Bangladesh represents a unique precedent where a country that was once a part of a larger Pakistan, accustomed to military coups, was itself born out of a military loss for Pakistan. Much of the discourse around the creation of Bangladesh rose from the discomfort that West Pakistan had with the limitations that East Pakistan wanted to introduce to the charter of social and political dominance by the bigger western limb. While one expected this genesis to have liberated Bangladesh from the ills of military law and military rule, paradoxically the experience that it has had has proved the contrary. Martial law has existed in Bangladesh over significant spans of time and the army has worked closely with the government in matters of civilian administration even in times of civilian governance. This has eaten into its vitals in many ways and takes one back to the basic premise that the absence of early democratic traditions and culture, coupled with an army that is prone to operating in unwelcome civilian spaces, often hinders the growth of democracy.

Henry Kissinger had infamously referred to Bangladesh in 1972 as an 'international basket case'. Notwithstanding the consistent military interference in its polity, Dasgupta observes, '(h)istory has proved him wrong. The former East Pakistan had lagged behind West Pakistan in economic development. But five decades later, Bangladesh has a *higher* per capita GDP (PPP) than Pakistan. It is also ahead of Pakistan in terms of important social indicators, such as life expectancy at birth, years of schooling, and the Gender Gap Index. Yesterday's 'basket case' holds out promise of emerging as an Asian success story.'[64] Jalal notices that,

> . . . (p)rimarily through rapid social development, Bangladesh has escaped the 'basket case' label it was unflatteringly bestowed soon after it separated from United Pakistan . . . (It) has moved far ahead of Pakistan in the rate of improvement of most human development indicators . . . Social development continues to lag in Pakistan, yet there is no generally agreed explanation for this important difference. Observers look for an answer mainly in the cultural differences between the two countries, but such partial explanations have not proven satisfactory. In Bangladesh, the simple hypothesis is that greater poverty led to widespread demand for social services, and *a permissive attitude toward the NGOs* allowed them to meet that demand. Once established, NGOs became part of Bangladesh's socio-economic fabric.[65]

The interesting lesson on hand is that despite the militarization of politics and inchoate democratic traditions, the countervailing force of civil society movements and NGO activism can offset the lopsided developmental growth in young democracies.

Bangladesh appears to have fared better than Pakistan in this regard and serves as a subtle reminder to India.

Milam cautions, for good measure, that the country's future is yet 'up for grabs' and the attempts by 'unelected military/civilian government to remake Bangladesh's political culture' could threaten 'traditional Bengali tolerance and diversity' as well as challenge the people's 'attachment to constitutionalism and democracy'. He suggests 'the alarming possibility' that such unelected governments 'could enjoy wielding power too much and stay too long', which could return the country to 'political and economic stagnation and human rights abuses' that characterize a government 'dominated by a corrupted military.'[66]

Will Bangladesh dispel such an unwelcome climax? Only time will tell.

Conclusion

> *'Before Independence the British had kept politics out of the Indian Army. Discussion of politics was taboo in officers' messes and the jawans and junior commissioned officers were carefully insulated from political influence.'*
>
> —Major K.C. Praval, *Indian Army after Independence*

The study of 'praetorianism' in India and Pakistan throws up some interesting contrasts. The Indian soldier was seen as belonging to an army reared by the British, lacking in 'social cohesion' and enjoying a 'detached relationship . . . [with] Indian society at large.'[1] This not only distanced the institution from society generally but gave the early Indian soldier a sense of being 'a second-class citizen'.[2] This would hold true for the counterparts in the Pakistan Army as well, as both were cut from the same cloth. However, the army in Pakistan was able to earn a socio-political legitimacy of sorts, by being seen as an efficient, mainstream and patriotic institution at a time when other institutions were half-cooked. This key distinction led to a radically different status and identity for the two armies, and thereby impacted their democratic future.

At the inception, the establishment in both countries appears to have also feared the army's intentions. Brigadier Z.A. Khan analyses the prevailing mindset in the Pakistan Army in the 1950s:

> . . . [W]hen we started our service, the terms of service of armed forces officers were radically changed. Compulsory retirement without assigning a reason was introduced and the right to ask for a trial, if an allegation affected the character of an officer, was withdrawn. These measures were presumably taken to discourage officers from trying to overthrow civilian governments but they did not prevent the three successful coups [as of 1990] that have taken place and *only resulted in shifting loyalty from the country to the superior officers.*[3] (Emphasis supplied.)

He refers, of course, to a distrust *within* the army's chain of command itself. But it reveals the acute awareness of the possibility of civilian governments being overthrown by the army, and this trust deficit would no doubt extend to the civilian leadership as well (which had itself given the army a foothold in internal law-and-order situations).

The Indian situation was piquant too. Lieutenant General Vas notes:

> Lawyers dominated the political scene in 1947. They were well informed about the social, economic, cultural problems facing India. They were not familiar with politico–military issues. Nehru, unlike his father, took little interest in military matters. He hoped to create a world of nations who instead of forming rival groups would learn to settle their disputes peacefully. He had great faith in the United Nations. Over-laying his idealism was a deep hatred for war and all things military. *Nehru's disinterest affected the thought and prejudices of four decades of politicians, intellectuals and civil servants who, taking their cue from him, failed to acquire an adequate understanding of the legitimate role of the military force in democratic governance.*[4] (Emphasis supplied.)

However, civil–military relations in both countries developed in dramatically different directions. The army in India remained passive in political matters, while its Pakistani counterpart held (and continues to hold) main stage in the political arena. Cohen, in his seminal work *The Pakistan Army,* finds that '[I]t is futile to debate whether the military has been pulled into politics [because of the incompetence of civilian leaders] or has pushed its way in [to ensure that civilians do not pursue policies anathematic to military interests].' 'Due weight must be given,' he comments, 'to the historical and doctrinal ethos of the Pakistan Army itself' which not only believes 'it defends society from external enemies, but a number of officers will argue that the military has an important role in ensuring that Pakistan society itself modernizes and yet remains pure and truly Islamic [and] *Pakistan society must remain worthy of the military.*' [5] In the end,

> A friendly critic would point out that . . . [though] the military has intervened on several occasions when it was dissatisfied with the power or performance of the bureaucracy or the political parties: *it will not permit the latter to become effective national institutions.*[6] (Emphasis supplied.)

Army coups in Pakistan have ostensibly taken place because of 'general dissatisfaction with corrupt and inefficient governments', though military rule has lingered for too long and 'made the return of democracy extremely difficult'.[7] The absence of strong, secular civilian institutions is the antithesis of a robust democracy. Hassan Abbas is candid in stating that 'the people of Pakistan still yearn for true democracy', which can only be obtained if Pakistan's military establishment takes a back seat, equally the Pakistan Army 'dare not confront' the extremist right-wingers in Pakistan who have many sympathizers within Pakistan, and indeed, within its army.[8] Allen McGrath notices that when democracy was first usurped in 1954, the blame paradoxically was placed on the *people* of Pakistan. He comments, 'When those who destroyed Pakistan's democracy wrote their histories, they placed a large part of the blame for the destruction on the victims. Supposedly it was the people, because they were not 'ready' for democracy, who were charged with being the underlying cause of the failure.'[9]

Husain Haqqani is insightful in observing that 'Pakistan's preoccupation with security may have its roots in the fact that the military was the only fully functional institution inherited by the country at the time of the country's founding.' While politicians and civil servants had to 'start from scratch', the army was well established in terms of infrastructure and standing at the British Indian Army Northern Command Headquarters in Rawalpindi, which gave it a head start in the inchoate circumstances of 1947.[10] This made the army, as Lieven notes, 'resilient and effective' in comparison with other British-inherited institutions and gave it a far greater role in Pakistan than the security apparatus in India.[11]

Pakistan's history could be seen as one of conflict between 'an underdeveloped political system and a well-organized army', with the army being disinclined to bringing about political stability as that would well undermine its position and 'charisma'.[12] The charisma of the army was often built on its well-oiled media outreach, coupled with the social media handles of its admirers. This was evident with the #ThankYouRaheelSharif campaign in 2015 which elevated the general's popularity far beyond his namesake prime minister. Some of this also has to do with the fact that the military in Pakistan sees itself as 'a breed apart' and belonging to a 'family different from (and vastly superior to) Pakistani civil society' as also 'morally superior to (the) feudal political class'[13]—a perspective that the citizenry has bought into from time to time.

The *New York Times* ironically called General Asif Nawaz the 'Champion of Democracy'[14] for his restrained approach as COAS. Perhaps no political leader in Pakistan had deserved or indeed earned such a title. Ayesha Siddiqa acknowledges that unless 'democratic forces bridge their internal divisions' and discard their own 'authoritarian principles', the military would continue to remain at the helm.[15] This is accentuated by the economic interests that the military enjoys. John Kenneth Galbraith in his work *How to Control the Military* argues that the military was never meant to be an 'unlimited partner' in the arms industry and stripping it of that economic interest would enable the military establishment to revert to 'its traditional position in the [American] political system.'[16]

Contrary to the scenario in Pakistan, in India it was civilian intervention that marginally blurred the political neutrality of the forces, as the relationship of Krishna Menon with General Kaul has shown. The forces have themselves refrained from any 'political activism'. The reasons, though varied, mark the key difference between the two nations and underscore the complex relationship between the army and democracy.

Referring to the Menon–Kaul nexus, Praval comments:

> The British may have sequestered the Army in imperial interest but the practice they established is usual in democratic countries. General Cariappa and his successors adhered to this policy, and the Indian Army remained apolitical, though in most other countries newly freed from colonial rule, the Army had taken to politics and even taken over the reins of government in some cases. It would have been in the interests of the country if the Indian Army had been kept free from politics and left to follow the established procedures and traditions *without interference from the politicians*. This was particularly undesirable as the latter

> had no experience of soldiering or war. Unfortunately, this interference began with Menon and surfaced into public view in 1959 after Kaul's promotion to Lieutenant General. The event created a furore in the Press and in Parliament.[17] (Emphasis supplied.)

The adverse effect of Menon's intervention in military promotions and strategies, and the disregard of bipartisan advice from the military leadership, resulted in the humiliation of 1962 at the hands of the Chinese. But the absence of any military manoeuvre in response to these events laid the canvas for improved relations between the institutions and space for democracy to grow, with all its stumbles, in a relatively young India. It cannot but be said that the military leadership itself, during the war with China, had disclosed chinks in its armour (without intending the pun).

Jairam Ramesh notes:

> A coup had taken place . . . in October 1958 in neighbouring Pakistan, and there was loose talk in the cocktail party circuit of whether India's turn would be next. A naturally paranoid defence minister would have found all this sinister, even though the *Times of India* of 4 January 1959 carried this report: 'No Possibility of Military "Coup" in India'. Ruling out the possibility of a military 'coup' in India, Mr. V.K. Krishna Menon, Defence Minister, said here today that 'whosoever attempted such a thing would come to grief . . .' Mr. Menon said: 'We have a strong parliamentary system of Government. Our soldiers are well educated and disciplined. They do not meddle in politics.' 'In fact,' Mr. Menon added, 'it is silly to think in terms of a military dictatorship.' 'The people,' he said, 'were conscious of their democratic rights

> and the prevailing social conditions widely varied from what led to military regime in other countries.'[18]

In another interview with the *Times of India* in 1968, in the context of the Chinese invasion, Menon admitted that there was 'pressure upon me from all sides . . . not to increase the Army efficiency and strength but to cut it down'.[19] The vexed issue of 'structuring' civil–military relations was paramount in the initial years of India's independence, but 'had become so warped' that someone of General Thimayya's stature 'could be reduced to a virtual non-entity' and 'success and survival in the military hierarchy depended on falling in line with the 'Chosen One' or at best by keeping one's mouth shut and sailing with the wind, as was the case with General Pran Thapar and Lieutenant General Bogey Sen.'[20]

The 'broad principles' for such civil–military structuring in a democracy have been expressed to include 'civil' control over military where the word 'civil' means *political* (and only political) and not bureaucratic; space to be left to the generals to 'plan and maneuver'; and responsibility and accountability of 'every cog in the defence structure'.[21]

Air Marshal Nehra goes on to state that: '[A]ll the above principles were violated with impunity in evolving the defence structure of independent India, in view of the lukewarm interest [and lack of capability] of the politicians, bureaucrats . . . set about designing a structure in which Generals were pushed on to the periphery from which they could neither participate in any meaningful way in the decision-making process nor protest over being excluded.'[22] This is an atypical perspective to the interface between the army and the civilian establishment, underlining the treatment of the forces by the bureaucracy (as opposed to the political leadership) in decision-making.

The treatment of soldiers by itself is a sensitive issue in India. The disparity in pay has been discussed in the foregoing parts. As Brigadier Gurmeet Kanwal notes, 'the slow and laborious handling of this issue has led to a dangerous 'them versus us' civil–military divide'.[23] Former CNS Admiral Nanda concludes:

> Undoubtedly, the Indian military has the best officer corps in the world and they always provide the highest quality of leadership to their dedicated men. What pains me is that the man in uniform is soon forgotten once a war is over. There are innumerable cases of soldiers, sailors and airmen, or their families running from pillar to post for their dues. They often come up against red tape, inherited from the days of the British Empire . . . But institutional help lines need to be strengthened so that the pride of the uniform is maintained by our retired colleagues throughout their life.[24]

Samuel Huntington's comment cited earlier rings true, in that military intervention in politics thrives in the absence of effective political institutions in society.[25] The backdrop to the 1971 elections provides a clear comparison. The dominance of the Congress alliance was confirmed by the rousing mandate it received in the 1971 elections. Democracy in India was able to gain greater legitimacy and utilize its developing processes to distance itself from the 'institutional infirmities' forthcoming.[26] These processes were scantily in existence in neighbouring Pakistan. Instead, the army was deciding what was best in the national interest.

Subordination to civilian power is at the centre of the ethos of the Indian Army, which senior generals warn ought not to 'degenerate into servility or sycophancy'.[27] Equally, senior political leaders caution against 'using the Army in settling the internal affairs of the country', thereby 'creating a distance between the Army and (the) countrymen' and causing 'long-term dangers' to India's national security.[28] On the contrary, the balance of power in Pakistan is such that the army has assumed a dominant position and has involved itself in matters of internal and external policy.

This comparison directly reflects on the 'success of the democratic system in India' which 'notwithstanding its shortcomings, is no less a triumph for our (India's) Armed Forces for having remained true to their time-honoured apolitical traditions.'[29] General Vas goes on to state:

> The military ensured internal stability and kept scrupulously aloof, even in *tailor-made coup situations* such as were prevailing during the Emergency. While the serving rank and file of the armed forces are constitutionally prohibited from active politics, an ex-serviceman can legitimately play a role in the political arena. Sixty thousand service personnel retire annually; at any one time there are about seven million ex-servicemen in the country and they constitute a trained, disciplined, hardworking and loyal segment of society.

He labours the point that ex-servicemen have generally kept away from the mainstream of political, economic and cultural life, and the Indian Ex-Services League has resolved not to participate in any political activity as an organization. Though this 'self-imposed ban may have been valid during its formative years' his parting shot is, 'but there are many who would like a new ex-servicemen's political organization to emerge.[30]

General Sinha credits the army for 'giving sustenance to our (India's) democratic polity' being 'the only apolitical Army of the Third World' and with a 'better apolitical record than that of some developed democracies'.[31] Per contra, Pakistan's subversion of democracy by its military and civil society alike, and its inclination towards theocracy, could lead it to 'sink into medievalism'.[32] Its recent history has belied such an alarmist inference.

The emphasis in comparative politics on institutions is trite. 'Hard' institutions such as the bureaucracy are pivotal in the development of the political system of the concerned nation state. However, in a democratic set-up, power must necessarily vest in a legitimate, elected, civilian leadership. Other institutions such as the army can only be unobtrusive facilitators for the growth of democratic space. India seems to have achieved this balance, partly by design and partly by circumstance. Pakistan, however, has constantly had the balance of power shift towards the military, with short intervals of civilian rule, again 'drawn mainly from the top echelons of the bureaucracy and the army'.[33] More so, the civilian leaders have in themselves proved autocratic and undemocratic, especially in the absence of democratic traditions and institutions, as the regimes of Bhutto and Nawaz Sharif showed.

In comparison with India, military regimes in Pakistan, it has been seen, have 'rewarded senior officers in the defence establishment with top positions in the state structure as well as in semi-government and autonomous organizations . . . (and) has at each step awarded its principal constituents with land grants, defence contracts, permits, licenses and ambassadorial appointments. This has allowed for much greater upward mobility for military officials than in India.'[34] Jalal notes further that while 'there can be no doubt that some civil and military officials in India were duly rewarded for their role in helping preserve the symbiosis with ruling parties, for instance by securing jobs in public sector enterprises or key diplomatic appointments' yet 'they have been far less successful than their

Pakistani and Bangladeshi counterparts in using government jobs as ladders to private fortune.[35]

It is also seen that civilian control of military institutions and the isolation of the military from politics results in the development of not only an apolitical military, but the marked growth of civilian institutions over time. The converse is also apparent, in that, a dominant and ambitious army hinders the growth of democratic systems. In studying the regime in Britain, Deborah Avant finds that 'domestic political institutions foster agreement', which can hinder 'military professional autonomy'.[36] There is therefore the thin line to be walked between civilian control and civilian suffocation of the armed forces. Scholars have seen this as the conflict between military obedience on the one hand and political wisdom, military competence, legality and morality on the other—all of which lead to 'conservative realism' in placing society and order above the individual at most times.[37] In Pakistan's case, the military was able to let go of this conservativism and 'resolve' these conflicts for itself with mostly repugnant outcomes.

Shuja Nawaz sums up the situation with his assessment:

> Pakistan remains a fragile and dysfunctional polity, still not recovered from the lingering effects of extended military rule under Gen. Pervez Musharraf and the detritus of previous military regimes that have left civilian administrations and the political system stunted, *unable to exercise the control that the constitution devolves upon them*. The military, and especially the all-powerful army, pays *ritualistic obeisance to the concept of civilian supremacy*, as evident in numerous statements from its headquarters over the years, but actual decision making on defence matters tends still to be largely in the hands of the men in uniform rather than a truly

civilianized MoD or the national government.[38] (Emphasis supplied.)

Professor Steven Wilkinson attributes the divergence in the civil–military relations in India and Pakistan to a combination of the superior strategic, socio-economic and military inheritance that India enjoyed at Independence, the 'greater political institutionalization' of the Congress Party and the 'coup-proofing and balancing measures' that the State undertook to curb the military.[39]

Subhas Chandra Bose held the view that 'a democratic system could not solve the problems of free India' which needed a 'State of authoritarian character' that would serve the masses, and not 'a clique' or 'a few rich individuals.'[40] This view underestimates the scope for constitutionalism, and resonates more with the trajectory that Pakistan has taken through much of its history. Hugh Byas refers to the Japanese army as a political entity comprising 'a corps of officers . . . who have made military service their profession'. That army, he continues, is a 'hierarchy on a democratic base'.[41] Where the army stands in that hierarchy and how it conducts itself determine the sustainability of the base on which it rests.

Acknowledgements

I am indebted to,

Dr Muzaffar Assadi, my PhD guide, for enabling me to submit a thesis of some worth, which ultimately became the basis for this book;

Karthik Venkatesh, my editor, who has ideated with me, refined those ideas and painstakingly reviewed them in print;

Pranati Madhav, for introducing me to Karthik (at Koshy's, where else!);

Manali Das from Penguin, for her keen attention to the manuscript;

Admiral Arun Prakash (Retd), for his pointed suggestions on the manuscript;

Aakriti Khurana, for the cover design;

Rashmi Devi, for conversations that led me to eventually publish this work, and for her thoughtful responses to the text;

Gautam, Maeen and Meghana, for their help with typing and research from time to time;

Lokessh Ahuja, my friend, for the author photograph on the jacket;

Ravina, my sister, for her love and good energy; and

Deepak Rao, my man Friday, for everything he does.

Thank you, all.

Notes

Introduction

1 Mark Pennington, *Theory, Institutions and Comparative Politics,* cited in Judith Bara and Mark Pennington (Eds.), (SAGE Publications, New Delhi, 2009), p.13.

2 Ibid., p. 14.

3 Harry H. Eckstein, *A Perspective on Comparative Politics, Past and Present (Comparative Politics: A Reader)*, Harry Eckstein and David E. Apter (Eds.) (The Free Press, New York, 1963), p. 3.

4 Ibid., pp. 6–7. Machiavelli's *The Prince* makes comparative references to the varying success of the mercenary armies of France, Rome, Sparta and the Swiss (Chapter XII, *The Prince,* cited in Eckstein, Ibid).

5 Pennington, op. cit.

6 Zoya Hasan (Ed.), *Democracy in Muslim Societies: The Asian Experience* (SAGE Publications, New Delhi, 2007), p. 13. The basic characteristics of democracy have been generally held to include open elections to office with rights of participation to the citizens, equal value for each vote, freedom of choice, and access to information and rule of law; See: Alan T. Wood, *Asian Democracy in World History* (Routledge, London and New York, 2004), p. 2.

7 Ayesha Siddiqa, *Military Inc.: Inside Pakistan's Military Economy* (Pluto Press, London, 2007), p. 32.

8 Alan T. Wood, op. cit., p. 16.

9 Dr Charulata Singh, *The Role of Military in Politics: A Case Study of Bangladesh* (Neha Publishers, New Delhi, 2008), p. 13.

10 Asha Gupta (Ed.), *Military Rule and Democratization: Changing Perspectives* (Deep & Deep Publications, New Delhi, 2003), p. 2.

11 Emajuddin Ahamed, *Military Rule and the Myth of Democracy* (University Press Ltd, Dhaka, 1988), pp. 1–3.

12 Siddiqa, op. cit., p. 34.

13 Ibid., p. 37.

14 Ibid., p. 58.

15 Pennington, op. cit., pp. 133–37.

16 Ahamed, op. cit., pp. 6–25.

17 Martin Edmonds, *Armed Services and Society* (Leicester University Press, Leicester, UK, 1988), p. 102.

18 Jacques Van Doorn (Ed.), *Armed Forces and Society: Sociological Essays* (Mouton, The Hague, Netherlands, 1968), pp. 28–30.

19 Gupta, op. cit., p. 14.

20 Samuel P. Huntington, *Political Order in Changing Societies* (Yale University Press, USA, 1968), p. 192. The word was adapted from 'praetor'—Roman for 'army commander' or 'general'.

21 Samuel P. Huntington, *The Soldier and the State* (The Belknap Press of Harvard University Press, Cambridge, Massachusetts, 1985; Hereinafter 'Samuel P. Huntington'), p. 95.

22 Stephen Peter Rosen, *Societies and Military Power: India and Its Armies* (Oxford University Press, New Delhi, 1996), p. 7.

23 Paul Brooker, *Non-Democratic Regimes* (Palgrave Macmillan, Hampshire, UK, 2009), pp. 1–12.

24 H.S. Bhatia, *Military History of British India* (Deep & Deep Publications, New Delhi, 2008), p. 15.

25 Pradeep P. Barua, *Gentlemen of the Raj: The Indian Officer Corps, 1817–1949* (Pentagon Press, New Delhi, 2008), pp. 3–9.

26 Apurba Kundu, *Militarism in India: The Army and Civil Society in Consensus* (Viva Books, New Delhi, 1998), pp. 10–15.

27 http://defencedestination.weebly.com/rimc.html.

28 Stephen P. Cohen, *The Indian Army, Its Contribution to the Development of a Nation* (University of California Press, Berkeley, 1984), p. 119. Alumni of the IMA included two future chiefs of the Pakistan Army—Field Marshal Ayub Khan and General Yakub Khan as well as a future President—Major General Iskander Mirza (each of them having passed the interview with distinction), who were not too shy to enter into the realm of politics, as this work will examine later.

29 Kundu, op. cit., pp. 19–20.

30 Philip Mason, *A Matter of Honour: An Account of the Indian Army, Its Officers and Men* (Natraj Publishers, Dehradun, 2004), p. 465. The rest of the credo states: 'The honour, welfare and comfort of the men you command come next. Your own ease, comfort and safety come last, always and every time.'

31 Lt Gen. S.K. Sinha (Retired), Foreword to Major K.C. Praval, *Indian Army after Independence* (Lancer International, New Delhi, 1987), p. vii. General Sinha also markedly comments on the fact that the concept of nationalism was alien to the Indian Army raised by the British, that the Indian Army was always apolitical and that the only military coup in the thousands of years of Indian history related to Army Commander Pushyamitra Sunga's assassination and the

overthrow of Mauryan Emperor Brihadratha in 185 BCE. The regimental realignment in the British–Indian army followed the Mutiny of 1857 when more of the martial races (the Gurkhas, Sikhs, Punjabis, Jats and Rajputs) were introduced into the ranks, although the Bengal, Bombay and Madras armies were retained as 'separate'. These regimental alignments and traditions continue till date in the Indian Army. See also: Percival Spear, *A History of India, Volume II* (Penguin Books India, New Delhi, 1990), pp. 145–46.

32 Praval, op. cit., p. 8.

33 Barua, op. cit., pp. 126–31.

34 Lt Gen. S.L. Menezes, *Fidelity and Honour: The Indian Army from the Seventeenth to the Twenty-First Century* (Oxford University Press, New Delhi, 1999), p. 423.

35 Kundu, op. cit., pp. 76–77.

36 Later known as the Free-India Army or *Azad Hind Fauj*.

37 See Kundu, op. cit., pp. 56–61.

38 Kundu, op. cit., p. 61. Perhaps Nehru was equally swayed by Mountbatten's advice that 'the people who will serve you well in your national army of the future are those who are loyal to their oath; otherwise if you become unpopular, a disloyal army may turn against you.' Cited in Menezes, op. cit., p. 402.

39 Arjun Subramaniam, *India's Wars: A Military History* (HarperCollins Publishers India, Noida, 2016), p. 60. The author refers to Nehru and others reaping 'enormous political mileage' by pushing for charges to be dropped against the undertrials from the INA.

40 Praval, op. cit., pp. 6–7.

41 Barua, op. cit., p. 131.

42 Ayesha Siddiqa, op. cit., p. 59.

43 Shuja Nawaz, *Crossed Swords: Pakistan, Its Army, and the Wars Within* (Oxford University Press, Karachi, 2008), p. 27.

44 Kundu, op. cit., p. 189.
45 See Maya Tudor, *The Promises of Power: The Origins of Democracy in India and Autocracy in Pakistan* (Cambridge University Press, Cambridge, 2013), pp. 51–53.
46 For more, see Barney White-Spunner, *Partition: The Story of Indian Independence and the Creation of Pakistan in 1947* (Simon & Schuster, London, 2017), pp. 284–87.
47 Robert W. Stern, *Democracy and Dictatorship in South Asia: Dominant Classes and Political Outcomes in India, Pakistan and Bangladesh* (Praegar Publishers, Westport, Connecticut, 2004), pp. 9–17.
48 Hamid Khan, *Constitutional and Political History of Pakistan* (Oxford University Press, Karachi, 2009), p. 50.
49 Ishtiaq Ahmed, *The Pakistan Military in Politics* (Amaryllis, New Delhi, 2013), p. 98. This speech of Jinnah had caused consternation among the right-wing Sunni sections—as the very purpose behind the separation was religious (Jinnah was himself Shia) and gave to the left-leaning liberals fodder in their pursuit of a vision for Pakistan that was indeed secular. Jinnah has himself been described as religious, but 'in a non-denominational way', yet someone who opted for Lincoln's Inn for the Bar as an inscription there listed 'Prophet Mohammad as one of the top lawgivers of the world.' Saad S. Khan with Sara S. Khan, *Ruttie Jinnah: The Woman Who Stood Defiant* (Penguin Random House India, Gurgaon, 2020), p. 174.
50 Ahmed, *The Pakistan Military in Politics,* p. 55.
51 Sikandar Hayat, *The Charismatic Leader: Quaid-i-Azam Mohammad Ali Jinnah and the Creation of Pakistan* (Oxford University Press, Karachi, 2008), pp. 337–38.
52 Hasan, op. cit., p. 14.
53 Ranabir Samaddar, *A Biography of the Indian Nation: 1947–1997* (SAGE Publications, New Delhi, 2001), pp. 138–39.

54 Meghnad Desai and Aitzaz Ahsan, *Divided by Democracy* (Roli, New Delhi, 2005), pp. 13–75.

55 Philip Oldenburg, *India, Pakistan, and Democracy: Solving the Puzzle of Divergent Paths* (Routledge, London, 2010), pp. 1–4.

Chapter 1: Kashmir (1947–48)

1 Anuradha M. Chenoy, *Militarism and Women in South Asia* (Kali for Women, New Delhi, 2002), p. 77.

2 Jagmohan, *My Frozen Turbulence in Kashmir* (Allied Publishers, Mumbai, 2007), p. 84.

3 The NWFP interestingly had a Congress government in place, despite having a Muslim majority. It was ceded to Pakistan by way of a referendum, spearheaded by British interests in Partition. See: Raghvendra Singh, *India's Lost Frontier: The Story of the North-West Frontier Province of Pakistan* (Rupa Publications, New Delhi, 2019).

4 Balraj Krishna, *India's Bismarck: Sardar Vallabhbhai Patel* (India Source Books, Mumbai, 2007), p. 154.

5 Srinath Raghavan, *War and Peace in Modern India* (Permanent Black, Ranikhet, 2010), p. 98.

6 Balraj Krishna, op. cit., p. 97.

7 Lieutenant General E.A. Vas, *Without Baggage: A Personal Account of the Jammu and Kashmir Operations 1947–49* (Natraj Publishers, Dehradun, 1987), pp. 3–12.

8 Major General L.S. Lehl (Retired), PVSM, VrC, *A Nation Divided and the 1947 Indo–Pak War*, (*The Indian Army: A Brief History;* Ed: Major General Ian Cardozo (Retired), op. cit., pp. 64–65.

9 Cardozo, op. cit.

10 Praval, op. cit., p. 23.

11 Ibid., p. 35.

12 Ibid.
13 Ibid.
14 Lehl, op. cit., p. 66. The 1948 offensive was etched in history for an extraordinary feat, by Air Commodore 'Baba' Mehar Singh, who landed a Dakota aircraft in virtually impossible conditions in Leh, and also for Major General (later General) K.S. Thimayya's unprecedented manoeuvre in taking Stuart Light Tanks to the heights of Zoji La in Kargil, which had a telling effect on the morale of the Pakistani troops.
15 S.N. Prasad and Dharam Pal, History Division, Ministry of Defence, Government of India, *Operations in Jammu and Kashmir 1947–48* (Natraj Publishers, Dehradun, 1987: 2005 reprint), p. 380.
16 Sisir Gupta, *Kashmir: A Study in India–Pakistan Relations* (Asia Publishing House, Bombay, 1966), p. 126.
17 Lieutenant General S.K. Sinha, cited in Foreword to Praval, op. cit., p. x.
18 Gen Vas, op. cit., pp. 146–47.
19 Balraj Krishna, op. cit., pp. 153–56.
20 Air Marshal R.K. Nehra (Retired), *Hinduism and Its Military Ethos* (Lancer Publishers, New Delhi, 2010), p. 331.
21 Ibid., pp. 328–29.

Chapter 2: The Nehru–Menon–Kaul Axis

1 Neville Maxwell, *India's China War* (Natraj Publishers, Dehradun, 1997), p. 198.
2 Stephen P. Cohen, *India: Emerging Power* (Oxford University Press, New Delhi, 2001; hereinafter 'Stephen P. Cohen'), pp. 127–55.
3 Ibid.

4 Till date, this dilemma continues to dog the Indian defence establishment, with a lopsided dependence on imports from the global market. One of India's two aircraft carriers—*INS Vikrant*—is assembled at Cochin Shipyard, a refreshing indigenous project.
5 Theo Farrell, cited in Risa A. Brooks and Elizabeth A. Stanley, *Creating Military Power: The Source of Military Effectiveness* (Stanford University Press, Stanford, California, 2007), p. 152.
6 Cohen, op. cit.
7 Ramachandra Guha, *India after Gandhi* (Picador India, 2007), pp. 760–61.
8 Air Marshal K.C. Cariappa (Retired), *Field Marshal K.M. Cariappa* (Niyogi Books, New Delhi, 2007), p. 80 and 133.
9 Brigadier C.B. Khanduri, *Field Marshal K.M. Cariappa: His Life and Times* (Lancer Publishers, New Delhi, 1995), pp. 331–35.
10 See Anit Mukherjee, *The Absent Dialogue: Politicians, Bureaucracy and the Military in India* (Oxford University Press, New Delhi, 2020), pp. 44–45, 197.
11 Ibid., pp. 55–57. Also see Praval, op. cit., pp. 161–64.
12 Guha, op. cit., p. 307.
13 Praval, op. cit., pp. 158–59.
14 Air Commodore Jasjit Singh (Retired), AVSM, VrC, VM, *The Icon: Marshal of the Indian Air Force Arjan Singh, DFC* (KW Publishers and Centre for Air Force Studies, New Delhi, 2009), p. 137. There also appears to have been very little information, and whatever little was available was scrappy, about the intentions of the Chinese, their objectives, plans and preparations. No one seems to have been able to assess, or even to recognize significantly, the real state of the military threat that was looming menacingly across India's Eastern border during the 1950s.
15 Praval, op. cit., p. 159.

16 For more on this episode, see Ibid., pp. 160–63.

17 Ibid.

18 Ibid., p. 160 (quoting Kaul from his autobiography).

19 Guha, op. cit. On his part, Lieutenant General Kaul states that Major General Gyani had not commanded a division and hence both Krishna Menon and General Thimayya *jointly* decided to promote Kaul over Gyani. See: Lieutenant General B.M. Kaul, *The Untold Story* (Allied Publishers, Mumbai, 1969) p. 218. General Kaul claims that the reason behind General Thimayya's resignation was his inability to 'get on temperamentally with Menon'. (p. 221) Either way, the civil–military relations were strained like never before in Indian polity.

20 Cited in Jairam Ramesh, *A Chequered Brilliance: The Many Lives of V.K. Krishna Menon* (Penguin Random House India, Gurgaon, 2019), p. 845. The letter was leaked to the foreign press and is traced in Jairam Ramesh's research to the fact that '(f)or over five years, the *Statesman* had a military correspondent who wrote on defence matters from time to time. This correspondent was no journalist really. He was none other than J.N. Chaudhuri, a top army officer whose articles would appear occasionally under the byline 'By Our Military Correspondent'. He would become chief of the Indian Army in November 1962.' pp. 847–48.

21 Guha, op. cit.

22 This episode is discussed in detail in Kundu, op. cit., Brigadier C.B. Khanduri (Retired), *Thimayya—An Amazing Life* (Knowledge World International, New Delhi, 2006) and Humphrey Evans, *Thimayya of India: A Soldier's Life* (Natraj, Dehradun, 1988). Nehru and Thimayya had gotten along fairly well until then, and the latter (a lieutenant general then), was in fact chosen by Nehru to command the United Nations' Neutral Nations Repatriation Commission (NNRC) after the Korea War, 1953–54. Here, Thimayya

and Nehru's confidante and political adviser to the NNRC, P.N. Haksar, often clashed over their leaning towards the UN point of view vis-à-vis China. See: Jairam Ramesh, *Intertwined Lives: P.N. Haksar and Indira Gandhi* (Simon & Schuster India, New Delhi, 2018), pp. 59–60. Nehru, nonetheless, appointed Thimayya as army chief in 1957.

23 Srinath Raghavan, op. cit., p. 268. Taking a contrarian view of the episode, Raghavan sees this as 'military intrusion into the realm of policy'. p. 269.

24 Ibid.

25 Guha, op. cit.

26 Praval, op. cit. p. 158.

27 Ibid., p. 162.

28 See Lieutenant General Raj Kadyan (Retired), PVSM, AVSM, VSM, *The Lies That Win: Army Promotions* (Manas Publications, New Delhi, 2005).

29 Arjun Subramaniam cites B.G. Verghese, op. cit., pp. 221–22.

30 Ibid., p. 252.

31 Air Chief Marshal P.C. Lal, *My Years with the IAF* (Lancer Publishers, New Delhi, 2008), p. 75, 85.

32 Ibid.

33 T.J.S. George, *Krishna Menon* (Taplinger Publishing Co. Inc., New York, 1965), p. 223.

34 Ibid., p. 228.

35 Srinath Raghavan, op. cit., p. 274.

36 Jairam Ramesh, *A Chequered Brilliance: The Many Lives of V.K. Krishna Menon* (Penguin Random House India, Gurgaon, 2019), pp. 812–13.

37 Shiv Kunal Verma, *1962: The War That Wasn't* (Aleph Book Company, New Delhi, 2016), p. 51–52.

38 Ibid.

39 Praval, op. cit., pp. 164–65.

40 Ibid.

41 Major General V.K. Singh, *India's External Intelligence: Secrets of RAW* (Manas Publications, New Delhi, 2007), p. 29.
42 Praval, op. cit.
43 Ibid., p. 166.
44 Kundu, op. cit., p. 112.
45 See: Lieutenant General M.L. Chibber, PVSM, AVSM, *Military Leadership to Prevent Military Coup* (Lancer International, New Delhi, 1986), pp. 107–08 The author also states that Menon was a 'committed democrat' who was keen on preventing any military adventurism by senior officers.
46 Cited in Neville Maxwell, op. cit., p. 197.
47 Ibid.

Chapter 3: War with China

1 Lieutenant General Chibber, op. cit.
2 Praval, op. cit., p. 174.
3 Lorne J. Kavic, *India's Quest for Security,* cited in Praval, Ibid., p. 175.
4 Lehl, op. cit., p. 92.
5 Praval, op. cit., p. 143.
6 Arjun Subramaniam, op. cit., p. 232 The author also refers to dominant leaders such as Roosevelt and Churchill deferring to advice from their military commanders during World War II. p. 436.
7 Praval, op. cit.
8 Ibid., p. 145.
9 See Praval, op. cit., p. 177.
10 Guha, op. cit., p. 312.
11 Lehl, op. cit.
12 Praval, op. cit., p. 175.
13 Ibid. Incidentally, Kaul was on vacation in Kashmir at the time of the first attack by the Chinese.

14 One can only contrast this indifference with the firm refusal of General (later Field Marshal) Sam Manekshaw to Prime Minister Indira Gandhi's proposal to get on the offensive against Pakistan in East Pakistan (Bangladesh) in 1971 until such time as the troops were ready and the monsoons had passed. The Field Marshal simultaneously offered to resign but was supported by Prime Minister Gandhi. For more fuller discussion, see Chapter on War with Pakistan 1971.
15 Neville Maxwell, op. cit., pp. 221–22.
16 Praval, op. cit., p. 189.
17 Ibid., p. 190.
18 Ibid., p. 192.
19 Ibid., p. 204.
20 Major General D.K. Palit, *War in the High Himalaya: The Indian Army in Crisis, 1962* (Lancer International, C. Hurst, London, 1991), pp. 301–02.
21 Praval, op. cit., p. 202.
22 Ibid., p. 221.
23 Shiv Kunal Verma, op. cit., pp. 393–94.
24 Ibid.
25 Foreword to Praval, Ibid., p. xi.
26 Lieutenant General V.K. Singh (Retired), *Winds of War: The 1962 and 1965 Conflicts*, cited in Cardozo, op. cit., p. 108.
27 D.R. Mankekar, *The Guilty Men of 1962* (Penguin Books India, New Delhi, 1998), pp. 151–52. General Kaul, however, states that he willingly reported to depose before General Brooks only to be told that 'his orders were not to examine me (Kaul)'. See Lieutenant General Kaul, op. cit., pp. 466–67.
28 Shiv Kunal Verma, op. cit., p. 425.
29 Ibid.
30 Guha, op. cit., p. 338.
31 Praval, op. cit., p. 141.

32 Sisir Gupta, *Great Power Relations, World Order and the Third World* (Vikas Publishing House, New Delhi, 1981), p. 288.

33 Major General D.K. Palit, op. cit., pp. 112–13. The operation was commanded by Major (later Lieutenant) General C.P. Candeth with 40,000 troops under his command, apart from air and sea support. The Indian government was able call upon its forces to dislodge a foreign power that had ruled Goa for over 450 years, within merely forty hours, showcasing the might of the military and the reliance of the civilian government on the forces in the conduct of sensitive operations of acute political ramifications.

34 Shrikant Y. Ramani, *Operation Vijay: The Ultimate Solution* (Broadway Book Centre, Goa, 2008), pp. 388–96.

35 V.K. Singh, op. cit. Other commanders from the operations have described the 1962 action as 'the defeat of a handful of troops of the Indian Army, comprising four Brigades, which attempted to combat four Chinese Divisions over a frontage of 600 miles of most inhospitable terrain'. See Lieutenant General L.P. 'Bogey' Sen, *Slender Was the Thread*, (Sangam Books—Orient Longman, New Delhi, 1973), p. 297. The general blames the Indian government for creating the wrong impression that a corps of the Indian Army had moved in to North–East Frontier Agency (NEFA) when in fact the government was reluctant to withdraw its troops that were deployed in the Punjab and Jammu and Kashmir.

36 Cited in Srinath Raghavan, op. cit., p. 278.

37 Neville Maxwell, op. cit., p. 440.

38 Major General Sukhwant Singh, *Defence of the Western Border, Vol. II* (Lancer Publishers, New Delhi, 1998), p. 252.

39 A. Balakrishna Nair, *Facets of Indian Defence* (S. Chand & Co., New Delhi, 1983), p. 115.

40 Kundu, op. cit., pp. 146–47. Probal Dasgupta in his book *Watershed 1967: India's Forgotten Victory over China*

(Juggernaut Books, New Delhi, 2020) refers to the singular decision-making of field/army commanders such as Lieutenant General Sagat Singh at Nathu La (and Cho La) and later, in 1986, of Lieutenant General V.N. Sharma (later, COAS) at Tawang that did not brook red tape. In the latter episode, the COAS General Sundarji stood by the advice of his army commander over that of the bureaucrats in New Delhi, leading to a field visit by Prime Minister Rajiv Gandhi that vindicated the position of the army. Such examples fortify civil–military relations, especially in operational matters. The book highlights an important victory in the 1967 Ops that has remained unsung in Indian military history. The balance of power shifted considerably in India's favour post-1967, leading to a broad peace along the Line of Actual Control for over fifty years, until the violent skirmishes at Galwan in 2020.

41 Ibid., p. 153.

42 Probal Dasgupta, *Watershed 1967: India's Forgotten Victory over China* (Juggernaut Books, New Delhi, 2020), p. 122.

Chapter 4: War with Pakistan (1965)

1 Neville Maxwell, op. cit., p. 440.

2 Lieutenant General Harbakhsh Singh, VrC, Padma Bhushan and Padma Vibhushan, *In the Line of Duty: A Soldier Remembers* (Lancer, New Delhi, 2000), p. 323.

3 Neville Maxwell, op. cit.

4 Praval, op. cit., p. 235.

5 Major General D.K. Palit, VrC, *Musings & Memories* (Lancer Publishers, New Delhi, 2004), p. 428.

6 Praval, op. cit.

7 Stephen P. Cohen, op. cit., p. 138.

8 V.K. Singh, op. cit., p. 110.

9 Praval, op. cit., p. 248.

10 V.K. Singh, op. cit.
11 See Praval, op. cit., pp. 250–52.
12 Ibid.
13 V.K. Singh, op. cit., p. 119.
14 Praval, op. cit., p. 302.
15 Ibid.
16 Jung Chang and Jon Halliday, *Mao: The Unknown Story* (Vintage Books, London, 2007), pp. 605–06.
17 Lieutenant General Harbakhsh Singh, VrC, *War Despatches: Indo–Pak Conflict 1965* (Lancer Publishers, New Delhi, 1991), pp. 204–05.
18 One such was the extraordinary success at Dograi and Batapore, where a handful of soldiers of 3 Jat were able to vanquish over 800 Pakistani soldiers in a battle that came down to fighting with fists, sticks and stones, earning the battalion the highest gallantry decorations in the war and their Commanding Officer—Major (later Brigadier) Desmond E. Hayde a Maha Vir Chakra. For more on this battle, see: Brigadier Desmond E. Hayde, MVC, *The Battle of Dograi and Batapore* (Natraj Publishers, Dehradun, 2005).
19 Group Captain Ranbir Singh, *Marshal Arjan Singh, DFC: Life and Times* (Ocean Books, New Delhi, 2002), p. 59.
20 See chapter on Kargil 1999.
21 B.C. Chakravorty's scathing 'official' history of the 1965 War seems to be unavailable, though an excerpt can be found at: https://www.bharat-rakshak.com/archives/Official History/1965War/1965Chapter00.pdf.
22 Major General Lachhman Singh Lehl, op. cit., pp. 385–86.

Chapter 5: War with Pakistan (1971)

1 Ayesha Jalal, op. cit., pp. 72–74.
2 Javeed Alam, *Democracy and the People*, cited in Arvind Sivaramakrishnan (Ed.), *Short on Democracy* (Imprint One, Gurgaon, 2007), pp. 241–43.

3 Major General Sukhwant Singh, *Liberation of Bangladesh, Vol. I* (Lancer Publishers, New Delhi, 1998), p. 17.
4 Lieutenant General Depinder Singh, *Field Marshal Sam Manekshaw: Soldiering with Dignity* (Natraj Publishers, Dehradun, 2002), pp. 128–30.
5 Gary J. Bass, *The Blood Telegram: India's Secret War in East Pakistan* (Random House India, Noida, 2013), p. 93.
6 Ibid. The author also refers to General J.F.R. Jacob's assertion that it was *he* who dissuaded the army chief from taking early action in Bangladesh.
7 Jairam Ramesh, op. cit., p. 241.
8 Frank, op. cit., p. 334.
9 Frank, op. cit., p. 336.
10 Ibid.
11 Cited in Stephen P. Cohen, op. cit.
12 Admiral S.M. Nanda, *The Man Who Bombed Karachi: A Memoir* (HarperCollins Publishers India, New Delhi, 2004), p. 255.
13 Vice Admiral S.H. Sarma (Retired), PVSM, *My Years at Sea* (Lancer Publishers, New Delhi, 2001), p. 202; For the contrarian view on the sinking of *Ghazi,* see: Lieutenant General J.F.R. Jacob, *An Odyssey in War and Peace* (Lotus Roli, New Delhi, 2011), pp. 97–98.
14 Cohen, op. cit.
15 Lieutenant General J.F.R. Jacob, *Surrender at Dacca: Birth of a Nation* (Manohar Publishers, New Delhi, 1997), p. 160. General Jacob also, like Cohen, suggests that there were no express orders for the capture of 'Dacca'—an assertion that is refuted by Lieutenant General I.S. Gill, the Director of Military Operations (DMO) of the 1971 Operations. See: S. Muthiah, *The Life of Lieutenant General Inderjit Singh Gill, PVSM, MC* (Penguin Books India, New Delhi, 2008), p. 203. Either way, the actions of the military were ratified by the PM and were not themselves a cause for friction.

16 Admiral Arun Prakash (Retired), PVSM, AVSM, VrC, VSM, *From the Crow's Nest: A Compendium of Speeches and Writings on Maritime and Other Issues* (Lancer Publishers, New Delhi, 2007), p. 221.

17 Cohen op. cit. Gary J. Bass argues that the nuclear detonation at Pokhran in 1974 was a direct outcome of the presence of the *Enterprise.* See: Gary J. Bass, op. cit., pp. 335–36.

18 Admiral Nanda, op. cit., p. 239.

19 Captain Prem Singh, *Civil Military Operation* (Prashant Publishing House, New Delhi, 2009), p. 6.

20 Arjun Subramaniam, op. cit., p. 427.

21 Air Chief Marshal P.C. Lal, op. cit., pp. 325–26. The author and his counterpart CNS separately refer to a tendency on the part of the army, and particularly the COAS, to underplay the role of the other services. The office of CDS prevalent in Britain rotated among the three Services, with a retired chief of the army, navy and air force acting as CDS under the 'advice' of the defence minister. However, the creation of a CDS in India has now come to be (in 2019), though its efficacy is awaited as one may yet find 'uncompromising loyalty to one's service at the cost of the good of the country'—(cited in) Air Chief Marshal Dilbagh Singh (Retired), PVSM, AVSM, VM, *On the Wings of Destiny* (KW Publishers and Centre for Air Force Studies, New Delhi, 2010), pp. 211–12.

22 Kotera M. Bhimaya, *Civil–Military Relations: A Comparative Study of India and Pakistan* (RAND, Santa Monica, CA, 1997), p. 85.

23 Ibid. The healthy and transparent relationship between the government and the officers is also apparent from the account of DMO Lieutenant General I.S. Gill's 'walkout' from a briefing to the prime minister and senior officers due to their 'ceaseless chatter'. See: S. Muthiah, op. cit., p. 202. This did not in any manner affect the role played by the DMO or strain the relations between the protagonists.

24 The military leadership itself was of a high quality and several generals led from the front in a comprehensive success for the forces. Notwithstanding the 'restricted' official history of the Bangladesh War released by the Ministry of Defence in 1992, the body of work on the operations comprises the individual, and often conflicting, accounts of senior officers. On this aspect, see: P.V. Rajgopal (Ed.), *The British, the Bandits and the Bordermen: From the Diaries and Articles of K.F. Rustamji* (Wisdom Tree, New Delhi, 2009), p. 309 for an account of how the BSF and its legendary chief K.F. Rustamji's role in the defection of Pakistan's deputy high commissioner to Bangladesh was underplayed and 'distorted' by 'a senior Indian Army officer' in the latter's book.

25 Lieutenant General J.F.R. Jacob, op. cit., p. 154.

Chapter 6: Emergency

1 *Kesavananda v. State of Kerala.* Reported in All India Reporter (AIR) 1973 Supreme Court (SC) 1535. After the judgment in *Kesavananda v. State of Kerala,* the right of Parliament to amend the Constitution has been whittled down to cases where the amendment is compatible with the 'Basic Structure' of the Constitution and the notion of 'Basic Structure' has been expanded from time to time by the Supreme Court itself to include democracy, secularism, supremacy of the Constitution, judicial review, inter alia. Lord Meghnad Desai acknowledges that the role of institutions such as the judiciary in the evolution of democracy is vital—Meghnad Desai and Aitzaz Ahsan, op. cit., pp. 37–38.

2 Lloyd I. Rudolph and Susanne Hoeber Rudolph, *Explaining Indian Democracy: A Fifty-Year Perspective, 1956–2006* (Oxford University Press, New Delhi, 2008), p. 184.

3 Granville Austin, *Working a Democratic Constitution: A History of the Indian Experience* (Oxford University Press, New Delhi, 2009), p. 148.

4 N.B. Sen (Ed.), *Wit and Wisdom of Indira Gandhi* (New Book Society of India, New Delhi, 1972), p. 258.

5 Significantly, the decision to impose Emergency itself was not challenged before the Supreme Court, though various related issues such as the right to detain citizens without warrants, etc. did reach the Courts.

6 Kotera Bhimaya, op. cit., p. 84. Military leaders in Pakistan have often used the absence of worthy civilian leadership as their justification for entering the political mainstream.

7 P.N. Dhar, *Indira Gandhi, the 'Emergency' and Indian Democracy* (Oxford University Press, New Delhi, 2000), p. 233.

8 Ibid., p. 225.

9 Shanti Bhushan, *Courting Destiny: A Memoir* (Penguin Books India, New Delhi, 2008), pp. 136–37.

10 Article 352 provides for such declaration in cases where 'the security of India or any part of its territory is threatened, whether by war or external aggression or internal disturbance'.

11 Stephen P. Cohen, op. cit., p. 140.

12 David Selbourne, *An Eye to India: The Unmasking of a Tyranny* (Penguin, Middlesex, London, 1977), pp. 328–30.

13 Selbourne, op. cit., p. 329.

14 Kundu, op. cit., p. 159. This demand of JP's was criticized by former chief justice of India P.B. Gajendragadkar as one that 'would lead to chaos'. See N. Raghunathan, *Memories, Men and Matters* (Bharatiya Vidya Bhavan, Mumbai, 1999), p. 189. He questioned the ability of the army, police and other such organizations to judge the legality of such an order passed by a government in power.

15 Katherine Frank, *Indira: The Life of Indira Nehru Gandhi* (HarperCollins Publishers India, New Delhi, 2001), p. 376.
16 B. Raman, *The Kaoboys of R&AW: Down Memory Lane* (Lancer Publishers, New Delhi, 2007) p. 49.
17 Ibid.
18 Justice Khanna had boldly dissented from the majority view of four judges in his judgment that the fundamental right to life could not be suspended by the imposition of Emergency (see *ADM Jabalpur v. Shivkant Shukla* reported in AIR 1976 SC 1207. This dissent would cost him his chief justiceship.).
19 Shanti Bhushan, op. cit., pp. 144–45; also H.R. Khanna, *Neither Roses nor Thorns* (Eastern Book Company, Lucknow, 2003), pp. 83–88.
20 M.C. Chagla, *Roses in December* (Bharatiya Vidya Bhavan, Mumbai, 1994), p. 484. By later judgments such as the *Supreme Court Advocates on Record Association v. Union of India*, reported in (1993) 4 SCC 441, the Supreme Court has 'reclaimed' the power to appoint judges unto itself and whittled down the powers of the government in such matters. By the creation of a Collegium system, though, often, the last word remains with the government.
21 Frank, op. cit., p. 387.
22 T.J.S. George, *Lessons in Journalism: The Story of Pothan Joseph* (Viva Books, New Delhi, 2007), p. 174.
23 Entry 2A was added to List 1 in 1976, providing for the deployment of the armed forces in any state in aid of civil power, though enactments deploying the forces in certain states were already in place. For more, see the chapter on AFSPA.
24 Selbourne, op. cit. Bansi Lal's own conduct as defence minister came under scrutiny before the Justice Jaganmohan Reddy Commission. See: P. Jaganmohan Reddy, *The Judiciary I Served* (Orient Longman, Hyderabad, 1999), p. 281.
25 Ibid.
26 Kundu, op. cit., p. 161.

27 John Dayal and Ajoy Bose, *For Reasons of State: Delhi under Emergency* (Penguin Random House India, Gurgaon, 2018), p. XXIII.
28 Samuel P. Huntington, op. cit., pp. 77–78.
29 John Dayal, op. cit., p. 163.
30 Selbourne, op. cit., p. 131.
31 Lieutenant General Depinder Singh, op. cit.; Major General Shubhi Sood, *Leadership: Field Marshal Sam Manekshaw* (SDS Publishers, Noida, 2009).
32 Ibid., p.115.
33 Kundu, op. cit.
34 Lieutenant General Sinha, op. cit., p. 247.
35 Guha, op. cit., p. 507. The post-Emergency polls, of course, belied this 'widespread support'.
36 Ibid.
37 Austin, op. cit., pp. 309–10.
38 S. Nihal Singh, *Ink in My Veins: A Life in Journalism* (Hay House, Delhi, 2011), p. 179.
39 H.Y. Sharada Prasad, *The Book I Won't Be Writing and Other Essays* (Chronicle Books, New Delhi, 2003), pp. 113–14.
40 Kundu, op. cit., p. 167.
41 Kotera Bhimaya, op. cit., p. 117.

Chapter 7: Operation Blue Star

1 Frank, op. cit., p. 454.
2 P.C. Alexander, *Through the Corridors of Power: An Insider's Story* (HarperCollins Publishers India, New Delhi, 2004), pp. 231–83, where the author discusses the history of the Akali agitation in detail.
3 Frank, op. cit., p. 455. Also see, Pupul Jayakar, *Indira Gandhi: A Biography* (Penguin Random House India, Gurgaon, 2017), p. 461, where she refers to Zail Singh's involvement in identifying Bhindranwale as a contender to the Akali Dal.

4 Lieutenant General K.S. Brar (Retired), *Operation Blue Star: The True Story* (UBSPD, New Delhi, 2008), pp. 20–21.
5 For more on this episode, see Ibid., pp. 21–27.
6 Frank, op. cit., pp. 454–56. The author traces how Bhindranwale was chosen to 'divide Sikhs and break up the Akali Dal', but went on to undertake targeted assassinations, while 'Hindus were murdered and cows were decapitated'. He became the 'Frankenstein (Zail) Singh and Sanjay (Gandhi) had created.'.
7 Ibid., p. 455.
8 Ibid., p. 462. His unfortunate pliability, despite being in the highest constitutional office, evident from his statement, 'If my leader [Indira Gandhi] had said I should pick up a broom and be a sweeper, I would have done that'. See: Frank, op. cit., pp. 462–63.
9 Ibid., p. 464.
10 For more on these negotiations, see Chand Joshi, *Bhindranwale: Myth and Reality* (Vikas Publishing House, New Delhi, 1984), pp. 70–75.
11 Brar, op. cit., p. 26.
12 Frank, op. cit., pp. 477–78.
13 Ibid., p. 478. Indira Gandhi's coterie of advisers was Minister for External Affairs (later Prime Minister) P.V. Narasimha Rao, her secretary P.C. Alexander, her son—Rajiv and his cousin Arun Nehru. And clearly not the home minister.
14 Brar, op. cit., pp. 163–64; The author also acknowledges the instances of revolt by some Sikh officers, as discussed later.
15 Kundu, op. cit., p. 177.
16 Guha, op. cit., p. 566.
17 Brar, op. cit., p. 6.
18 Ibid., pp. 64–68.
19 Khushwant Singh, *Truth, Love and a Little Malice* (Ravi Dayal and Penguin Books India, New Delhi, 2002), p. 324.
20 Alexander, op. cit., pp. 295–96.

21 Raman, op. cit., p. 97.
22 Frank, op. cit., p. 464.
23 Brar, op. cit., pp. 52–53. The author refutes versions that he had himself slipped into the temple disguised as a devotee to get a first-hand picture of the circumstances.
24 Jad Adams and Phillip Whitehead, *The Dynasty: The Nehru–Gandhi Story* (TV Books, New York, 1997), p. 272.
25 Frank, op. cit., p. 467.
26 Guha, op. cit., p. 568.
27 Kirpal Dhillon, *Time Present and Time Past* (Penguin Books India, New Delhi, 2013), pp. 230–31. The author also attributes the failure of the operation, possibly, to the 'intellectual arrogance' of General Sundarji.
28 Ibid.
29 Kundu, op. cit., p. 181.
30 Alexander, op. cit., p. 303.
31 Ibid., p. 304.
32 Comprising about 15 per cent in the Indian Army and highly regarded for their valour.
33 Dilip Bobb and Asoka Raina, *The Great Betrayal: Assassination of Indira Gandhi* (Vikas Publishing House, New Delhi, 1985), p. 47.
34 Lieutenant General S.K. Sinha, op. cit., pp. 298–302.
35 General K.V. Krishna Rao, op. cit., pp. 245–46. Some commentators have pointed to General Vaidya's criticism of non-Congress regimes in his capacity as Eastern Army Commander, which endeared him to the political establishment. See: Kotera Bhimaya, op. cit., p. 73.
36 Air Chief Marshal O.P. Mehra (Retired), PVSM, *Memories: Sweet and* Sour (KW Publishers and Centre for Air Power Studies, New Delhi, 2010), pp. 154–59.
37 Frank, op. cit., p. 484.
38 Raman, op. cit., p. 107.
39 Major General V.K. Singh, op. cit., p. 109.

40 See: Manoj Mitta and H.S. Phoolka, *When a Tree Shook Delhi: The 1984 Carnage and Its Aftermath* (Roli Books, New Delhi, 2007), p. 3. The book records the chilling statement made by Prime Minister Rajiv Gandhi, in response to the events: 'When a large tree falls, the ground is bound to shake.' It is further noted that President Zail Singh pleaded helplessness and P.V. Narasimha Rao, senior minister at the time (and later prime minister), displayed indifference in responding to the situation.

41 Ibid., p. 75, 84. For a hard-hitting account of the anti-Sikh riots of 1984, also see: Jyoti Grewal, *Betrayed by the State: The Anti-Sikh Pogrom of 1984* (Penguin Books India, New Delhi, 2007). The author refers to a joint publication of People's Union for Democratic Rights (PUDR) and People's Union for Civil Liberties (PUCL) titled 'Who are the Guilty? Report of a Joint Inquiry into the Causes and Impact of the Riots in Delhi from October 31, 1984 to November 10, 1984' which expressly lists the names of political leaders, police personnel and private perpetrators (p. 179).

42 Brar, op. cit., p. 164, 170.

43 Kotera Bhimaya, op. cit., p. 90.

44 See chapter titled 'The AFSPA Experiment'.

45 Bobb, op. cit., pp. 47–48.

Chapter 8: IPKF in Sri Lanka and Admiral Bhagwat's Dismissal

1 Gautam Das and M.K. Gupta-Ray, *Sri Lanka Misadventure: India's Military Peace-Keeping Campaign 1987–1990* (Military Affairs Series, Har Anand Publications, New Delhi, 2008), p. 27.

2 Ibid., pp. 21–23. The Indian government was alleged to have been covertly training Tamil militants and even considered

sending Indian troops to *resist* the operations of the Sri Lankan army.

3 V.K. Murthi and Gautam Sharma, *Rajiv Gandhi: Challenges and Choices* (Radiant Publishers, New Delhi, 1986), p. 133.

4 A.G. Noorani, *Shocking Disclosures* (*Frontline*, Vol. 24, No. 18, 8–21 September 2007), review of Major General Harkirat Singh's (Retired) *Intervention in Sri Lanka: The IPKF Experience Retold* (Manohar, Delhi, 2007).

5 Lieutenant General S.C. Sardeshpande, UYSM, AVSM, *Assignment Jaffna* (Lancer Publishers, New Delhi, 1992), pp. 196–97.

6 Lieutenant General Depinder Singh, op. cit., p. 160.

7 Ibid.

8 Major General Ashok Krishna, AVSM, *India's Armed Forces: Fifty Years of War and Peace* (Lancer Publishers, New Delhi, 1998), pp. 127–28.

9 Gautam Das, op. cit., p. 303.

10 Rohan Gunaratna, *Indian Intervention in Sri Lanka* (South Asian Network on Conflict Resolution, Colombo, 1993), p. 237.

11 Lieutenant General Satish Nambiar, PVSM, AVSM, VrC, *For the Honour of India: A History of Indian Peacekeeping* (Centre for Armed Forces Historical Research/Army HQ, New Delhi, 2009), p. 413.

12 Lieutenant General Sardeshpande, op. cit., p. vii.

13 Anit Mukherjee, op. cit., pp. 202–04.

14 Ibid. The author refers to the prevailing state of affairs, prior to Admiral Bhagwat's tenure, as unprecedented 'subservience of the military to civilian authority', with particular reference to Defence Minister Mulayam Singh Yadav's regime in the United Front coalition government.

15 Admiral Vishnu Bhagwat, *Betrayal of the Defence Forces: The Inside Truth* (Manas Publications, New Delhi, 2001),

pp. 209–10. The book has substantial material on conceptual relations between the military and civilian establishments and discloses the author's intellectual bent and discomfort towards the bureaucracy.

16 Ibid.

17 B.G. Deshmukh, *A Cabinet Secretary Looks Back* (HarperCollins Publishers India, New Delhi, 2004), p. 166.

18 See Wilson John, *An Admiral Falls: The True Account of Vishnu Bhagwat's Dismissal* (Har Anand Publications, New Delhi, 1999).

19 Earlier, Admiral Bhagwat had filed a writ petition in the Bombay High Court when he was denied promotion as fleet commander, wherein he is alleged to have made 'all sorts of allegations against all senior naval officers' (Deshmukh, op. cit., p. 273). The petition was ultimately withdrawn when the ACR of the Admiral was revised.

Chapter 9: Kargil (1999), Operation Parakram and Mumbai 26/11

1 See chapter on Kashmir 1948.

2 See chapter on 1965 War.

3 Lieutenant General V.K. Singh (Retired), *Times of Trial,* cited in Cardozo, op. cit., p. 188.

4 See Rajendra Nath (ed.), *Kargil: Musharraf's War* (Lancer Books, New Delhi, 2003).

5 Myra MacDonald, *Heights of Madness: One Woman's Journey in Pursuit of a Secret War* (Rupa & Co., New Delhi, 2007), p. 46.

6 Lieutenant General V.R. Raghavan (Retired), *Siachen: Conflict Without End* (Penguin Books India, New Delhi, 2002), p. 36.

7 Ibid., pp. 79–81.

8 Foreword to Lieutenant General Raghavan, Ibid., p. ix. Incidentally, the USA and India had earlier 'collaborated' on a secret intelligence mission involving the IB and CIA and expert mountaineers to plant a 'nuclear-powered sensing device' in the Himalayas (specifically, the twin peaks of Nanda Devi) to peek 'behind the Bamboo Curtain' and get an idea of China's nuclear capability. See M.S. Kohli and Kenneth Conboy, *Spies in the Himalayas: Secret Missions and Perilous Climbs* (HarperCollins Publishers India, New Delhi, 2002).

9 Praveen Swami, *The Kargil War* (LeftWord, New Delhi, 2000), pp. 27–28.

10 Major General Ashok Kalyan Verma, *Kargil: Blood on the Snow (Tactical Victory Strategic Failure)* (Manohar Publishers, New Delhi, 2002), p. 105. The General, in his book, also credits the Indian generalship with a robust response to the crisis.

11 Colonel (later Brigadier) Gurmeet Kanwal, *Kargil '99: Blood, Guts and Firepower* (Lancer Publishers, New Delhi, 2000), pp. 72–73.

12 Lieutenant General Y.M. Bammi (Retired), *Kargil 1999: The Impregnable Conquered* (Natraj Publishers, Dehradun, 2002), pp. 331–37. The intrepid performance saw the army amass as many as 293 gallantry awards, including four Param Vir Chakras, ten Maha Vir Chakras and seventy Vir Chakras—India's highest gallantry awards in wartime. This was clearly not treated as a peacetime operation.

13 Report available at https://eparlib.nic.in/bitstream/123456789/63945/1/15_Defence_2.pdf It recommended the creating of a federal intelligence agency for better coordination.

14 General V.P. Malik, *Kargil: From Surprise to Victory* (HarperCollins Publishers India, New Delhi, 2006), p. 78.

15 Praveen Swami, op. cit., pp. 43–44.

16 Cited in General Malik, Ibid., pp. 415–18. Critics have described the KRC as being akin to the script of a 'Hindi pop film... replete with inconsistencies and contradictions'. See Praveen Swami, op. cit., pp. 106–07.

17 *Brigadier Devinder Singh v. Union of India & others*—judgment dated 17 May 2010 in W.P. © No. 17493/2006 transferred from the Delhi High Court, reported at http://www.aftdelhi.nic.in/benches/principal_bench/judgments/court_1/may/ta2722010brigdevindersingh17052010.pdf.

18 Paras 15 and 16 of the judgment in Brigadier Devinder Singh's case, op. cit.

19 Ibid., para 14.

20 *Union of India v. Brigadier Devinder Singh* https://indiankanoon.org/doc/170918532/.

21 Amarinder Singh, *A Ridge Too Far: War in the Kargil Heights 1999* (Motibagh Palace, Patiala, 2001), p. 101.

22 Praveen Swami, op. cit., p. 107.

23 See Lieutenant General (Retired) V.K. Sood and Pravin Sawhney, *Operation Parakram: The War Unfinished* (Sage Publications, New Delhi, 2003).

24 General S. Padmanabhan (Retired), PVSM, AVSM, VSM, *A General Speaks* (Manas Publications, New Delhi, 2010), p. 29.

25 Lieutenant General V.K. Sood (Retired) and Pravin Sawhney, *Operation Parakram: The War Unfinished* (SAGE Publications, New Delhi, 2003), p. 171.

26 Ibid., p. 13.

27 Brigadier Rahul K. Bhonsle (Retired), *Mumbai 26/11: Security Imperatives for the Future* (Vij Books, New Delhi, 2009), p. 2.

28 The Director General of NSG during the 26/11 operations was J.K. Dutta, IPS, while the Director General (Operations) was Brigadier G.S. Sisodia, supported by two colonels from

the army as Force Group commanders respectively—Baweja, op. cit., p. 69.

29 Including Major Sandeep Unnikrishnan, Ashok Chakra, Special Action Group, NSG (earlier 7 Bihar).

30 Brigadier Rahul Bhonsle, op. cit., pp. 180–202. Intelligence agencies in India function under antiquated executive orders and, till date, do not have any constitutional or even statutory status or oversight (except for parliamentary/administrative committees). This gives rise to larger questions of legitimacy of such critical institutions that are at the heart of India's national security, as also the exercise of 'police' powers that are not expressly vested in their officers.

31 Julio Riberio, IPS, cited in Harinder Baweja (Ed.), *26/11: Mumbai Attacked* (Roli Books, New Delhi, 2009), p. 189. Ironically, even the police force has been pressing for independence from political interference in matters of their appointment, transfer, operations and service conditions. The Supreme Court of India in *Prakash Singh's case*—reported in AIR 2006 SC 1117—has issued express directions to all states to take steps to ensure the autonomy of the Indian police. Many states are yet to implement these directions.

32 Baweja, op. cit., p. 9. And whose death cast aspersions on the efficiency of, and coordination among, the top brass of the Mumbai Police in the response to the attack. See: Vinita Kamte (with Vinita Deshmukh), *To the Last Bullet: The Inspiring Story of Braveheart—Ashok Kamte* (Amesha Prashasan, Pune, 2009), pp. 56–61(The author is the widow of the officer.).

33 S.M Mushrif, *Who Killed Karkare?* (Pharos Media and Publishers, New Delhi, 2010), pp. 185–244. While Mushrif's conspiracy theory regarding the assassination of Karkare per se remains uncorroborated, it is clear that there were

serious questions about (a) who led Karkare and his team of Kamte and Salaskar to CST station, owing to glaring blanks in communication and operational command—See Vinita Kamte, op. cit., pp. 37–63; and (b) that compelling intelligence prior to the 26/11 attacks had been suppressed or otherwise disregarded. See Mushrif, op. cit., p. 14.

34 See: https://www.dnaindia.com/india/report-26-11-answer-sm-mushrif-queries-high-court-tells-govt-1475265 The affidavit filed by the commissioner of police refuted the allegations of involvement of any right-wing Hindu outfits. See: https://www.hindustantimes.com/mumbai/court-summons-ex-igp-over-karkare-book/story-aKAYGHzAplF0MshZpuZI7M.html The writ petitions were ultimately disposed of without ordering an investigation into the matter. See: https://www.livelaw.in/bombay-hc-refuses-order-probe-26-11-martyr-hemant-karkares-death/.

35 Ibid., p. 266.

Chapter 10: AFSPA

1 Section 3. Powers to declare areas to be disturbed areas—If, in relation to any state or Union Territory to which this act extends, the Governor of that State or the administrator of that Union Territory or the Central Government, in either case, if of the opinion that the whole or any part of such State of Union territory, as the case may be, is in such a disturbed or dangerous condition that the use of armed forces in aid of the civil power is necessary, the Governor of that State or the Administrator of that Union Territory or the Central Government, as the case may be, may by notification in the Official Gazette, declare the whole or such part of such State or Union territory to be a disturbed area.

2 Which is an order passed under Section 144 of the Code of Criminal Procedure, 1908.

3 As indicated in the preamble to the Act, which provides 'for special powers to be conferred upon members of the armed forces in disturbed areas in the State (sic) of Arunachal Pradesh, Assam, Manipur, Meghalaya, Mizoram, Nagaland and Tripura'.

4 Sumantra Bose, *Kashmir at the Crossroads: Inside A 21st Century Conflict* (Picador India, New Delhi, 2021), pp. 76–77.

5 Ibid., p. 78.

6 Ibid., p. 81, 168. The 2018 Report of the UNHCR also alludes to human rights violations by army officers under the guise of the implementation of AFSPA.

7 B.G. Verghese *First Draft: Witness to the Making of Modern India* (Tranquebar Press, Chennai, 2010), p. 361. The author adds that the inquiry 'team' recommended the monitoring of the misuse of AFSPA and 'criticised the decision to keep out foreign media and international human rights organisations from J&K'. Ibid.

8 See: https://www.livelaw.in/machil-fake-encounter-aft-gives-bail-5-ex-army-men-life-termsays-victims-dressed-like-terrorist-pathan-suit-read-order/.

9 Anuradha Bhasin, *A Dismantled State: The Untold Story of Kashmir after Article 370* (HarperCollins Publishers India, Gurgaon, 2023), pp. 111–12.

10 Arif Ayaz Parrey, 'Kashmir: Three Metaphors for the Present,' cited in Sanjay Kak, *Until My Freedom Has Come: The New Intifada in Kashmir* (Penguin Books India, New Delhi, 2011), p. 233. Kashmir was in the spotlight in August 2019 when Article 370 of the Constitution of India was abrogated by the Union Government, removing the special status given to the state.

11 (1998) 2 SCC 109. The court held that Parliament was competent to enact the law in exercise of its powers under Entries 2, 2A and 97 of the Union List and Article 248, and that the law was not one dealing simpliciter with 'law and order', which is a State subject. Interestingly, the insertion of Entry 2A which provides for the deployment of armed forces in any State in aid of civil power with the attendant powers of such officers, was itself inserted by the 42nd amendment to the Constitution in 1976, several years after AFSPA was enacted.

12 Radha Kumar, *Paradise at War: A Political History of Kashmir* (Aleph Book Company, New Delhi, 2018), p. 248.

13 A.S. Dulat, op. cit., p. 231.

14 Radha Kumar, op. cit., p. 314. This was something the Second Administrative Reforms Committee too had recommended in 2007.

15 Verghese, op. cit., p. 285. Irom Sharmila went on a staggering sixteen-year hunger strike from 2000, seeking the removal of AFSPA in Manipur, which ultimately happened in many parts of the state by 2022. For more, see Anubha Bhonsle, *Mother Where's My Country? Looking for Light in the Darkness of Manipur* (Speaking Tiger, New Delhi, 2016). The state of Manipur slipped into violent ethnic clashes in 2023.

16 Sangeeta Barooah Pisharoty, *Assam: The Accord, The Discord* (Penguin Random House India, Gurgaon, 2019), p. 136.

17 See Pisharoty, op. cit., for instances where the officers are alleged to have torn orders of the court on production.

18 Pisharoty, op. cit., p. 138. For other instances of abuse by the armed forces/police, see Nandita Haksar, *The Many Faces of Kashmiri Nationalism: From the Cold War to the Present Day* (Speaking Tiger Books, New Delhi, 2020).

19 Article 34. Restriction on rights conferred by this Part while martial law is in force in any area: Notwithstanding anything in the foregoing provisions of this Part, Parliament may by law indemnify any person in the service of the Union or of a State or any other person in respect of any act done by him in connection with the maintenance or restoration of order in any area within the territory of India where martial law was in force or validate any sentence passed, punishment inflicted, forfeiture ordered or other act done under martial law in such area.

20 For a general discussion, see Charles Chasie and Sanjoy Hazarika, *The State Strikes Back: India and the Naga Insurgency* (East West Centre, Washington, 2009), pp. 11–13.

21 Anuradha Bhasin, op. cit., pp. 250–51. In 2003, the army vacated several such spaces in a gesture of goodwill.

22 Which are governed by public international law.

23 See fn 9 *supra.*

24 Dulat, op. cit., p. 232.

25 Ibid.

26 *Naga People's Movement of Human Rights* v. *Union of India, supra.* The Supreme Court also directed a six-monthly periodic review of the declaration issued under the Act so that it does not apply ad nauseum.

27 Available at https://www.academia.edu/67570123/National_Security_Laws_in_India_The_Unraveling_of_Constitutional_Constraints.

28 Ibid.

29 *Extra Judicial Execution Victim Families Association vs Union of India* reported in (2016) 14 SCC 578. The report submitted by the Court appointed panel found at least six such instances.

Chapter 11: Martial Law (1953)

1 Stephen P. Cohen, *The Pakistan Army* (hereinafter 'Stephen Cohen'; Oxford University Press, Karachi, 1984), pp. 34–35.
2 Owen Bennett Jones, *Pakistan: Eye of the Storm* (Penguin Books India, New Delhi, 2002), p. 231. The table does not mention the acting heads of state who held office at various points in time.
3 Musharraf was chief executive from October 1999 onwards. He was replaced by a civilian President, Asif Ali Zardari, in 2008.
4 Sikandar Hayat, *The Charasmatic Leader: Quaid-i-Azam Mohammad Ali Jinnah and the Creation of Pakistan* (Oxford University Press, Karachi, 2008), p. 338.
5 Rafiq Zakaria, *The Man Who Divided India: An Insight into Jinnah's Leadership and Its Aftermath* (Popular Prakashan, Mumbai, 2002), pp. 178–81.
6 Hayat, op. cit., p. 345.
7 Shuja Nawaz, op. cit., p. 77.
8 Nawaz, op. cit., p. 78.
9 Ibid., p. 78.
10 Brian Cloughley, *A History of the Pakistan Army: Wars and Insurrections* (Lancer Publishers/OUP, New Delhi, 2002), p. 32.
11 Nawaz, op. cit., p. 83.
12 Ibid., pp. 83–84.
13 Ibid., p. 87.
14 Deepa Agarwal and Tahmina Aziz Ayub, *The Begum: A Portrait of Ra'ana Liaquat Ali Khan, Pakistan's Pioneering First Lady* (Penguin Random House India, Gurgaon, 2019), p. 120.
15 Ayesha Jalal, *Democracy and Authoritarianism in South Asia* (Cambridge University Press, Cambridge, UK, 1995), p. 19.

16 Oldenburg, op. cit., p. 17.
17 Ian Talbot, *Pakistan: A Modern History* (Oxford University Press, New Delhi, 1998) p. 140.
18 The Ahrars, founded as an 'Indian Muslim' group, opposed to imperialism and feudalism, were at loggerheads with the Ahmadiyyas, a more missionary Islamist group that has faced persecution in Pakistan for being 'infidels'.
19 Stephen Cohen, op. cit., pp. 49–50.
20 Cloughley, op. cit., p. 38.
21 *Civil-Military Relations: A Comparative Study of India and Pakistan* (RAND, Santa Monica, CA, 1997), op. cit., p. 91.
22 Nawaz, op. cit., p. 88.
23 Ibid. Per contra, the army in India offers allegiance to the popular government in power without looking to the executive for approval on the legitimacy of the government. The final arbiter in this regard in India, unlike in Pakistan, is the Supreme Court.
24 Jones, op. cit., p. 230.
25 Immigrants from India at Partition.
26 Talbot, op. cit., pp. 106–07.
27 Stephen Cohen, op. cit., p. 50.

Chapter 12: Ayub Khan's Coup

1 Samuel Huntington, *Political Order in Changing Societies*, cited in Nawaz, op. cit., p. 139.
2 Cited in Stephen P. Cohen, *The Idea of Pakistan* (Hereinafter 'Cohen'; Oxford University Press, New Delhi, 2004), p. 58. For a detailed study of the 1954 episode, see Allen McGrath, *The Destruction of Pakistan's Democracy* (Oxford University Press, Karachi 1996).
3 Ibid.

4 Talbot, op. cit., p. 142.
5 Stephen P. Cohen, op. cit., p. 50.
6 *Federation of Pakistan v. Maulvi Tamizuddin Khan* reported in PLD 1955 FC 240—the Federal Court reversed the judgment of the High Court of Sindh, which found the imposition of emergency to be illegal.
7 Talbot, op. cit.
8 Mohammed Ayub Khan, *Friends Not Masters: A Political Autobiography* (University Press Limited, Dhaka, 2008) pp. 186–91.
9 Generally, see Cohen, op. cit., pp. 7–8.
10 One school of thought in force was that elections were postponed since Liaquat Ali's regime as the incumbent office-bearers were uncertain of their own electability or, indeed, of favourable constituencies. See: Ishtiaq Ahmed, op. cit., p. 98.
11 Stephen P. Cohen, op. cit., p. 60.
12 The One Unit Scheme was devised in 1955 to merge the four provinces in West Pakistan—Punjab, Sindhi, Balochistan and NWFP—into a single unit to broadly match the size, economy and unity of East Pakistan. This was in the teeth of the sharp linguistic and ethnic diversity of these provinces. Despite strong resistance, it managed to remain in force till 1970 when it was abrogated by General Yahya Khan and the four provinces reverted to their erstwhile status.
13 Nawaz, op. cit., p. 140.
14 Ibid.
15 Ibid., p. 149.
16 Cloughley, op. cit., p. 48.
17 Ibid., p. 153 Interestingly, these reactions from the US were solicited by President Iskander Mirza himself, as he was building up a case for a military takeover with himself at the helm, using the failure of democracy as the justification for the precipitous action.

18 Cohen, op. cit., pp. 59–61.
19 Nawaz, op. cit., p. 142.
20 Ishtiaq Ahmed, op. cit., pp. 109–10.
21 Cohen, op. cit.
22 Nawaz, op. cit.
23 Ibid., p. 62.
24 Ibid., p. 143.
25 See Ibid., section titled 'Insiders vs. Outsiders' pp. 144–46.
26 Ibid., p. 160.
27 Ibid., p. 161.
28 Cohen, op. cit., p. 64.
29 Ibid.
30 See *State v. Dosso* LEX/SCPK/0042/1958. This judgment was subsequently overruled by the Supreme Court of Pakistan in *Asma Jilani v. Government of Punjab* (1972). https://rb.gy/7zy7h, whereby the second imposition of martial law by General Yahya Khan was invalidated.
31 Cohen, op. cit., p. 65.
32 Ambassador Arshad Sami Khan, SJ, *Three Presidents and an Aide: Life, Power and Politics* (Pentagon Press, New Delhi, 2008) p. 19.

Chapter 13: War with India (1965)

1 Edward Luttwak, *Coup d'etat: A Practical Handbook,* cited in Nawaz, op. cit., p. 139.
2 Nawaz, op. cit., p. 164.
3 Mohammad Ayub Khan, op. cit., p. 58.
4 Ibid.
5 Nawaz, op. cit., p. 193.
6 Ibid., p. 194 onwards.
7 See Cohen, op. cit., pp. 73–75.
8 Cohen, op. cit., p. 73.
9 Nawaz, op. cit., pp. 202–03.

10 Ibid., pp. 206–07.

11 As the corresponding chapter on India demonstrates, See *supra.*

12 The navy chief was conspicuous by his absence, as the blueprint at the time did not take into account a significant role for the navy. It was only in the 1971 War that India actually utilized her full naval prowess in both the Eastern and Western Theatres to great success.

13 Nawaz, op. cit., p. 220.

14 Ayub Khan's son Gohar has, in his book *Glimpses into the Corridors of Power,* sought to insinuate that Field Marshal Sam Manekshaw, had, around the time of the 1965 conflict, 'sold' the operational plans of the Indian Army to Pakistan—See Gohar Ayub Khan, op. cit., p. 88—a charge that remains unsubstantiated and is ridiculed by Indian and Pakistani authors alike. See Nawaz, op. cit., p. 228.

15 Nawaz, op. cit., pp. 235–38.

16 Ibid., pp. 238–41.

17 Cohen, op. cit.

18 Ibid. Major General Akhtar Malik—an army commander—accused Yahya Khan of unilaterally altering operational plans and commanders, resulting in great damage to Pakistan's chances in the conflict. Whether this was sabotage or mere lack of acumen is another matter.

19 Altaf Gauhar, *Ayub Khan: Pakistan's First Military Ruler* (Sang-e-Meel Publications, Lahore, 1998), p. 435.

20 Another factor that may have contributed to the overthrow of Ayub was a growing peasant-worker movement in 1968–69 that promised 'revolutionary socialism'. Many of these mass leaders would join the Pakistan People's Party, which was founded in December 1967 and seek democratic substitutes to authority. For more on this intriguing and lesser-known part of Pakistan's history, see Lal Khan, *Pakistan's Other Story: The 1968-9 Revolution* (Aakar Books, New Delhi, 2009).

21 Nawaz, op. cit. Ironically, Ayub Khan had himself chosen Yahya Khan in preference to other Generals because he believed that Yahya had 'come to hit the bottle hard [and]... had no time for politics' and was considered a loyal and harmless person! Cited in Gauhar, op. cit., pp. 407–08.

Chapter 14: Yahya Khan's Tenure

1 A coup by a State agency, to protect the State from perceived downfall.
2 Cloughley, op. cit., p. 144.
3 Nawaz, op. cit., p. 249.
4 Ibid.
5 For more, see Ibid., pp. 251–52.
6 Ayesha Siddiqa', op. cit.
7 Jones, op. cit., p. 280.
8 These were:
   1. There should be a Federation of Pakistan on the basis of the Lahore Resolution (Passed in 1940, it provided for the status of 'Independent States' for Muslim dominated areas with the right to seek their own constitution and commonwealth with neighbouring provinces;.
   2. Federal government should be limited to Defence and Foreign Affairs;.
   3. There should be two separate currencies for the two wings or measures to stop capital flight from East to West;.
   4. The centre should have no tax-raising powers;.
   5. Foreign exchange earnings of each wing should remain with each wing;.
   6. A militia or paramilitary force for East Pakistan should be set up. Ibid., p. 162.
9 Nawaz, op. cit., p. 260.
10 Ibid., pp. 261–62.

11 Ibid., p. 267.
12 For more on this, see Ibid., p. 267–68.
13 Telegram dated 5 March 1971, cited in Nawaz, Ibid., p. 266.
14 Cloughley, op. cit., pp. 146–47.
15 Dennis Kux, *The United States and Pakistan 1947–2000: Disenchanted Allies* (Woodrow Wilson Centre Press, Washington, 2001), pp. 196–97.

Chapter 15: War with India (1971)

1 Benazir Bhutto, *Reconciliation* (Pocket Books, London, 2008), pp. 176–77.
2 See Frank, op. cit., pp. 330–31 and Nawaz, op. cit., pp. 256–63.
3 Frank, op. cit., p. 330.
4 Ibid., p. 331.
5 Cohen, op. cit.
6 Cited in Golam W. Choudhury, op. cit., p. 31.
7 Ibid.
8 Craig Baxter (Ed.), *Diaries of Field Marshal Mohammad Ayub Khan 1966*–1972 (Oxford University Press, Karachi, 2007), p. 499.
9 Cohen, op. cit., pp. 75–76.
10 Nawaz, op. cit., p. 308.
11 Arshad Sami Khan, op. cit., pp. 213–14.
12 Ibid.
13 Brigadier Z.A. Khan (Retired), *The Way It Was: Inside the Pakistan Army Indo–Pak Wars 1965 and 1971* (Natraj Publishers, Dehradun, 2007) p. 349. For details of the 1971 War, see pp. 320–83.
14 Ibid.
15 Lieutenant General A.A.K. Niazi, *The Betrayal of East Pakistan* (Oxford University Press, Karachi, 2006) p. 276.

For other perspectives on whether the break-up of Pakistan was pre-planned or otherwise, see: Major General Hakeem Arshad Qureshi, *The 1971 Indo–Pak War: A Soldier's Narrative* (Oxford University Press, Karachi 2004), pp. 269–72 and Brigadier A.R. Siddiqi, *East Pakistan: The Endgame* (Oxford University Press, Karachi, 2004), pp. 216–18. Apart from describing the break-up of Pakistan as 'the consequence of a premeditated—insouciant, if you will, political mischief and machination', Brigadier Siddiqi also castigates the civil society of West Pakistan for its 'deep... deliberate silence'.

16 S. Nihal Singh, op. cit., p. 121.

17 Gary J. Bass, op. cit., p. 276.

18 Arshad Sami Khan, op. cit., pp. 187–90.

19 Nawaz, op. cit., p. 320.

20 Ibid., p. 313. The Commission itself has been criticized as being 'disgusting' for its 'preconceived idea that Yahya (Khan) was a drunkard and a womanizer' and with a 'hidden agenda to blame Yahya'. See Arshad Sami Khan, op. cit., pp. 213–14.

21 This desire came to some fruition vide the covert support to the Sikh separatist (Khalistani) movement, the militant Kashmiri separatists and ultimately the overt operation in Kargil (1999).

22 Cloughley, op. cit., p. 238.

Chapter 16: The Bhutto Years

1 Cohen, op. cit., p. 73.

2 Nawaz, op. cit., p. 323.

3 See Cohen, op. cit., pp. 78–79 The report indicted officers for their 'lust for wine and women, and greed for lands and houses.'.

4 One can roughly compare such a development to the establishment of the Border Security Force in India.
5 Nawaz, op. cit., pp. 339–42. Later these assets came under direct army control under General Zia's succeeding regime and have continued thus.
6 Cohen, op. cit. It was, in fact, rare and refreshing to see an army chief in Pakistan resisting the temptation of having his troops being deployed in matters of settling internal political scores, which was one of the key reasons for the army getting a foothold in the politics of the state.
7 Ibid., p. 79.
8 Ibid., p. 75.
9 Taseer, op. cit., pp. 135–44. India appears to have been taken in by this argument.
10 Nawaz, op. cit., p. 323.
11 Cloughley, op. cit., p. 251.
12 Nawaz, op. cit., p. 333-34.
13 Ibid., p. 336.
14 M. Asghar Khan, *My Political Struggle* (Oxford University Press, Karachi, 2008), p. 21.
15 Taseer, op. cit., p. 161.
16 Nawaz, op. cit., pp. 344–45.
17 Ibid., p. 346.
18 Taseer, op. cit., p. 163.
19 Nawaz, op. cit., p. 348.
20 Nawaz, op. cit., p. 348.
21 Taseer, op. cit., p. 203.
22 Cloughley, op. cit., p. 239.
23 Recently, the Supreme Court of Pakistan on a presidential reference opined that Bhutto did not receive a fair trial in the Lahore High Court.

Chapter 17: Zia's Reign

1 Jones, op. cit., pp. 232–233.
2 Article 6 reads: '*High Treason: (1) Any person, who abrogates or attempts or conspires to abrogate, subverts or attempts to subvert the Constitution by the use of force or show of force or by other unconstitutional means shall be guilty of high treason.*'.
3 Nawaz, op. cit., p. 359.
4 Cohen, op. cit., p. 84.
5 Ibid.
6 Nawaz, op. cit., p. 360 .
7 Cited in Cloughley, op. cit., p. 278.
8 Ibid.
9 Nawaz, op. cit., p. 384.
10 Bidanda M. Chengappa, *Pakistan: Islamization, Army and Foreign* Policy (A.P.H. Publishing Corporation, New Delhi, 2004), p. 59.
11 Benazir Bhutto, *Pakistan: The Gathering Storm* (Vikas Publishing House, New Delhi, 1983), p. 55.
12 Known popularly as 'Operation Khalifa'.
13 Cohen, op. cit., p. 108.
14 Ibid., p. 85.
15 Generally, see Ibid., pp. 112–15.
16 Cloughley, op. cit., p. 292.
17 Cohen, op. cit.
18 See Nawaz, op. cit., pp. 381–84.
19 *Kesavananda Bharati v. State of Kerala* reported in (1977) 4 SCC 225, referred supra.
20 Cohen, op. cit., p. 100.
21 Nawaz, op. cit., p. 388.
22 Ibid., pp. 388–91.

23 For more, see section titled 'A Fateful Air Crash', Ibid., pp. 393–96.
24 Cohen, op. cit., pp. 97–130.
25 Ibid.
25 Nawaz, op. cit., p. 398.
26 Ibid.
27 Benazir Bhutto, op. cit., pp. 187–88.

Chapter 18: 'Decade of Democracy'

1 Cited in Stephen P. Cohen, op. cit., p. 131.
2 Cohen, op. cit., p. 86. The castigation of the Election Commission contrasts with the position in India where the Election Commission has historically been pivotal to the conduct of free and fair elections.
3 The stated threat from India and the alleged persecution of Kashmiri Muslims by the Indian State were the basis for the Pakistan Army to legitimize its active role in the governance of Pakistan.
4 Nawaz, op. cit., p. 411.
5 Nawaz, op. cit.
6 Jones, op. cit., pp. 245–46.
7 Nawaz, op. cit., p. 415.
8 Beg, being a Mohajir, appeared 'more loyal than the King' and possibly undertook such posturing largely to please his Punjabi colleagues.
9 For more, see Cohen, op. cit., pp. 79–81, p. 146.
10 Benazir Bhutto, op. cit., p. 197.
11 Ibid., p. 201.
12 Nawaz, op. cit., p. 425.
13 Nawaz, op. cit., p. 430.
14 Such an amendment in India would possibly fall foul of the 'basic structure' doctrine and would most likely be quashed by the Supreme Court. Even existing provisions for removal

of democratically elected governments, by way of emergency powers under Article 356 of the Constitution of India, cannot be exercised whimsically and are subject to judicial review.

15 Nawaz, op. cit., p. 434.

16 Of whom Brigadier Zahir Alam Khan authored *The Way It Was*—a hard-hitting critique of the Pakistan Army's failures in the 1965 and 1971 wars and referred to earlier.

17 See section titled 'Selecting a New Army Chief', Nawaz, op. cit., pp. 440–43.

18 Nawaz, op. cit., p. 444 (Incidentally, Shuja Nawaz is the brother of General Nawaz.).

19 Cloughley, op. cit., p. 326.

20 'Milbus' or military interest in business had grown 'exponentially' by now, with prevalent housing schemes, public sector opportunities and infrastructure opportunities that brought the military even closer to the economy. See Ayesha Siddiqa, op. cit., pp. 153–55.

21 Akin to the binding nature of the advice given by the Council of Ministers to the President of India under Article 84 of the Constitution of India.

22 Nawaz, op. cit., p. 452 The author refers to General Nasir as 'a born-again Muslim with a rakish past'.

23 Cloughley, op. cit., p. 328.

24 See Michael Parenti, *History as Mystery* (City Lights Publishers, California, 1999), p. 236.

25 Nawaz, op. cit., p. 458.

26 Ibid., p. 469.

27 See *Mian Muhammad Nawaz Sharif v. President of Pakistan* LEX/SCPK/0023/1993.

28 Cloughley, op. cit., pp. 334–35.

29 Nawaz, op. cit., p. 477.

30 Ibid., pp. 481–82.

31 Ibid., pp. 484–86.

32 Ibid., p. 487.

33 Cloughley, op. cit., p. 336.
34 Nawaz, op. cit., pp. 487–89.
35 Cohen, op. cit., p. 10.

Chapter 19: Musharraf's Coup

1 Nawaz, op. cit., p. 501.
2 Ibid., p. 508.
3 The details of the Indian response have already been discussed in the Chapter 'Kargil (1999)' *supra.*
4 Musharraf, op. cit., p. 98.
5 Nawaz, op. cit., p. 510.
6 Musharraf, op. cit., p. 96.
7 Nawaz, op. cit., p. 519.
8 Jones, op. cit., p. 108.
9 'Unofficial' as the involvement of the army was never officially conceded by Pakistan, despite conspicuous evidence thereof. The website of the Pakistan Army—www.pakistanarmy.gov.pk had, put up a list of 453 soldiers who were killed in action in Kargil 1999.
10 Musharraf, op. cit., p. 86. He also lands a low blow on Sharif, 'I must say that I was quite amused by his style of working: I never saw him reading or writing anything.'.
11 Mary Anne Weaver, *Pakistan: In the Shadow of Jihad and Afghanistan* (Farrar, Straus & Giroux, New York, 2002), p. 30.
12 Musharraf, op. cit., p. 109.
13 Cited in Nawaz, op. cit., p. 528.
14 Ibid.
15 In contrast to India, where the army owes its allegiance to the Constitution and constitutionally elected governments, and not to its own conceptions of national good.
16 Musharraf, op. cit., p. 137.

17 Cohen, op. cit., p. 90. During this time, the government's support for the Afghan Taliban and for Islamic militants in Indian-administered Kashmir boomeranged with the Taliban collaborating with the Al-Qaeda, which compelled the United States to clip the wings of General Musharraf with its 'War on Terror', whereby Pakistan was compelled to undertake the elimination of terror and distance itself from the Taliban.

18 Murtaza Razvi, *Musharraf: The Years in Power* (HarperCollins Publishers India, Noida, 2009), p. 57.

19 Husain Haqqani, *Pakistan: Between Mosque and Military* (Carnegie Endowment for International Peace, Washington, 2005), p. 165.

20 Benazir Bhutto, op. cit., p. 214.

21 Shuja Nawaz, *The Battle for Pakistan: The Bitter US Friendship and a Tough Neighbourhood* (Penguin Random House India, New Delhi, 2019), pp. 325–26 The author notes that his successor, General Kayani, recalled most of these officers from civilian posts and 'forbade meetings of serving officers with politicians, including President Musharraf'.

22 Ibid.

23 William B. Milam, *Bangladesh and Pakistan: Flirting with Failure in South Asia* (Hurst Publishers, London, 2011), pp. 233–34.

24 Wilson John, *The General and Jihad* (Pentagon Press, New Delhi, 2007), p. 2.

25 Musharraf, op. cit., p. 167.

26 Cohen, op. cit., p. 88.

27 Ibid., p. 12.

Chapter 20: 'An Army's Nation'

1 Cohen, op. cit., p. 88.
2 Sudhir Kumar Singh, *Human Rights in Pakistan* (Pentagon Press, New Delhi, 2007), pp. 199–203.
3 See Lieutenant Colonel Rajkumar Pattu and Brigadier Man Mohan Sharma, FRGS, *Indian Prisoners of War in Pakistan* (Trishul Publications, Noida, 2006).
4 Whose murder accused have been acquitted by the High Court at Sindh. The government has preferred an appeal to the Supreme Court.
5 Benazir Bhutto, op. cit., p. 215.
6 Dennis Cux, op. cit., pp. 354–55.
7 Musharraf, op. cit., pp. 154–55.
8 Cited in Shyam Bhatia, *Goodbye Shahzadi: A Political Biography of Benazir Bhutto* (Lotus Collection: Roli Books, New Delhi, 2008), pp. 114–15.
9 Hassan Abbas, *Pakistan's Drift into Extremism* (Pentagon Press, New Delhi, 2005), p. 234.
10 Murtaza Razvi, op. cit., p. 61.
11 Ibid., p. 66–67.
12 Richard V. Weekes, *Pakistan: Birth and Growth of a Muslim Nation* (Royal Book House, Karachi, 2004; 1964 manuscript), p. 266.
13 Hassan Abbas, op. cit., p. 197.
14 Zahid Hussain, *Frontline Pakistan: The Struggle with Militant Islam* (Penguin Books India, New Delhi, 2007), p. 188.
15 Shyam Bhatia, op. cit., pp. 86–87, 115.
16 Benazir Bhutto, op. cit., p. 222.
17 Razvi, op. cit., p. 232.
18 Imran Khan, *Pakistan: A Personal History* (Transworld Publishers, London, 2011), p. 111.
19 Razvi, op. cit., p. 179.

20 Wilson Jones, *Pakistan: Four Scenarios* (Pentagon Press, New Delhi, 2007), pp. 41–48.
21 Ibid., p. 76.
22 Shyam Bhatia, op. cit., p. 117.
23 Benazir Bhutto, op. cit., pp. 1–2.
24 Shyam Bhatia, op. cit., p. 120.
25 Mushrif, op. cit., p. 45.
26 Shyam Bhatia, op. cit., p. 121.
27 Heraldo Muñoz, *Getting Away with Murder: Benazir Bhutto's Assassination and the Politics of Pakistan* (W.W. Norton, New York, 2014), p. 165.
28 Meena Menon, *Reporting Pakistan* (Penguin Random House India, Gurgaon, 2017), p. 253.
29 Razvi, op. cit., p. 224.

2008 and After: The Flux

1 'Sharif claims victory in Pakistan elections', Al Jazeera, 12 May 2013, https://www.aljazeera.com/news/2013/5/12/sharif-claims-victory-in-pakistan-elections.
2 'Nawaz Sharif blames Gen Bajwa & Gen Faiz for Pakistan's current turmoil', *The Hindu*, 20 January 2023, https://www.thehindu.com/news/international/nawaz-sharif-blames-gen-bajwa-gen-faiz-for-pakistans-current-turmoil/article66413716.ece.
3 Nadeem F. Paracha, 'Smokers' Corner: 'Hybrid Regimes' and Their Discontents', *Dawn*, 11 October 2020, https://www.dawn.com/news/1584372/smokers-corner-hybrid-regimes-and-their-discontents.
4 PTI, 'Pak Army chief backs Imran Khan's peace initiatives', *Deccan Herald*, 23 December 2018, https://www.deccanherald.com/world/pak-army-chief-backs-imran-709522.html.

5 Secunder Kermani, 'Imran Khan: What led to charismatic Pakistan PM's downfall', BBC, 10 April 2022, https://www.bbc.com/news/world-asia-61047736.

6 For more, see Khurram Hussain, 'The Generals and Their Captain', *Caravan*, 1 May 2023, https://caravanmagazine.in/politics/imran-khan-pakistan-military-general-bajwa. Imran Khan would later accuse General Bajwa of being responsible for the disqualification of Nawaz Sharif in the Panama Papers case and point to the continuing covert influence of the army over Pakistani politics.

7 Niyati Singh, 'Army tightens grip on Pakistan as Imran Khan's popularity wanes', *Hindustan Times*, 10 June 2020, https://www.hindustantimes.com/world-news/army-tightens-grip-on-pakistan-as-imran-khan-s-popularity-wanes/story-8SwnFXn3TlQ3r1EnQOu7rL.html.

8 Neena Gopal, 'In Pakistan, the Military, the Mian, and the Messiah', *Deccan Herald*, 18 April 2023, https://www.deccanherald.com/opinion/in-pakistan-the-military-the-mian-and-the-messiah-1210621.html.

9 *Chief of Defence Staff: A Historic Reform in Higher Defence Organisation*, https://static.pib.gov.in/WriteReadData/specificdocs/documents/2021/oct/doc202110501.pdf.

10 See: Sushant Singh, 'On the Defensive', *Caravan*, 1 June 2024, https://caravanmagazine.in/security/military-modi-political-project. The piece details the increasing politicization of the armed forces and the inclination of senior officers to affiliate with mainstream political and religious policies. Recently, Air Chief Marshal R.K.S. Bhadauria, who retired in 2021, joined the BJP describing his years serving under its regime as 'the best time of my service'. See: 'Lok Sabha elections 2024: Former Indian Air Force chief R K S Bhadauria joins BJP, says "best time of my service was..."', Mint, 24 March 2024, https://www.livemint.com/politics/news/lok-sabha-elections-2024-

former-indian-air-force-chief-r-k-s-bhadauria-joins-bjp-11711261767431.html.

11 Ibid., *Caravan*.

12 Amit Cowshish and Rahul Bedi, 'A Host of Complex Issues Threaten the Formation of the Military's Integrated Theatre Commands', Wire, 8 July 2021, https://thewire.in/security/military-integrated-theatre-commands-bipin-rawat-air-force-army-issues.

13 Mayank Singh, 'Public spat as CDS calls Air Force a support arm, Air Chief says it is not', *New Indian Express*, 3 July 2021, https://www.newindianexpress.com/nation/2021/Jul/03/public-spat-as-cds-calls-air-force-a-support-arm-air-chief-says-it-is-not-2324831.html.

14 https://static.mygov.in/indiancc/2021/11/mygov-999999999630641418.pdf (Interestingly the page refers to the air strikes as having been 'conducted by the Indian army'.).

15 'Defence Ministry takes a dig at former navy chief, deletes tweet later', *India Today*, 26 October 2018, https://www.indiatoday.in/india/story/ministry-of-defence-takes-a-dig-at-former-navy-chief-deletes-tweet-later-1375885-2018-10-26.

16 'Kashmiris now share intel on terrorists, says Gen. Bipin Rawat', *The Hindu*, 13 November 2021, https://www.thehindu.com/news/national/kashmiris-now-share-intel-on-terrorists-says-gen-bipin-rawat/article37475888.ece. Also see: Akash Bisht, 'Fear in Kashmir as top general talks of "deradicalization" camps', Al Jazeera, 24 January 2020, https://www.aljazeera.com/news/2020/1/24/fear-in-kashmir-as-top-general-talks-of-deradicalisation-camps.

17 Ananth Krishnan, 'China lodges protest over Gen. Rawat comments on "security threat"', *The Hindu*, 25 November 2021, https://www.thehindu.com/news/national/china-

lodges-protest-over-gen-rawat-comments-on-security-threat/article37684787.ece.

18 'Galwan Valley: China and India clash on freezing and inhospitable battlefield', BBC, 17 June 2020, https://www.bbc.com/news/world-asia-india-53076781. For the statement of the defence minister, see: 'Text of Raksha Mantri Shri Rajnath Singh Statement in Rajya Sabha on September 17', Press Information Bureau, 17 September 2020, https://www.pib.gov.in/PressReleseDetailm.aspx?PRID=1655521.

19 See Lieutenant General H.S. Panag's pieces published in ThePrint: i) 'Pulwama mosque, Manipur incidents bad for Army's image. There's need for course correction', 6 July 2023, https://theprint.in/opinion/pulwama-mosque-manipur-incident-bad-for-armys-image-theres-need-for-course-correction/1656958/ ii) 'Army deciding common dress code for officers just a cosmetic change. Malaise runs deeper', 18 May 2023, https://theprint.in/opinion/army-deciding-common-dress-code-for-officers-just-a-cosmetic-change-malaise-runs-deeper/1579580/.

20 See: Sushant Singh, 'Tour of Duty model could add to majoritarian violence and affect army efficiency', *Caravan*, 21 April 2022, https://caravanmagazine.in/security/tour-of-duty-pensions-lead-to-majoritarian-violence-hindutva-army-efficiency; Rahul Bedi, 'Why Veterans, Defence Experts View Agnipath as "Incompetent, Unworkable and Inimical"', Wire, 28 June 2022, https://thewire.in/security/veterans-defence-agnipath-cricism; 'The Tour of Duty: Give the Agniveers a chance', Observer Research Foundation, 20 June 2022, https://www.orfonline.org/expert-speak/the-tour-of-duty-give-the-agniveers-a-chance.

21 Vijay Mohan, '17-year old anomaly, where generals were getting lower pay than juniors, ends as government finally implements High Court orders', *Tribune India*, 20 June, https://www.tribuneindia.com/news/nation/17-year-old-

anomaly-where-generals-were-getting-lower-pay-than-juniors-ends-as-government-finally-implements-high-court-orders-518793.

22 S.G. Vombatkere, 'Whither India's Armed Forces: Politicisation by Default or Design?' 8 November 2023, Wire, https://thewire.in/security/india-armed-forces-politicisation-by-default-or-design.

23 Rahul Bedi, 'Politicisation of the Military Is Happening in Full Public View, Veterans Raise Concerns', Wire, 25 October 2023, https://thewire.in/security/politicisation-of-indian-military-veterans-helplessly-watch-on; M.G. Devasahayam, Commandeering Civil Services and Armed Forces for Propaganda Could Make India a Failed State', Wire, 3 November 2023.

24 Imran Khan, op. cit., p. 171.

25 It is reported that the IAF handled private air traffic at the Jamnagar air base during the Ambani family pre-wedding celebrations, based on a request made by the Reliance Group to the defence secretary who conveyed the same to the chief of air staff. See: Dinakar Peri, 'IAF stepped in to handle air activity at Jamnagar airport during Ambani's pre-wedding bash', *The Hindu*, 14 April 2024, https://www.thehindu.com/news/national/iaf-stepped-in-to-handle-air-activity-at-jamnagar-airport-during-ambanis-pre-wedding-bash/article68061860.ece.

Bangladesh: The Experiment

1 Anthony Mascarenhas, *The Rape of Bangla Desh* (Vikas Publications, New Delhi, 1971), p. 139 (The book was said to have been banned in Bangladesh.).

2 Chandrashekhar Dasgupta, *India and the Bangladesh Liberation War* (Juggernaut Books, New Delhi, 2021), pp. 247–48.

3 Ayesha Jalal, op. cit., pp. 85–86.
4 Dasgupta, op. cit., p. 13.
5 Ayesha Jalal, op. cit., p. 87.
6 Milam, op. cit., p. 36.
7 Ibid., pp. 85–89.
8 Milam, op. cit., p. 38.
9 Ayesha Jalal, op. cit.
10 Salil Tripathi, *The Colonel Who Would Not Repent* (Aleph Book Company, New Delhi, 2014), p. 264.
11 Ibid., p. 240.
12 A similar prejudice to that faced by Mohajirs in Pakistan.
13 Milam, op. cit., p. 35.
14 Ali Riaz, *Bangladesh: A Political History since Independence* (Bloomsbury India, New Delhi, 2019), pp. 62–63.
15 B.Z. Khusru, *The Bangladesh Military Coup and the CIA* (Rupa Publications, New Delhi, 2014), p. 226. The book develops a theory that the coup was orchestrated by the CIA who wanted Bangladesh to fail as a democracy.
16 Tripathi, op. cit., p. 245.
17 Charulata Singh, *The Role of Military in Politics: A Case Study of Bangladesh* (Neha Publishers, New Delhi, 2008), p. 275.
18 Ayesha Jalal, op. cit., p. 115–16.
19 Charulata Singh, op. cit., p. 79.
20 Marcus F. Franda, *Bangaldesh: The First Decade* (South Asian Publishers, Michigan, 1982), p. 239.
21 Milam, op. cit., p. 52.
22 Ibid.
23 Joseph Allchin, *Many Rivers, One Sea: Bangladesh and the Challenge of Islamist Militancy* (Penguin Random House India, Gurgaon, 2019), p. 45.
24 Mascarenhas, op. cit., p. 11.
25 Milam, op. cit. p. 55.
26 Ayesha Jalal, op. cit., pp. 117–18.

27 Milam, op. cit., pp. 62–63.
28 Milam, op. cit., p. 58.
29 Ibid. Ziaur Rahman would regularly meet 'formation commanders' to ensure that the army was involved in civilian policymaking. This was still not enough to keep all military factions on his side.
30 Ibid.
31 Ibid
32 Milam, op. cit., p. 64.
33 Milam, op. cit., p. 64.
34 Ayesha Jalal, op. cit., p. 118.
35 Charulata Singh, op. cit., p. 279.
36 Ayesha Jalal, op. cit., p. 142.
37 Milam, op. cit., pp. 66–67.
38 Jalal, op. cit., pp. 116–20.
39 Charulata Singh, op. cit., p. 85.
40 Ibid.
41 See Milam, op. cit., pp. 95–106.
42 Milam, op. cit., p. 103.
43 See Riaz, op. cit., pp. 73–75.
44 For more, see Milam, op. cit., pp. 107–09.
45 Ayesha Jalal, op. cit., p. 120.
46 This fructified in successful anti-incumbency results in 1996 and 2001.
47 To BNP's credit, it did not permit anti-Hindu violence to spread after the Babri Masjid demolition in India. For more on this, see Milam, op. cit., p. 120.
48 Milam, op. cit., p. 124.
49 The operation was called 'Operation Clean Heart', perhaps betraying a Freudian political intention.
50 Milam, op. cit., p. 131.
51 Allchin, op. cit., p. 82.
52 Ali Riaz, *Bangladesh: A Political History Since Independence* (Bloomsbury India, New Delhi, 2019), pp. 88–89.

53 Ibid., p. 90.
54 For a detailed account of the 'genocide' of the time, see Mascarenhas *supra*. As per his account in *The Rape of Bangla Desh*, the ethnic cleansing of thousands of Hindus in East Pakistan in 1971 was reminiscent of Hitler's 'final solution' and saw over eight million refugees migrate to India. The violent murders of common (Muslim) Bangladeshis were equally horrific. Also see, Salil Tripathi *supra* who refers to the official Bangladesh claim on the number of deaths at three million, which Mujib had himself echoed in interviews to foreign correspondents.
55 Riaz, op. cit., p. 99.
56 Ibid.
57 Generally, see Kudret Bülbül, Md. Nazmul Islam, Md. Sajid Khan (Ed.), *Rohingya Refugee Crisis in Myanmar, Ethnic Conflict and Resolution* (Springer, Singapore, 2022).
58 Charulata Singh, op. cit., p. 280.
59 Cited in Charulata Singh, op. cit., pp. 82–83.
60 Ayesha Jalal, op. cit., p.121: The author extends the contrast to India, albeit in the absence of military rule and notes, 'Yet most perturbing for the subcontinent, even relatively autonomous political processes in India have not generated the kind of pressures needed to force the state structure into undertaking major redistributive measures. Alliances between dominant castes and classes both within the ruling parties and the non-elected institutions of the state have used the democratic rubric to perpetuate economic inequalities and social injustices. Populism in India quite as much as in Pakistan and Bangladesh proved to be a mirage and merely provided grounds for a greater reassertion of authoritarian tendencies rooted in the state structure and the political economy. That after years of diverging political developments, these tendencies are co-existing with formal

democracy in all three countries in the 1990s is a matter less of relief than of consternation.'.

61 Ibid.

62 Milam, op. cit., p. 227.

63 Anam Zakaria, *1971: A People's History from Bangladesh, Pakistan and India* (Penguin Random House India, Gurgaon, 2019), pp. 277–78.

64 Dasgupta, op. cit., p. 250.

65 Jalal, op. cit., pp. 141–44.

66 Milam, op. cit., pp. 241–42.

Conclusion

1 Arjun Subramaniam, op. cit., p. 68.

2 Ibid., citing General K. Sundarji.

3 Brigadier Z.A. Khan, op. cit., p. 384. The brigadier was himself passed over for promotion for his critical take on the leadership of the army in 1971.

4 Lieutenant General E.A. Vas (Retired), cited in *Field Marshal K.M. Cariappa Memorial Lectures 1995–2000* (Directorate General on Infantry in association with Lancer Publishers and Distributors, New Delhi, 2001), p. 134.

5 Stephen P. Cohen, op. cit., p. 131.

6 Ibid.

7 Cloughley, op. cit., p. 408. Khalid Mahmud Arif, in his piece 'The Role of the Military in Politics: Pakistan 1947–97', states that the martial regimes of Ayub Khan, Yahya Khan and Zia-ul-Haq were 'initially hailed by a vast majority of the public' that was frustrated with governments, and as the coups were 'bloodless, and by and large, benign'. Cited in Hafeez Malik (Ed.), *Pakistan: Founder's Aspirations and Today's Realities* (Oxford University Press, Karachi, 2003) p. 123.

8 Hassan Abbas, op. cit., pp. 240–41.
9 McGrath, op. cit., p. 231.
10 Husain Haqqani, *Reimagining Pakistan: Transforming a Dysfunctional Nuclear State* (HarperCollins Publishers India, Noida, 2018), p. 160.
11 Anatol Lieven, *Pakistan: A Hard Country* (Public Affairs, New York, 2012), p. 173. He interestingly contrasts India with Pakistan in moral–cultural terms by saying, 'The difference with Pakistan is that in India there is no coherent and unified cultural alternative to the modern state and its legal structures, which also operates as a standing moral reproach to those structures. In Pakistan, in the view of many believers, there is the way of Islam reflected in the Shariah.' (At page 123). This position could be challenged in India today in the light of an evergrowing political Hindutva.
12 McGrath, op. cit., pp. 165–67.
13 Lieven, op. cit., p. 160.
14 Nawaz, op. cit., p. 458.
15 Ayesha Siddiqa, op. cit., p. 249.
16 John Kenneth Galbraith, *How to Control the Military* (Signet Books, New York, 1969), p. 75.
17 Praval, op. cit., p. 160.
18 Jairam Ramesh, *A Chequered Brilliance,* op. cit., pp. 849–50.
19 Shiv Kunal Verma, op. cit., pp. 425–26.
20 Ibid.
21 Air Marshal Nehra, op. cit., p. 332.
22 Ibid. The author also criticizes the military leadership for failing to 'be heard' and for creating space for the bureaucrat to come closer to the political leadership.
23 Gurmeet Kanwal, Neha Kohli (Ed.), *Defence Reforms: A National Imperative* (IDSA, New Delhi, 2018), p. 12. The author refers to the fact that for the longest time, the Department of Ex-servicemen's Welfare in the Ministry of Defence did not have a single ex-serviceman in it!.

24 Admiral Nanda, op. cit., p. 295.

25 Samuel Huntington, op. cit.

26 Javeed Alam, op. cit., pp. 241–43.

27 Lieutenant General S.K. Sinha, cited in *Field Marshal K.M. Cariappa Memorial Lectures 1995–2000* (Directorate General on Infantry in association with Lancer Publishers and Distributors, New Delhi, 2001), p. 59.

28 Jaswant Singh, cited in *Field Marshal K.M. Cariappa Memorial Lectures 1995–2000*, Ibid., p.125.

29 Lieutenant General E.A. Vas, *The Search for Security: Controlling Conflict and Terrorism,* (Natraj Publishers, Dehradun, 1989), pp. 264–65.

30 Ibid. Apart from the absence of a formal organization (or 'party') of ex-servicemen, the instances of retired officers running for elections are also few and far between. Major General Khanduri (Retired) was one who became Chief Minister of Uttarakhand, and former chief General V.K. Singh, a union minister. But such examples are rare in India.

31 Lieutenant General Sinha, op. cit., pp. 53–54 This, despite what the author describes as 'an unfortunate coup syndrome among our (India's) decision-makers', leading to the army's isolation and to the development of 'the most irrational higher defence organization in the world'.

32 M.J. Akbar, *Tinderbox: The Past and Future of Pakistan* (HarperCollins Publishers India, Noida, 2011), p. 312.

33 Ayesha Jalal, *The State of Martial Rule* (Sang-e-Meel Publications, Lahore, 1999), p. 295. This is not to say that democracy is perfect in concept or implementation. Critics see it as being 'subversive', 'unworkable' and with the risk that 'too much democracy can kill off democracy'. See: Sushila Ramaswamy, *Political Theory: Ideas and Concepts* (Macmillan, New Delhi 2007), p. 406. The author also alludes to the fact that even in working democracies, power structures emerge by way of corporations, the military etc.

that dominate public policy leading to a 'military–industrial complex'. (At p. 68).

34 Jalal, op. cit., p. 142. The Fauji Foundation, run by the army, owns tax-exempt manufacturing units in the realm of sugar, fertilizers, gas, cereals and metals and is a parallel economy in itself.

35 Ibid.

36 Cited in Risa A. Brooks, op. cit., p. 101.

37 Samuel P. Huntington, op. cit., pp. 76–79. In what he describes as the 'military mind'.

38 Shuja Nawaz, *The Battle for Pakistan*, p. 346. Ishtiaq Ahmed cites LePorte to describe Pakistan as 'a garrison state' where along with the military, the ISI and other intelligence services have expanded their roles 'far beyond their formal remits'. Ishtiaq Ahmed, op. cit., pp. 442–43. Others have described it as 'a semi-state', continuing to 'wonder what kind of state it wants to be'. Khaled Ahmed, *Pakistan's Terror Conundrum* (Penguin Random House India, Gurgaon, 2020), p. 249

39 Steven I. Wilkinson, *Army and Nation: The Military and Indian Democracy since Independence* (Orient Blackswan, New Delhi, 2015), p. 9. According to the author, having 'fixed class' but multi-ethnic battalions was one such measure.

40 Reba Som, *Gandhi, Bose, Nehru, and the Making of the Modern Indian Mind* (Penguin Books India, New Delhi, 2004), p. 197. It is interesting that Bose 'began life as a politician' but ended as a soldier in the quest for independence, with the INA as the bedrock. This goes to show the role of the martial factor in pre-Independence India, which is often glossed over in highlighting the civilian traditions that pervaded the early decades after 1947. See Peter Ward Fay, *The Forgotten Army: India's Armed Struggle for Independence 1942–1945* (Rupa Publications, New Delhi, 1994), p. 523.

41 Hugh Byas, *Government by Assassination* (Alfred A. Knopf, New York, 1942), p. 133.

Bibliography

A. Balakrishnan Nair, *Facets of Indian Defence* (S. Chand & Company Ltd, New Delhi, 1983).

Aditya Sondhi, *Unfinished Symphony* (Penguin Books India, New Delhi, 2003).

Admiral Arun Prakash, *From the Crow's Nest: A Compendium of Speeches and Writings on Maritime and Other Issues* (Lancer Publishers, New Delhi, 2007).

Admiral S.M. Nanda, *The Man Who Bombed Karachi: A Memoir* (HarperCollins Publishers India, New Delhi, 2004).

Admiral Vishnu Bhagwat, *Betrayal of the Defence Forces: The Inside Truth* (Manas Publications, New Delhi, 2001).

Ahmed Rashid, *Descent into Chaos: How the War against Islamic Extremism Is Being Lost in Pakistan, Afghanistan and Central Asia* (Penguin Books India, New Delhi, 2008).

Air Chief Marshal Dilbagh Singh (Retired), PVSM, AVSM, VM, *On the Wings of Destiny* (KW Publishers and Centre for Air Force Studies, New Delhi, 2010).

Air Chief Marshal O.P. Mehra (Retired), PVSM, *Memories: Sweet and* Sour (KW Publishers and Centre for Air Power Studies, New Delhi, 2010).

Air Chief Marshal P.C. Lal, *My Years with the IAF* (Lancer, New Delhi, 1986).

Air Commodore Jasjit Singh, *Nuclear India* (K.W. Publishers, New Delhi, 1998).

Air Commodore Ranvir Kumar, AVSM, *Legal Safeguards for Defence Personnel* (Manas Publications, New Delhi, 2007).

Air Marshal K.C. Cariappa (Retired), *Field Marshal K.M. Cariappa* (Niyogi Books, New Delhi, 2007).

Alan T. Wood, *Asian Democracy in World History* (Routledge, London and New York, 2004).

Alex Von Tunzelmann, *Indian Summer: The Secret History of the End of an Empire* (Pocket Books, 2008).

Altaf Gauhar, *Ayub Khan: Pakistan's First Military Ruler* (Sang-e-Meel Publications, Lahore, 1998).

Amarinder Singh, *A Ridge Too Far: War in the Kargil Heights 1999* (Motibagh Palace, Patiala, 2001).

Ambassador Arshad Sami Khan, SJ, *Three Presidents and an Aide: Life, Power and Politics* (Pentagon Press, New Delhi, 2008).

Anatol Lieven, *Pakistan: A Hard Country* (Public Affairs, New York, 2012).

Anit Mukherjee, *The Absent Dialogue: Politicians, Bureaucracy and the Military in India* (Oxford University Press, New Delhi, 2020).

Anubha Bhonsle, *Mother Where's My Country? Looking for Light in the Darkness of Manipur* (Speaking Tiger, New Delhi, 2016).

Anuradha M. Chenoy, *Militarism and Women in South Asia* (Kali for Women, New Delhi, 2002).

Apurba Kundu, *Militarism in India: The Army and Civil Society in Consensus* (Viva Books, New Delhi, 1998).

Arjun Subramaniam, *India's Wars: A Military History* (HarperCollins Publishers India, Noida, 2016).

Arvind Sivaramakrishnan (Ed.), *Short on Democracy* (Imprint One, Gurgaon, 2007).

A.S. Dulat with Aditya Sinha, *Kashmir: The Vajpayee Years* (HarperCollins Publishers India, New Delhi, 2015).

Asha Gupta (Ed.), *Military Rule and Democratization: Changing Perspectives* (Deep & Deep Publications, New Delhi, 2003).

Ashok Parthasarathi, *Technology at the Core: Science and Technology with Indira Gandhi* (Dorling Kindersley (India), New Delhi, 2007).

Ayesha Jalal, *Democracy and Authoritarianism in South Asia: A Comparative and Historical Perspective* (Cambridge University Press, Cambridge, England, 1995).

Ayesha Jalal, *The State of Martial Rule* (Sang-e-Meel Publications, Lahore, 1999).

Ayesha Siddiqa, *Military Inc.: Inside Pakistan's Military Economy* (Pluto Press, London, 2007).

B. Raman, *The Kaoboys of R&AW: Down Memory Lane* (Lancer Publishers, New Delhi, 2007).

Balraj Krishna, *India's Bismarck: Sardar Vallabhbhai Patel* (India Source Books, Mumbai, 2007).

Barney White-Spunner, *Partition: The Story of Indian Independence and the Creation of Pakistan in 1947* (Simon & Schuster, London, 2017).

Benazir Bhutto, *Pakistan: The Gathering Storm* (Vikas Publishing House, New Delhi, 1983).

Bharat Karnad, *Nuclear Weapons and Indian Security: The Realist Foundations of Strategy* (Macmillan India Ltd., New Delhi, 2002).

Bidanda M. Chengappa, *Pakistan: Islamisation, Army and Foreign Policy* (APH Publishing Corporation, New Delhi, 2004).

Brian Cloughley, *A History of the Pakistan Army: Wars and Insurrections* (Lancer Publishers/OUP, New Delhi, 2002).

Brigadier Z.A. Khan (Retired), *The Way it Was: Inside the Pakistan Army—Indo–Pak Wars 1965 and 1971* (Natraj Publishers, New Delhi, 2007).

Brigadier Chandra B. Khanduri, *Field Marshal K.M. Cariappa: His Life and Times* (Lancer Publishers, New Delhi, 1995).

Brigadier Chandra B. Khanduri, FICHR, FABI, *Thimayya: An Amazing Life* (Knowledge World, New Delhi, 2006).

Brigadier R.A. Singh (Retired), VSM, *Military Governance in Pakistan* (Raj Publications, New Delhi, 2007).

Brigadier Rahul K. Bhonsle (Retired), *Mumbai 26/11: Security Imperatives for the Future* (Vij Books, New Delhi, 2009).

Brigadier Kim Yadav, *British Lions and the Indian Tigers: Triumph of the Sepoy against the British Sword* (Manas Publications, New Delhi, 2004).

Brigadier Vijai K. Nair (Retired), *Nuclear India* (Lancer International, New Delhi, 1992).

Captain Bharat Verma, Vice Admiral G.M. Hiranandani (Retired), Air Marshal B.K. Pandey (Retired), *Indian Armed Forces* (Lancer Publishers, New Delhi, 2008).

Captain Prem Singh, *Civil Military Operation* (Prashant Publishing House, New Delhi, 2009).

Chand Joshi, *Bhindranwale: Myth and Reality* (Vikas Publishing House, New Delhi, 1984).

Colonel Gurmeet Kanwal, *Kargil '99: Blood, Guts and Firepower* (Lancer Publishers, New Delhi, 2000).

Colonel R.D. Palsokar, MC, PSC, *Shivaji: The Great Guerrilla* (Natraj Publishers, Dehradun, 2003).

Craig Baxter (Ed.), *Diaries of Field Marshal Mohammad Ayub Khan 1966–1972* (Oxford University Press, Karachi, 2007).

D.R. Mankekar, *The Guilty Men of 1962* (Penguin Books India, New Delhi, 1998).

Deepa Agarwal and Tahmina Aziz Ayub, *The Begum: A Portrait of Ra'ana Liaquat Ali Khan, Pakistan's Pioneering First Lady* (Penguin Random House India, Gurgaon, 2019).

Dennis Kux, *The United States and Pakistan 1947–2000: Disenchanted Allies* (Woodrow Wilson Centre Press, Washington, 2001).

Dilip Bobb, Asoka Raina, *The Great Betrayal: Assassination of Indira Gandhi* (Vikas Publishing House, New Delhi, 1985).

Dr Anil Kumar Singh, *Military and Media* (Lancer Publishers and Distributors, New Delhi, 2006).

Dr Charulata Singh, *The Role of Military in Politics: A Case Study of Bangladesh* (Neha Publishers, New Delhi, 2008).

Dr R.M. Kasliwal and Dr R.R. Kasliwal, *The Impact of Netaji and INA on India's Independence* (UBS Publishers' Distributors, New Delhi, 2005).

Emajuddin Ahamed, *Military Rule and the Myth of Democracy* (University Press Ltd, Dhaka, 1988).

Feroza H. Seervai, *Evoking H.M. Seervai: Jurist and Authority on the Indian Constitution* (Feroza H. Seervai, 2005).

Field Marshal K.M. Cariappa Memorial Lectures 1995–2000 (Directorate General on Infantry in association with Lancer Publishers and Distributors, New Delhi, 2001).

Gary J. Bass, *The Blood Telegram: India's Secret War in East Pakistan* (Random House India, Noida, 2013).

Gautam Das and M.K. Gupta-Ray, *Sri Lanka Misadventure: India's Military Peace-keeping Campaign 1987–1990* (Military Affairs Series, Har Anand Publications, New Delhi, 2008).

General K.S. Thimayya, *Experiment in Neutrality* (Vision Books, New Delhi, 1981).

General S. Padmanabhan, *India Checkmates America 2017* (Manas Publications, New Delhi, 2004).

General S. Padmanabhan (Retired), PVSM, AVSM, VSM, *A General Speaks* (Manas Publications, New Delhi, 2010).

General V.P. Malik, *Kargil: From Surprise to Victory* (HarperCollins Publishers India, New Delhi, 2006).

General V.P. Malik (Retired), PVSM, AVSM, *Defence Planning: Problems and Prospects* (Manas Publications, New Delhi, 2006).

George Perkovich, *India's Nuclear Bomb: The Impact on Global Proliferation* (Oxford University Press, New Delhi, 1999).

Gohar Ayub Khan, *Glimpses into the Corridors of* Power (Oxford University Press, Karachi, 2007).

Golam W. Choudhury, *Pakistan: Transition from Military to Civilian Rule* (Scorpion Publishing Ltd., Essex, 1988).

Gordon Corera, *Shopping for Bombs: Nuclear Proliferation, Global Insecurity, and the Rise and Fall of the A.Q. Khan Network* (C. Hurst & Co. (Publishers) Ltd., London, 2006).

Gurmeet Kanwal, Neha Kohli (Ed.), *Defence Reforms: A National Imperative* (IDSA, New Delhi, 2018).

Granville Austin, *Working a Democratic Constitution: A History of the Indian Experience* (Oxford University Press, New Delhi, 2009).

Group Captain Jacob Chakko, *Memoirs* (Jacob K. Chakko, Los Angeles, USA, 1999).

Group Captain Ranbir Singh (Retired), Wing Commander Ranjit Kumar Mandal, *Eternal Principles of War* (Kritika Books, New Delhi, 2002).

Group Captain Ranbir Singh (Retired), *Marshal Arjan Singh, DFC: Life and Times* (Ocean Books, New Delhi, 2002).

H.R. Khanna, *Making of India's Constitution* (Eastern Book Company, Lucknow, 1981).

H.R. Khanna, *Neither Roses nor Thorns* (Eastern Book Company, Lucknow, 1987).

H.S. Bhatia, *Military History of British India* (Deep & Deep Publications, New Delhi, 1977).

Hamid Khan, *Constitutional and Political History of Pakistan* (Oxford University Press, Karachi, 2009).

Harinder Baweja (Ed.), *26/11: Mumbai Attacked* (Roli Books, New Delhi, 2009).

Harry Eckstein and David E. Apter (Eds.), *Comparative Politics: A Reader* (The Free Press, New York, 1963).

Hassan Abbas, *Pakistan's Drift into Extremism: Allah, the Army and America's War on Terror* (Pentagon Press, Delhi, 2005).

Hugh Byas, *Government by Assassination* (Alfred A. Knopf, New York, 1942).

Husain Haqqani, *Pakistan: Between Mosque and Military* (Carnegie Endowment for International Peace, Washington, 2005).

Husain Haqqani, *Reimagining Pakistan: Transforming a Dysfunctional Nuclear State* (HarperCollins Publishers India, Noida, 2018).

Humphrey Evans, *Thimayya of India: A Soldier's Life* (Natraj Publishers, Dehradun,1988).

Ian Talbot, *Pakistan: A Modern History* (Oxford University Press, New Delhi, 1998).

Imran Khan, *Pakistan: A Personal History* (Transworld Publishers, London, 2011).

Ishtiaq Ahmed, *The Pakistan Military in Politics* (Amaryllis, New Delhi, 2013).

J. Clement Vaz, *Profiles of Eminent Goans: Past and Present* (Concept Publishing Company, New Delhi, 1997).

Jacques Van Doorn (Ed.), *Armed Forces and Society: Sociological Essays* (Mouton, The Hague, Netherlands, 1968).

Jad Adams and Phillip Whitehead, *The Dynasty: The Nehru–Gandhi Story* (TV Books, New York, 1997).

Jagmohan, *My Frozen Turbulence in Kashmir* (Allied Publishers, Mumbai, 2007).

Jairam Ramesh, *A Chequered Brilliance: The Many Lives of V.K. Krishna Menon* (Penguin Random House India, Gurgaon, 2019).

Jairam Ramesh, *Intertwined Lives: P.N. Haksar and Indira Gandhi* (Simon & Schuster India, New Delhi, 2018).

Javeed Alam, *Who Wants Democracy?* (Orient Longman, New Delhi, 2004).

John Dayal and Ajoy Bose, *For Reasons of State: Delhi under Emergency* (Penguin Random House India, Gurgaon, 2018).

John Kenneth Galbraith, *How to Control the Military* (Signet Books, New York, 1969).

Joseph E. Stiglitz and Linda J. Bilmes, *The Three Trillion Dollar War: The True Cost of the Iraq Conflict* (Penguin Books, New York, 2008).

Judith Bara and Mark Pennington (Eds.), *Comparative Politics* (SAGE Publications, New Delhi, 2009).

Jung Chang and Jon Halliday, *Mao: The Unknown Story* (Vintage Books, London, 2007).

K.V. Krishna Rao, *In the Service of the Nation: Reminiscences* (Penguin Books India, New Delhi, 2001).

Katherine Frank, *Indira: The Life of Indira Nehru Gandhi* (HarperCollins Publishers India, New Delhi, 2001).

Kenneth S. Davis, *Soldier of Democracy: A Biography of Dwight Eisenhower* (Doubleday, Doran & Company, Inc., Garden City, New York, 1945).

Khaled Ahmed, *Pakistan's Terror Conundrum* (Penguin Random House India, Gurgaon, 2020).

Khushwant Singh, *Truth, Love & a Little Malice* (Ravi Dayal and Penguin Books India, New Delhi, 2002).

Kishore Mahbubani, *The New Asian Hemisphere: The Irresistible Shift of Global Power to the East* (BBS Public Affairs, New York, 2008).

Kirpal Dhillon, *Time Present and Time Past* (Penguin Books India, New Delhi, 2013).

Kudret Bülbül, Md. Nazmul Islam, Md. Sajid Khan (Ed.), *Rohingya Refugee Crisis in Myanmar, Ethnic Conflict and Resolution* (Springer, Singapore, 2022).

Lal Khan, *Pakistan's Other Story: The 1968-9 Revolution* (Aakar Books, New Delhi, 2009).

L.K. Advani, *My Country: My Life* (Rupa & Co., New Delhi, 2008).

Lieutenant Colonel Gautam Sharma (Retired), *Indian Army: A Reference Manual* (Reliance Publishing House, New Delhi, 2000).

Lieutenant Colonel Rajkumar Pattu, Brigadier Man Mohan Sharma, FRGS, *Indian Prisoners of War in Pakistan: Hapless & Helpless Victims of a Perverted Concept of Civil Supremacy* (Trishul Publications, Noida).

Lieutenant Colonel R.J. Dickinson, *Officers' Mess: Life and Customs in the Regiments* (Bookmart, New Delhi, 2008).

Lieutenant Colonel Rajkumar Pattu and Brigadier Man Mohan Sharma, FRGS, *Indian Prisoners of War in Pakistan* (Trishul Publications, Noida; year of publication not mentioned; circa 2006).

Lieutenant General Harbakhsh Singh (Retired), VrC, *In the Line of Duty: A Soldier Remembers* (Lancer Publishers and Distributors, New Delhi,2000).

Lieutenant General K.S. Brar (Retired), *Operation Blue Star: The True Story* (UBSPD, New Delhi, 2008).

Lieutenant General S.K. Sinha (Retired), *Changing India: Straight from the Heart* (Manas Publications, New Delhi, 2007).

Lieutenant General V.K. Sood (Retired) and Pravin Sawhney, *Operation Parakram: The War Unfinished* (SAGE Publications, New Delhi, 2003).

Lieutenant General Y.M. Bammi (Retired) *Kargil 1999: The Impregnable Conquered* (Natraj Publishers, Dehradun, 2000).

Lieutenant General Depinder Singh, PVSM, VSM, *Field Marshal Sam Manekshaw: Soldiering with Dignity* (Natraj Publishers, Dehradun, 2002).

Lieutenant General Depinder Singh, PVSM, VSM, *Indian Peacekeeping Force in Sri Lanka* (Natraj Publishers, New Delhi, 2001).

Lieutenant General E.A. Vas, PVSM, *The Search for Security: Controlling Conflict and Terrorism* (Natraj Publishers, Dehradun, 1989).

Lieutenant General E.A. Vas, PVSM, *Without Baggage: A Personal Account of the Jammu and Kashmir Operations 1947–49* (Natraj Publishers, Dehradun, 1987).

Lieutenant General Harbakhsh Singh (Retired), VrC, *War Despatches: Indo–Pak Conflict 1965* (Lancer Publishers, New Delhi, 1991).

Lieutenant General Harbaksh Singh (Retired), VrC, *War Despatches: Indo–Pak Conflict 1965,* (Lancer International, New Delhi, 1991).

Lieutenant General J.F.R. Jacob, *Surrender at Dacca: Birth of a Nation* (Manohar Publishers, New Delhi, 1997).

Lieutenant General J.F.R. Jacob, *An Odyssey in War and Peace* (Lotus Roli, New Delhi, 2011).

Lieutenant General K.P. Candeth (Retired), PVSM, *The Western Front: Indo–Pakistan War 1971* (The English Book Depot, Dehradun, 1997).

Lieutenant General M.L. Chibber, PVSM, AVSM, *Military Leadership to Prevent Military Coup* (Lancer International, New Delhi, 1986).

Lieutenant General Raj Kadyan, *The Lies that Win: Army Promotions* (Manas Publications, New Delhi, 2005).

Lieutenant General S.C. Sardeshpande, UYSM, AVSM, *Assignment Jaffna* (Lancer Publishers, New Delhi, 1992).

Lieutenant General S.L. Menezes (Retired), *Fidelity and Honour: The Indian Army from the Seventeenth to the Twenty-first Century* (Oxford University Press, New Delhi, 1999).

Lieutenant General S.K. Sinha (Retired), PVSM, *A Soldier Recalls* (Lancer International, New Delhi, 1992).

Lieutenant General Satish Nambiar, PVSM, AVSM, VrC, *For the Honour of India: A History of Indian Peacekeeping*

(Centre for Armed Forces Historical Research/Army HQ, New Delhi, 2009).

Lieutenant General V.R. Raghavan, *Siachen: Conflict Without End* (Penguin Books India, New Delhi, 2002).

Lieutenant General Vijay Oberoi, PVSM, AVSM, and Colonel Utkarsh S. Rathore, *Indian Army Aviation 2025* (KW Publishers, New Delhi).

Lloyd I. Rudolph and Susanne Hoeber Rudolph, *Explaining Indian Democracy: A Fifty-Year Perspective, 1956–2006* (Oxford University Press, New Delhi, 2008).

M.S. Kohli and Kenneth Conboy, *Spies in the Himalayas: Secret Missions and Perilous Climbs* (HarperCollins Publishers India, New Delhi, 2003).

M. Asghar Khan, *My Political Struggle* (Oxford University Press, Karachi, 2008).

M.S. Kohli, *Sherpas: The Himalayan Legends (*UBS Publishers' Distributors, New Delhi, 2003).

M.Y. Effendi, *Punjab Cavalry: Evolution, Role, Organisation and Tactical Doctrine* (Oxford University Press, 2007).

Madhavi S. Mahadevan, *The Madras Sappers: An Enduring Legacy* (Madras Engineer Group and Centre, 2002).

Major General E. D'Souza (Retired), PVSM, *A 'Royal' Tribute: A History of the 5th Battalion, The Maratha Light Infantry* (ARB Interactive, Mumbai, 2005).

Major General Harkirat Singh (Retired), *Intervention in Sri Lanka: The IPKF Experience Retold* (Manohar Publishers, Delhi, 2007).

Major General Ian Cardozo (Retired), AVSM, SM, *The Indian Army: A Brief History* (Centre for Armed Forces Historical Research, New Delhi, 2005).

Major General Lachhman Singh Lehl (Retired), PVSM, VrC, *Missed Opportunities: Indo–Pak War 1965* (Natraj Publishers, Dehradun, 1997).

Major General Shubhi Sood (Retired), *Leadership Field Marshal Sam Manekshaw* (SDS Publishers, Noida, 2006).

Major General Ashok Kalyan Verma, *Kargil: Blood on the Snow (Tactical Victory Strategic Failure)* (Manohar Publishers, New Delhi, 2002).

Major General Ashok Krishna, AVSM, *India's Armed Forces: Fifty Years of War and Peace* (Lancer Publishers and Distributors, New Delhi, 1998).

Major General D.K. Palit VrC, *Musings & Memories—Vol. I*, (Palit & Palit and Lancer Publishers, 2004).

Major General D.K. Palit VrC, *Musings & Memories—Vol. II*, (Palit & Palit and Lancer Publishers, 2004).

Major General J.F.C. Fuller, *The Generalship of Alexander the Great* (Wordsworth Editions Ltd., Hertfordshire, UK, 1998).

Major General P.K.D. Kapur, VSM, *Footprints and Milestones—A Story of Army Service Corps* (Kapse Printers, Bangalore, 1990).

Major General Sukhwant Singh, *Defence of the Western Border* (Lancer Publishers, New Delhi, 1981).

Major General Sukhwant Singh, *The Liberation of Bangladesh: India's Wars since Independence* (Lancer Publishers, New Delhi, 1980).

Major General V.K. Singh, *India's External Intelligence: Secrets of Research and Analysis Wing (RAW)* (Manas Publications, New Delhi, 2007).

Major General V.K. Singh, *Leadership in the Indian Army: Biographies of Twelve Soldiers* (SAGE Publications, New Delhi, 2005).

Major Jodh Singh and P.N. Khera, *Indira's India* (Indian School Supply Depot, New Delhi, 1972).

Major K.C. Praval, *Indian Army after Independence* (Lancer International, New Delhi, 1987).

Manoj Mitta and H.S. Phoolka, *When a Tree Shook Delhi: The 1984 Carnage and Its Aftermath* (Roli Books, New Delhi, 2007).

Martin Edmonds, *Armed Services and Society* (Leicester University Press, Leicester, UK, 1988).

Meena Menon, *Reporting Pakistan* (Penguin Random House India, Gurgaon, 2017).

Meghnad Desai and Aitzaz Ahsan, *Divided by Democracy* (Roli, New Delhi, 2005).

Murtaza Razvi, *Musharraf: The Years in Power* (HarperCollins Publishers India, Noida, 2009).

Myra MacDonald, *Heights of Madness: One Woman's Journey in Pursuit of a Secret War* (Rupa & Co., New Delhi, 2007).

N.R. Madhava Menon, *Rule of Law in a Free Society* (Oxford University Press, New Delhi, 2008).

Neville Maxwell, *India's China War* (Natraj Publishers, Dehradun, 1970).

Owen Bennett Jones, *Pakistan: Eye of the Storm* (Penguin Books India, Delhi, 2002).

P.C. Alexander, *Through the Corridors of Power: An Insider's Story* (HarperCollins Publishers India, New Delhi, 2004).

P.M. Nair, *The Kalam Effect: My Years with the President* (HarperCollins Publishers India, New Delhi, 2008).

P.V. Rajgopal (Ed.), *The British, the Bandits and the Bordermen: From the Diaries and Articles of K.F. Rustamji* (Wisdom Tree, New Delhi, 2009).

Paul Brooker, *Non-Democratic Regimes* (Palgrave Macmillan, Hampshire, UK, 2009).

Pervez Musharraf, *In the Line of Fire: A Memoir* (Pocket Books, London, 2006).

Philip Mason, *A Matter of Honour: An Account of the Indian Army, its Officers and Men* (Natraj Publishers, Dehradun, 2004).

Philip Oldenburg, *India, Pakistan, and Democracy: Solving the Puzzle of Divergent Paths* (Routledge, London, 2010).

Pupul Jayakar, *Indira Gandhi: A Biography* (Penguin Random House India, Gurgaon, 2017).

Pradeep P. Barua, *Gentlemen of the Raj: The Indian Army Officer Corps, 1817–1949* (Praeger Publishers, Westport, CT, 2008).

Praveen Swami, *The Kargil War* (LeftWord, New Delhi, 2000).

Probal Dasgupta, *Watershed 1967: India's Forgotten Victory Over China* (Juggernaut Books, New Delhi, 2020).

Rafiq Zakaria, *The Man Who Divided India: An Insight into Jinnah's Leadership and its Aftermath* (Popular Prakashan, Mumbai, 2002).

Rajeev Sharma, *Pak Proxy War: A Story of ISI, bin Laden and Kargil* (Kaveri Books, New Delhi, 1999).

Raghvendra Singh, *India's Lost Frontier: The Story of the North-West Frontier Province of Pakistan* (Rupa Publications, New Delhi, 2019).

Ramachandra Guha, *India after Gandhi: The History of the World's Largest Democracy* (Macmillan, London, 2007).

Ranabir Samaddar, *A Biography of the Indian Nation: 1947–1997* (SAGE Publications, New Delhi, 2001).

Rear Admiral K. Sridharan (Retired), AVSM, *A Maritime History of India* (Director, Publications Division, Ministry of Information and Broadcasting, Government of India, New Delhi, 1982).

Richard V. Weekes, *Pakistan: Birth and Growth of a Muslim Nation* (Royal Book House, Karachi, 2004; 1964 manuscript).

Risa A. Brooks and Elizabeth A. Stanley, *Creating Military Power: The Source of Military Effectiveness* (Stanford University Press, Stanford, California, 2007).

Robert Pinkney, *Democracy in the Third World* (Viva Books, New Delhi, 2008).

Robert W. Stern, *Democracy and Dictatorship in South Asia: Dominant Classes and Political Outcomes in India, Pakistan and Bangladesh* (Praegar Publishers, Westport, CT, 2004).

Rohan Gunaratna, *Indian Intervention in Sri Lanka* (South Asian Network on Conflict Resolution, Colombo, 1993).

R.S.N. Singh, *The Military Factor in Pakistan* (Lancer Publishers, New Delhi, 2008).

S. Muthaiah, *Born to Dare: The Life of Lieutenant General Inderjit Singh Gill PVSM, MC* (Penguin Books India, New Delhi, 2008).

S. Nihal Singh, *Ink in my Veins: A Life in Journalism* (Hay House, Delhi, 2011).

Sudhir Kumar Singh and M.H. Syed, *Human Rights in Pakistan* (Pentagon Press, New Delhi, 2007).

S.M Mushrif, *Who Killed Karkare?* (Pharos Media and Publishers, New Delhi, 2010).

S.N. Prasad and Dharam Pal, History Division, Ministry of Defence, Government of India, *Operations in Jammu & Kashmir 1947–48* (Natraj Publishers, Dehradun, 1987: 2005 reprint).

Saad S. Khan with Sara S. Khan, *Ruttie Jinnah: The Woman Who Stood Defiant* (Penguin Random House India, Gurgaon, 2020).

Salmaan Taseer, *Bhutto: A Political Biography* (Vikas Publishing House, Karachi, 1980).

Samuel P. Huntington, *Political Order in Changing Societies* (Yale University Press, USA, 1968).

Samuel P. Huntington, *The Soldier and the State* (The Belknap Press of Harvard University Press, Cambridge, Massachusetts, 1985).

Sanjay Kak, *Until My Freedom Has Come: The New Intifada in Kashmir* (Penguin Books India, New Delhi, 2011).

Shankar Roychowdhury, *Officially at Peace* (Penguin Books India, New Delhi, 2002).

Shiv Kunal Verma, *1962: The War That Wasn't* (Aleph Book Company, New Delhi, 2016).

Shrikant Y. Ramani, *Operation Vijay: The Ultimate Solution* (Broadway Book Centre, Goa, 2008).

Shuja Nawaz, *Crossed Swords: Pakistan, its Army, and the Wars Within* (Oxford University Press, Karachi, 2008).

Shuja Nawaz, *The Battle for Pakistan: The Bitter US Friendship and a Tough Neighbourhood* (Penguin Random House India, New Delhi, 2019).

Shyam Bhatia, *Goodbye Shahzadi: A Political Biography of Benazir Bhutto* (Lotus Collection: Roli Books, New Delhi, 2008).

Sikandar Hayat, *The Charismatic Leader: Quaid-i-Azam Mohammad Ali Jinnah and the Creation of Pakistan* (Oxford University Press, Karachi, 2008).

Sisir Gupta, *Kashmir: A Study in India–Pakistan Relations* (Asia Publishing House, Bombay, 1966).

Sisir Gupta, *Great Power Relations, World Order and the Third World* (Vikas Publishing House, New Delhi, 1981).

Srinath Raghavan, *War and Peace in Modern India* (Permanent Black, Ranikhet, 2010).

Srinjoy Chowdhury, *Despatches from Kargil* (Penguin Books India, New Delhi, 2000).

Stephen P. Cohen, *The Indian Army, Its Contribution to the Development of a Nation* (University of California Press, Berkeley, 1984).

Stephen P. Cohen, *India: Emerging Power* (Oxford University Press, New Delhi, 2001).

Stephen P. Cohen, *The Pakistan Army* (Oxford University Press, Karachi, 1984).

Stephen Peter Rosen, *Societies and Military Power: India and Its Armies* (Oxford University Press, New Delhi, 1996).

Stephen P. Cohen, *The Idea of Pakistan* (Oxford University Press, New Delhi, 2004).

Steven I. Wilkinson, *Army and Nation: The Military and Indian Democracy since Independence* (Orient Blackswan, New Delhi, 2015).

Strobe Talbott, *Engaging India: Diplomacy, Democracy, and the Bomb* (Penguin Books India, New Delhi, 2004).

Sudhir Kumar Singh, *Human Rights in Pakistan* (Pentagon Press, New Delhi, 2007).

T.J.S. George, *Krishna Menon: A Biography* (Taplinger Publishing Co. Inc., New York, 1965).

V.K. Murthi and Gautam Sharma, *Rajiv Gandhi: Challenges and Choices* (Radiant Publishers, New Delhi, 1986).

Vice Admiral S.H. Sarma (Retired), PVSM, *My Years at Sea* (Lancer Publishers and Distributors, New Delhi, 2001).

Vinita Kamte (with Vinita Deshmukh), *To the Last Bullet: The Inspiring Story of Braveheart—Ashok Kamte* (Amesha Prashasan, Pune, 2009).

Wasim Akram, *Sultan: A Memoir* (Hardie Grant Books, Melbourne, 2022).

William B. Milam, *Bangladesh and Pakistan: Flirting with Failure in South Asia* (Hurst Publishers, London, 2011).

Wilson John, *An Admiral Falls: The True Account of Vishnu Bhagwat's Dismissal* (Har Anand Publications, New Delhi, 1999).

Wilson John, *Pakistan: Four Scenarios* (Pentagon Press, New Delhi, 2008).

Wilson John, *The General and Jihad* (Pentagon Press, New Delhi, 2007).

Zahid Hussain, *Frontline Pakistan: The Struggle with Militant Islam* (Penguin Books India, New Delhi, 2007).

Zareer Masani, *Indian Tales of The Raj* (BBC Books, London, 1987).

Zoya Hasan, *Democracy in Muslim Societies: The Asian Experience* (SAGE Publications India, New Delhi, 2007).

Zoya Hasan, E. Sridharan, R. Sudarshan, *India's Living Constitution: Ideas, Practices, Controversies* (Permanent Black, New Delhi, 2002).

Index

Scan QR code to access the
Penguin Random House India website